Tapestry in Time

Tapestry in Time

The Story of the Dominican Sisters
Grand Rapids, Michigan, 1966 – 2012

Edited by

MARY NAVARRE, OP

WILLIAM B. EERDMANS PUBLISHING COMPANY
Grand Rapids, Michigan / Cambridge, U.K.

© 2015 Mary Navarre
All rights reserved

Published 2015 by
Wm. B. Eerdmans Publishing Co.
2140 Oak Industrial Drive N.E., Grand Rapids, Michigan 49505 /
P.O. Box 163, Cambridge CB3 9PU U.K.

Printed in the United States of America

20 19 18 17 16 15   7 6 5 4 3 2 1

Library of Congress Cataloging-in-Publication Data

Tapestry in time: the story of the Dominican sisters,
Grand Rapids, Michigan, 1966-2012 / edited by Mary Navarre, OP.
pages   cm
Includes bibliographical references and indexes.
ISBN 978-0-8028-7255-5 (pbk.: alk. paper)
1. Congregation of Our Lady of the Sacred Heart (Grand Rapids, Mich.)
2. Congregation of Our Lady of the Sacred Heart (Grand Rapids, Mich.) — Biography.
I. Navarre, Mary, 1943-   editor.

BX4337.24.T37 2015

271'.972077456 — dc23

2015017963

www.eerdmans.com

*Dedicated to the 1,709 women
who have entered the
Dominican Sisters ~ Grand Rapids, Michigan, since 1877.
Some stayed a day,
others a lifetime,
each left her mark of grace,
her desire to know the living God.
For each one, we are grateful.*

CONTENTS

A Word about the Title   ix
Introduction   x
Notes for the Reader   xiii
Contributors   xiv
Preamble: Tapestry for a New Time   xix

PART I

Prayer: Essential to Dominican Life   1

New Moments in Prayer   3
Dominicans at Prayer   22
New Places for Prayer: Chapels — Renovated, New, and Restored   36

PART II

Study: Essential to Dominican Life   51

Study Transforms the Community   53
Into a Period of Intense Study and Personal Renewal   64
Formation — Becoming a Sister   89
Theological and Professional Study   98

PART III

Common Life: Essential to Dominican Life   115

Life in Common — Structures That Hold us Together   118
Living and Loving Day by Day   134
Concentric Circles   150

CONTENTS

PART IV

MINISTRY: ESSENTIAL TO DOMINICAN LIFE   181

Aquinas College in Changing Times   183
New Mexico — Dominicans in the Land of Enchantment   196
Chimbote, Peru — The Challenge of the Andes   210
Dominican Center at Marywood   230
Social Consciousness and Ministry   238
Horizons Broaden and Ministries Flourish   259

CONCLUSION

THE VIEW FROM HERE   281

Appendix 1: Working Assumptions
for the History Project Task Force   287
Appendix 2: Statement of Policy and Investment Objectives   288
Appendix 3: Lists   291
Bibliography   293
Glossary   296
Index of Names   301
Index of Subjects   307

A WORD ABOUT THE TITLE

The title of the first volume of our history, *Period Pieces,* works as a metaphor for the pieces of a quilt which when sewn together make a large and useful whole, much like the chapters of the book itself. Also, since a *period piece* is thought of as an object or work set in or reminiscent of an earlier historical period, it is a suitable title for the first part of our story which covers the earliest years from 1877 to the new era beginning with the close of Vatican Council II in 1965.

This title of the second volume of our history, *Tapestry in Time,* describing our lives from 1966 to 2012, also works as a metaphor, but this time it is likened to the stitches of a tapestry. Like a quilt, a tapestry is usually the work of many hands, and it tells a story. This book is our story, told through many writers and storytellers whose words have been recorded in oral history and stitched together over time. Like a tapestry it creates an image of our continuing story.

Appropriately enough, many Sisters who tell the stories in this volume also left their handiwork in the stitchery to create the seven liturgical tapestries that seasonally adorn the Dominican Chapel/Marywood. Two of these are depicted on the cover of this book.

Both quilts and tapestries are often the work of women, and this is the story of women who joined their lives to serve God, strengthened by the bonds of sisterhood in the Order of St. Dominic and lived out in service with the ever ancient, yet ever renewing Catholic Church.

INTRODUCTION

THE COMPLETION OF this book is the work of many hands. We can always accomplish more together than any one of us can do individually. Never was this truer than in the production of the book you hold in your hand. It began in 2008 when the Prioress at that time, Sister Nathalie Meyer, suggested that the next volume of the history of the Congregation needed to be written.

So we did what good Dominicans always do — we formed a committee to study the possibilities. The original committee of seven members met monthly, utilized experts, listened to consultants, and began to discuss what could be in this book and who could help us write it. None of the committee members had published a book before and there was a brief temptation to hire an outsider to do the writing, but we soon realized that this was our story to tell and we had to be the ones to tell it.

Each time we met as a committee we called upon all those Sisters who had now joined the great cloud of witnesses and were numbered among the Communion of Saints to inspire us in our work to tell the unvarnished truth of our journey in faith for the past fifty plus years as the Catholic Church, and Religious Life in particular, were transformed in response to Vatican Council II.

The original members of the core group were *Sisters Amata Fabbro, Genevieve Galka, Jean Milhaupt, Mary Navarre, Michael Ellen Carling, Rose Marie Martin,* and *Teresa Houlihan.* We were assisted at this time by the able and conscientious *Rosemary Steers,* who took meticulous notes and helped keep us organized.

Our archivists, Sisters Rose Marie Martin and Michael Ellen Carling, recommended that we consult with Margaret Susan Thompson, PhD, a professor of Women's History at Syracuse University whom they had met at a conference for archivists of Dominican Congregations. Dr. Thompson met with us October 25, 2008, giving us valuable insights and raising questions of audience and style, context, framework, and format. She also recommended

Introduction

a trip to visit the IHM (Sisters, Servants of the Immaculate Heart of Mary) Sisters in Monroe, Michigan, who had completed a history of their congregation. And thus the work began.

On November 20, 2008, Sisters Rose Marie Martin, Michael Ellen Carling, Mona Schwind (the author of the first volume of the Congregational history, *Period Pieces*), and Mary Navarre traveled to Monroe, Michigan, to meet with the group of IHM Sisters who had written their text, entitled *Building Sisterhood,* which was published by Syracuse University in 1997. These Sisters shared the process they used for writing their story, including pitfalls and cautions. They also generously shared their working assumptions which we adopted in a modified form for our own process (see Appendix).

The working committee, eventually renamed the History Project Task Force, accumulated a list of books, articles, and dissertations to read and discuss on the topic of religious life — its history and evolution. There were also readings and suggestions on the craft of writing as well as guidelines for publishing. Sisters from the Congregation were solicited to contribute essays in their field of interest and expertise. The Task Force met every month for several years carefully discussing options, encouraging the writers, and editing the submitted texts of the writers.

God called Sister Jean Milhaupt home on November 2, 2011. Although not a member of the Task Force, Sister Mona Schwind, the former archivist, resource person and writer of the first volume, died January 14, 2013. Three other members of the Task Force faced health problems that necessitated their resignation from the committee. This left three members of the original seven to see the project to completion — however, most of the "heavy lifting" of planning and organizing had been done prior to these last three departures.

I know that I am speaking on behalf of many when I express my gratitude for each member of the Task Force. Sister Jean, master of word and syntax, offered a careful eye and ready wit to the process for as long as she was able to do so. Sister Mona's history, *Period Pieces,* became our "go to" source for facts and history to give background to the current work. Sister Amata added her depth of knowledge of Scripture, an "ear" for good writing, and a ready humor to steady us at endless meetings; Sister Teresa always knew the right verb to convey meaning with freshness and clarity. Sister Genevieve kept the big picture before us; her analytical mind, deep research, and meticulous oral

INTRODUCTION

histories of the Sisters — recorded, transcribed, and organized — provided invaluable resource material for every chapter. Sister Rose Marie kept us focused at every meeting and offered leadership as well as the superbly accessible archives material ever at the ready for the use of writers. Sister Michael Ellen is our walking history book. She has a keen eye for every "jot and tittle," dates, spelling of names, accuracy of dates, and just the right photograph to complete every passage. Without each of these talented, generous women, the final product would be much less in every way.

As the essays from the contributors came in, it became apparent that the style, voice, and scope of each varied considerably. A single narrative voice was needed to provide context, continuity, and cohesion to the finished product. The newly elected Leadership Team of 2012 commissioned me to that task and to bring the project to completion.

Here is our story based on many contributors from Sisters who lived the reality of the past fifty years, and wrote from their perspective of that reality. It has been sifted through many readings, meetings, suggestions, and drafts, shaped by one author and offered to you for your delight.

Sr. Mary Navarre

NOTES FOR THE READER

1. All interviews of Sisters in the Oral History project were conducted by Sister Genevieve Galka and transcripts are located in the Marywood Archives.

2. To save space, the title Sister is abbreviated to S. in the footnotes.

3. Members of the Dominican order are entitled to use the initials OP after their names to indicate membership in the Order of Preachers. To avoid peppering each page with the OP initials after a Sister's name, the reader is to assume the post-nominal initials OP after a Sister's name, unless otherwise noted.

4. All Scripture quotations, unless otherwise noted, are taken from the *New American Bible* in the publication referred to as the *Anselm Academic Study Bible* (Anselm Academic, 2013).

5. The word *Church* when capitalized refers to the Roman Catholic Church.

6. The word *Congregation* when capitalized refers to an autonomous unit of Women Religious with a central office in a Motherhouse, e.g., Grand Rapids Dominicans; Adrian Dominicans.

7. Direct quotations are verbatim, although for the sake of consistency, some words are capitalized that were not so in the original, e.g., Church, Congregation.

CONTRIBUTORS

Mary Ann Barrett, OP, is currently serving on the Leadership Team for the Dominican Sisters ~ Grand Rapids 2012–2018. She received her Master's degree in Pastoral Studies in 1990. Prior to her election she was the Pastoral Associate at St. Francis de Sales Parish in Holland, Michigan. Eleven years as a high school teacher, nine years in vocation work, and twelve years in campus ministry — all gave her insights and experience to write the chapters on common life. Sister Mary Ann has remarkable gifts for both living the common life well and writing about it.

Mary Patricia Beatty, OP, is currently serving as librarian for the Dominican Sisters ~ Grand Rapids where she organizes, purchases books, and administers the Marywood Library. Sister Mary Pat received a Master of Science degree in Library Science from the University of Michigan in 1970, and a Master of Arts degree in Religious Education from the Aquinas Institute of Religious Studies in 1977. Eighteen years in library work, fifteen years as bookstore manager in the Grand Rapids Catholic Diocese and later at Marywood, seven years in parish work — all gave her a "third eye" for social justice advocacy and made her the right choice to gather the data for the chapter "Horizons Broaden and Ministries Flourish."

Margaret Mary Birchmeier, OP, is nearing the completion of her fiftieth year as administrator, midwife, and missionary in Chimbote, Peru. Sister Margaret Mary is a registered nurse/midwife, earning her R.N. Certification from Mercy Central in 1962 and her Certification in midwifery from the Catholic Maternity Institute in 1965. She earned a Bachelor of Arts degree from Aquinas College in 1980. In addition to her skills in nursing, administration, and intercultural missionary work, Sister Margaret Mary is also a fine writer with a remarkable memory for the political, social, medical, and spiritual evolution that is told in the compelling story of that city by the sea and challenge of the Andes — Chimbote, Peru.

Mary Donnelly, OP, is currently in her seventh year as Rector at Pangborn Hall at the University of Notre Dame in South Bend, Indiana. Prior to that post, Sister Mary was the novice director for the Congregation and before that she served for ten years as Pastoral Associate and Campus Minister at the St. Paul Campus Church at Ferris State University in Big Rapids, Michigan. Sister Mary earned a Master's degree in Pastoral Studies at the Aquinas Institute in St. Louis, Missouri. In 2000, she earned a Doctor of Ministry from Western Theological Seminary in Holland, Michigan. Her experience and reflections contributed greatly to the chapter on formation as well as the chapter on professional and theological study.

Orlanda Leyba, OP, has served for thirty years in Catholic schools as a teacher, principal, and director of Christian Ministry. She received her Master's in Administration of Schools in 1978 from the University of Michigan. Sister Orlanda currently lives in Inkster, Michigan, where she volunteers her services with the national organization, Dominican Sisters Conference; she also volunteers at a local soup kitchen and Manna Meals. A life-long advocate for social justice, Sister Orlanda wrote the chapter on the rise of social consciousness. In addition to her gifts for teaching and administration, Sister Orlanda is a superb photographer and artist in her own right. With one eye on social justice, she keeps her other eye on the beauty all about her and adds to both — beauty and justice each day of her life.

Marie Celeste Miller, OP, teaches Art History at Aquinas College. She received a PhD in Art History from Emory University in Atlanta, Georgia, in 1983. With eleven years of high school teaching and twenty-eight years as professor at Aquinas College (three years as founding director of the Humanities Program and four years as Dean of Curriculum), Sister Celeste was the best person to write the chapter on the "jewel" that Aquinas College continues to be for the Dominican Sisters ~ Grand Rapids.

CONTRIBUTORS

Mary Ellen McDonald, OP, is currently serving on the pastoral care team of the Marywood Campus. The team's work includes the spiritual companioning program for the Marywood Home Health Care service of the Marywood Circle.[1] A life-long learner, Sister Mary Ellen's early encounter with liberation theology and its founder Gustavo Gutierrez, OP, influenced her commitment to work for justice for all peoples. Sister Mary Ellen earned a Master of Arts in Religious Studies from the Aquinas Institute of Religious Studies in 1967 and she received a certificate in Theological Studies in 1984 from the Catholic Theological Union in Chicago. Sister Mary Ellen has served in parishes in the Saginaw Diocese in Michigan for thirty-five years; twenty-four of those were in the role of pastoral administrator in parishes where there were no priests. Sister Mary Ellen contributed to the chapter on lifelong learning — a reality she has lived.

Megan McElroy, OP, is currently the co-director at the Collaborative Dominican Novitiate in St. Louis, Missouri, where she guides the newest members along the path of formation in Religious Life according to the Dominican tradition. Sister Megan received a Master's degree in Divinity in 2006 from the Catholic Theological Union in Chicago. She has served as a pastoral associate for thirteen years and a high school teacher of religion for four years. In addition to her work as a co-director at the novitiate, Sister Megan is studying at Aquinas Institute to complete her Doctor of Ministry in Preaching. A contemplative person to the core, Sister Megan was the right choice to compose the chapter "New Moments in Prayer."

Mary Navarre, OP, served as a Councilor on the Leadership Team of the Grand Rapids Dominicans from 2006 to 2012, after which she accepted the challenge of serving as the general editor for the completion of this book, telling the story of the Dominican Sisters ~ Grand Rapids from 1966 forward. Before her election to the Council, she taught in Catholic schools throughout

---

1. Marywood Circle is a collaborative joint venture with Porter Hills Retirement Community and Services providing an array of life services and spiritual support to older adults in the greater Grand Rapids area.

Contributors

Michigan. For the last twenty-nine years of her teaching career, she taught in both the Humanities and Education Departments at Aquinas College. Sister Mary received her doctorate from Boston University in 1984. Mary is a storyteller for all ages. She believes stories are the "glue" that holds us together as a people and her ardent wish is that, to paraphrase the Hebrew prophet Habakkuk, she has heard the command to "write the story down, make it plain on the pages of this book."

Mary Kay Oosdyke, OP, is currently the director of Associate Life for the Dominican Sisters ~ Grand Rapids, a position she has held since 2008. Sister Mary Kay received her doctorate in theology from Boston College in 1987 and served as both teacher and administrator at Aquinas College, Grand Rapids; Ursuline College, Cleveland, Ohio; and at the Aquinas Institute, St. Louis, Missouri. Sister Mary Kay was one of the many Sisters who worked collaboratively with four Dominican Congregations to bring to fruition the beautifully published prayer book known as *Dominican Praise: A Provisional Book of Prayer for Dominican Women* published in 2005. She was the right person to compose the chapter on renewed traditions of Dominican prayer.

Eva Silva, OP, taught high school for eighteen years, was vocation director for four years, and served in parish work for five years before launching into her current career as a psychotherapist. Sister Eva received a Master's degree in Spanish language and culture from Michigan State University in 1976; and a Master's in counseling in 1996. She practiced as a psychotherapist with the Samaritan Center in Albuquerque for seven years. For the past ten years she has been in private practice in Albuquerque, New Mexico. As a native New Mexican and Latina woman, Sister Eva was the best person to write the chapter on the "jewel" known as New Mexico.

Carmelita Switzer, OP, is currently on the staff at Dominican Center at Marywood where she has served in the capacity of teaching, coordinating the spiritual formation program, and providing spiritual direction. Prior to that, Sister Carmelita taught high school for eighteen years, served as formation director for four years and pastoral associate/administrator for fifteen years, first in parishes and then six years at Marywood as the Pastoral Life Coordinator for the campus. Sister Carmelita provided just the right resources for the needed references about Vatican Council II.

Sue Tracy, OP, currently serves as a staff chaplain at Spectrum Hospital in Grand Rapids. As a four-time cancer survivor, Sister Sue brings understanding and humor to her chaplaincy work for the past twenty years. Before that Sister Sue taught for eleven years in Catholic junior high and high schools, served as director of vocations for the Congregation for seven years, and in a parish for eight years. She earned a Master's degree in Religious Education from Aquinas College in 1971. In addition to her work at the hospital, Sister Sue is in constant demand as a public speaker. She gives innumerable presentations every year on many topics — although one thread runs through them all and that is humor. Her gregarious nature and vast circle of friends made her the natural choice to complete the chapter "Concentric Circles."

Diane Zerfas, OP, is currently on the staff at Dominican Center at Marywood and also serves as the Director for novices and for those in the initial years of formation who have not yet taken final vows. Prior to this role, Sister Diane served on the Leadership Team of the Dominican Sisters ~ Grand Rapids from 2000 to 2006. Sister Diane taught high school for fifteen years and served in formation ministry and in direct pastoral work. She served five years at Marywood as the Director of Pastoral Life for the Campus. Diane contributed her insights and experience to the chapter on Dominican Center/Marywood.

PREAMBLE: TAPESTRY FOR A NEW TIME

Introduction

AT THE TIME our story begins in the latter half of the twentieth century, angst and turmoil described much of the world and that for several reasons. Two world wars had occurred in the first half of the century, claiming the lives of eighty million people, most of them noncombatants. The second of those wars included the genocide of the Jewish people resulting in six million deaths of that population alone. The United States' invention and deployment of atomic bombs on Japan brought with it heretofore unheard of catastrophe and the realization that we humans now had the capacity to annihilate ourselves. Western hegemony collapsed with decolonization in Africa and the Eurasian continent as well as parts of the southern hemisphere in the Americas. The Cold War with its threat of the spread of atheistic communism pervaded the consciousness of Americans. The United States' involvement in the Vietnam War escalated throughout the 1960s. All of these occurrences shaped the mindset of everyone — American citizens and world citizens alike in that decade.

In the same month as the opening of the Vatican Council II, October 1962, Americans shuddered with horror as the leaders of the United States and the Soviet Union came within a hair's breadth of nuclear war and the mutual extermination of millions.

The seclusion of convent living could not hold out against such earth-shaking events. Sisters, young and old, joined a grief-stricken citizenry watching the sad funeral procession of the first Catholic president of the United States, John F. Kennedy, who was assassinated November 22, 1963. His was the first of three violent assassinations the country would experience, as the Reverend Martin Luther King, Jr., and Robert F. Kennedy were shot five years later. Vatican Council II closed in 1965 and for American Catholic Sisters, a new day began. The serene protection of convent rules would not prevail. Apostolic Women Religious throughout the United States, including the Grand Rapids Dominicans, were about to see their semi-monastic life change utterly.

One such change vividly foretold of much to come:

Soon after the close of the Council, the Latin language for liturgies of Mass and the Office changed to English in what seemed to be an overnight occurrence. For years the major superior had intoned the Angelus Prayer at 6:00 a.m., 12:00 noon, and 6:00 p.m. "Angelus Domini nuntiavit Mariae," she intoned; to which all who were present replied: "Et concepit de Spiritu Sancto." Then one day, Mother Victor, in her sixteenth year as Mother General of the Grand Rapids Dominicans, intoned: "The angel of the Lord declared unto Mary." And all present replied: "And she conceived of the Holy Spirit." Such a simple event signaled momentous changes to come.

Mother Victor Flannery (left) and Sr. Aquinas Weber, 1966; a new moment in the history of the Congregation.

Clearly this Vatican Council had *not* maintained the status quo. Change was in the air just as surely as the mother tongue of English now filled the air of a chapel that had known only Latin for decades. The change in the specific language of prayer signaled another language change — that of discourse style. While the documents of previous Church councils had been marked by the language of commands, laws, definitions, and prescriptions, the language of this Council's documents was suggestive of invitation, persuasion, dialogue, service, inclusion, and pastoral care. Several new terms became hallmarks of this Council and were incorporated into the lives of the Sisters. Words like *aggiornamento* (adaptation to contemporary times), *ressourcement* (return to the original sources), *collegiality* (collaboration with peers), and *subsidiarity* (those affected by decisions need to be part of the making of those decisions) became part of the vocabulary and eventually the lived reality of the Sisters. Change is difficult. Many apostolic Women Religious who had been on the cusp of internal renewal even before the Council was called, took to this new relational style with the alacrity of a deer thirsting for running waters. Others resisted change. Still others found ways to be at peace with the changes in a gradual transition. The remarkable feature of it all is that the Sisters remained together, praying with and for each other, studying and working side by side, loving and living in sisterly affection whatever the garb, prayer style, ministry or understanding of religious life as it was evolving in this new time.

Preamble

One of the strongest symbols of this unity can be seen in the beautiful liturgical tapestries that provide color, texture, and interest to the north wall of Dominican Chapel/Marywood. With the renovation of the chapel in 1985, the Sisters were called upon to hand stitch the pieces of the tapestry over the course of many months whenever they could spare the time. Month after month through all seasons of the year, the Sisters came in from their missions and spent a few hours stitching. Those who were not apt at the task were coached and encouraged by those who were so skilled. Some were able to spend little time at this task, while others devoted large amounts of time. It did not matter. What did matter was that each contributed as much as she was able; and together these seven tapestries continue to delight and inspire the Sisters as well as all who call Marywood their liturgical home. Together, we are so much more than any one person individually. Large and small, neat and not so neat, we are all part of the fabric of life. In the pages that follow, the past fifty years of that story is told — it is a story of prayer, study, community, and service; it is a tapestry stitched in truth and love, a tapestry in this time.

Tapestry stitched by all the Sisters, symbolic of our communal life and work.

PART I

Prayer: Essential to Dominican Life

Most Sisters educated prior to Vatican Council II can repeat verbatim the Baltimore Catechism definition of prayer as lifting our minds and hearts to God. They memorized it as children, taught it to the next generations, and lived it in their daily lives. In the decades following Vatican Council II, this understanding of prayer remained the same in substance, but different in sound and style. Prayer has always been both communal and private, and for most Catholics until recently, prayer has been primarily the recitation of memorized prayers or readings of approved words in booklets or from prayer cards. In the two chapters that follow, the shift from these formulaic prayers to a more spontaneous and intimate form of prayer is described as it evolved slowly but surely in the post-Conciliar years. Cherished traditions of Dominicans at prayer went through shifts and renewal; finally, the chapel at the Motherhouse underwent a renovation reflecting the post-Conciliar understanding of a new way of celebrating the Mass, now often referred to as the Eucharistic Celebration.

New ways of praying are described in the first essay. These emanated both from the teaching of the Church following Vatican Council II, and the recognition of changing times in the twentieth century. Adjusted times for prayer were only the beginning as prayer became more personal, included liturgical dance, inclusive language, and yes, even preaching. The Charismatic Renewal became a source of refreshment for some and annual retreats changed to accommodate the individual's needs.

In the second chapter the evolution of prayer in the Dominican tradition is described. From its centuries-old foundation through the changes following Vatican Council II to contemporary practices with the emphasis on Liturgies of Word and Eucharist, the Dominican Order has expressed prayer in its own unique way. While Dominicans have always been ecclesial in the traditions of the Roman Catholic Church rites, they have also found ways to recognize the incarnational reality of human persons. Dominicans have been innovative in adapting to the needs of the mission and loyal to their own traditions inherited from the earliest years of the Order's foundation.

For the Dominican Sisters of Grand Rapids, singing has played an essential and joyous part of their prayer together. Blessed with gifted musicians from the earliest days to the present, the Sisters made the transition from the ethereal beauty of Gregorian chant, through the awkward stage of the early renewal songs — many more appropriate for a campfire setting — to contemporary choral music and newly composed songs that lift minds and hearts to God in full-bodied praise in English, and occasionally in Spanish and Latin.

There is some repetition in these essays in Part I as each author viewed the changes through her distinctive lens. For example, both writers describe the changes in praying the Office. The first chapter describes the changes using oral histories of the Sisters, while the second chapter focuses on the forms and prayer books that evolved. Both chapters discuss the change to using language that is inclusive of women. The overlap in topics is varied in perspective, tone, and emphasis, developing a fuller appreciation of the events for the reader.

Finally, the third chapter of Part I describes the renovation of the Marywood Chapel, taking into account the principles elucidated in the United States Bishops' Commission on the Liturgy.

As well, some events described in this part will be revisited in the chapters on study, common life, and ministry. Life seldom fits neatly into the boxes humans create for it. The interdependence of the four essential elements of Dominican Life, i.e., prayer, study, common life, and ministry, reflect the complexity and the joy of the life in all of its manifestations.

New Moments in Prayer

Sing to the Lord a new song;
Sing to the Lord, all the Earth.

PSALM 96:1

ONE OF THE unexpected blessings and surprises of the Second Vatican Council was how quickly and seriously the Church embraced the teachings of the Council Fathers. Though there were clergy, Religious, and laity who desired that the Church continue to hold on to the traditions that had been handed on from the Council of Trent four centuries earlier, it was clear the Holy Spirit was active in the changes that were taking place in churches, homes, seminaries, and convents throughout the world. Society and church witnessed the exterior changes, such as Mass said in the vernacular language, the presider facing the congregation, receiving Communion under both Species, that is both bread and wine, an openness to people of other faiths and traditions, changes in habit and horarium. Less evident but no less transformational, however, was the very identity of the Church from the metaphor of a Church Militant *(Ecclesia Militans)*[1] to one of the Pilgrim People of God, inspired by the Holy Spirit and guided by the teachings of the Church.

from the Church Militant to the Pilgrim People of God

---

1. A pre–Vatican Council II definition of the Church as the Christians on earth struggling against sin and darkness.

The path upon which they walked the journey to God was called *holiness.*

As pilgrims, the members of the Church were called to journey to God, and the path upon which they walked the journey was called *holiness.* Once told what to believe and how to recite prayers, now all the baptized were invited to take personal responsibility for their faith and their relationship with God. This stood in contrast to the notion which prevailed at the time many women joined Religious Life when the choice for religious life was the path of perfection leading to a holy life worthy of God. What the Council emphasized, however, was that it is Baptism that draws us into relationship with God and Baptism that starts the believer on that pilgrim path of holiness. Once the realm of those who lived lives of perfection, most notably the saints, the life of holiness became a universal call at the Second Vatican Council:

The life of holiness became a universal call.

> Therefore in the Church, everyone whether belonging to the hierarchy, or being cared for by it, is called to holiness, according to the saying of the Apostle: "For this is the will of God, your sanctification."[2]

As the Church embarked on this new discovery of itself as a Pilgrim People of God, professed Religious also engaged in a renewal unique to their own state in life. In The Decree on the Appropriate Renewal of Religious Life *(Perfectae Caritatis),* the Council Fathers invited Women and Men Religious to rediscover the original spirit of their founders in order to respond to the signs of the times:

> It redounds to the good of the Church that institutes have their own particular characteristics and work. Therefore let their founders' spirit and special aims they set before them as well as their sound traditions — all of which make up the patrimony of each institute — be faithfully held in honor.... Institutes should promote among their members an adequate knowledge of the social conditions of the times they live in and of the needs of the Church. In such a way, judging current events wisely in the light of faith and burning with apostolic zeal, they may be able to assist men [sic] more effectively.[3]

---

2. http://www.vatican.va/archive/hist_councils/ii_vatican_council/documents/vat-ii_const_19641121_lumen-gentium_en.html, Chapter V, #39.

3. http://www.vatican.va/archive/hist_councils/ii_vatican_council/documents/vat-ii_decree_19651028_perfectae-caritatis_en.html, #2.

Thus called to renewal in the spirit of the founder, religious orders began to recover the treasure of each institute's *charism*. Women Religious in apostolic communities needed to further adapt their way of life from the customs of the nineteenth century. Although the full rigor of the monastic life had been somewhat changed in the late nineteenth century to accommodate the work of teaching and nursing, now even greater changes were called forth to adapt again to new ministries.

For the Sisters in Grand Rapids at the Motherhouse, the schedule prior to the changes of Vatican Council II called for them to rise early in the morning in order to be in chapel by 5:30 a.m. Matins and Lauds were prayed, followed by a half hour of meditation in common. Mass was celebrated, followed by exposition of the Blessed Sacrament before breakfast, and then the Sisters ate breakfast and went off to ministry. While the postulants were in school and the professed Sisters were at ministry, the novices chanted the Little Office at noon.[4] Upon returning from ministry, the sisters prayed rosary and Vespers at 5:00 p.m. The day ended with Compline at 7:00 p.m. According to the oral history given by Sister Margaret Hillary, though never intended to be so, the sense of prayer was simply "getting it in." She reflected, "The more that we were told by Vatican Council II to be 'in the world' (to become involved in the social issues of the world), the more we were out of the monastic structure. That had an effect on the coming together to pray according to the monastic model."[5]

With the enlightened awareness that each one was called to a more personal relationship with God, the Sisters in the Congregation entered into numerous opportunities that deepened that relationship, both individually and communally. Chief among these opportunities was the possibility of praying the Mass and Divine Office in English.[6] In her Circular Letter of

Each Sister was called to a more personal relationship with God.

---

4. S. Rosemary O'Donnell, Oral History, May 16, 2011, Marywood Archives, Folder 2011.196.

5. Margaret Hillary interviewed by G. Galka, Oral History, September 8, 2009, Marywood Archives Folder 2009.063.

6. http://www.vatican.va/holy_father/paul_vi/motu_proprio/documents/hf_p-vi_motu-proprio_19660806_ecclesiae-sanctae_en.html. "Although Religious who recite a duly approved Little Office perform the public prayer of the Church . . . it is nevertheless recommended to the institutes that in place of the Little Office they adopt the Divine Office either in part or in whole so that they may participate more intimately in the liturgical life of the Church. . . ."

January 20, 1967, the Prioress, Sister Aquinas Weber, wrote to the members of the Congregation:

> The Committee on Prayer Life has recommended that we experiment in our houses with the saying of the Divine Office. Any house that wishes to do this may do so. I do, however, wish to be notified of the houses where this will be done. I make this request so that all of the Office books can be ordered through Marywood and thus reduce the initial cost, as the outlay of money will be considerable.[7]

Sister Aquinas's letter of April 20, 1967, indicates that the response was so overwhelming that Divine Office books were ordered for the entire community.[8] A third letter reveals some of the resistance to the changes: "By the time you receive this letter you will be quite proficient in executing the recitation of the Divine Office. In our preparation meetings, it was learned that not all houses are singing the *Salve* and *O Lumen* in English."[9]

In recounting her memories, Sister Elaine LaBell commented, "I remember when we got our new Office books to say the Office in English ... it sounded so strange. They took the melody of the *O Lumen* and the *Salve Regina* and put English words to it, and it just didn't make it."[10] Although most prayers and hymns are now sung in English, these two time-honored traditional hymns of the Dominican family, *O Lumen* and *Salve Regina,* are now sung in Latin as they are two hymns that, in the words of Sister Elaine, "just didn't make it" in English.

Praying the psalms and having Mass celebrated in English was an exhilarating experience. Sister Amata Fabbro recounted,

> We went to Mass one Sunday and the priest said everything in English, and we sang the hymn *Praise My Soul the King of Heaven*. I'll never forget that. I thought it was just marvelous. I was just thrilled to hear those words. We

---

7. S. Aquinas Weber, Circular Letters, July 1966–July 1968, Marywood Archives.
8. Weber, April 20, 1967.
9. Weber, May 12, 1967.
10. S. Elaine LaBell, Oral History, June 27, 2007, Marywood Archives, Folder 2009.0423, p. 23.

were all excited. The liturgy changes were really coming fast and furious. It was great.[11]

To hear Scripture proclaimed in one's mother tongue was thrilling for those whose home language was English. The same was true for those who spoke Spanish as their first language. Sister Teresa Houlihan recalled the time when this happened:

> I remember the Gospel was read in Spanish and the Hispanic Sisters wept. That was the first time they had ever heard Spanish in the Motherhouse chapel. It was wonderful. It was spectacular. It was a lovely day. Oh, they were so pleased and so was our Council.[12]

With the experience of communal prayer in the vernacular, a new awareness was developing among Women Religious. It was one thing to pray the Office in Latin with minimal understanding of what the words meant; however, as the ancient saying *Lex orandi, lex credendi, lex vivendi*[13] articulates, prayer indicates what a community believes, and belief influences how the community lives. As the Office was translated into English, Sisters were taking to heart the words they were praying. They became aware of how words shape and form them consciously and subconsciously. "Language is always influential and formative, but it may be especially influential in times of prayer because at these times the whole person is ideally involved — through speech and hearing, through sight and touch and movement."[14]

> **Prayer indicates what a community believes, and belief influences how the community lives.**

Inclusive Language

Living in a patriarchal society and worshiping in a patriarchal church, Sisters became aware of the importance of language in prayer. Praying by only using male references for God and male pronouns for humanity found the Sisters

---

11. S. Amata Fabbro, Oral History, July 7, 2010, Marywood Archives, Folder 2011.019, p. 58.
12. S. Teresa Houlihan, Marywood Archives, November 25, 2008, Folder 2009.0421, p. 7.
13. Loosely translated: As we pray/worship, so we believe and so we live.
14. Pat Kozak, CSJ, and Janet Schaffran, CDP, *More Than Words* (Rocky River, OH: Creative Offset Printing, 1986), p. 4.

wrestling with the question of inclusion and who God is and, ultimately, who they were. Admittedly, for some Sisters, it was not an issue; for others, it was becoming more and more difficult to use only male language in prayer. The more Sisters drank in the Scriptures and discovered other metaphors for God beyond Father, the richer was their relationship with God. The discovery of a more expansive concept of God led the Sisters to a deeper awareness of themselves as created in the image and likeness of God. Confirmed in this belief, the Sisters began to take seriously what it meant to be a daughter of God, a sister of Jesus, a sister to others in the Body of Christ, a sister in the Dominican Family.

Taking seriously what it meant to be a daughter of God and a sister of Jesus, of others in the Body of Christ, and in the Dominican Family

With consciousness raised, Women Religious (and women in general) became aware of their nearly complete exclusion from the text and the preaching of the Scriptures. Were they included in the message or not? Who else was being left out? Was such exclusion part of the emerging understanding of what it meant to be *church*? "Inclusive language is not merely a matter of taste or literary sophistication but a matter of faithfulness to God and to our moral responsibility for our neighbors."[15]

In light of this growing awareness, there was a gradual, though intentional, movement toward the use of inclusive language in the community's communal prayer. The Sisters engaged in study based on biblical and theological scholarship. Grounded in study and scriptural reflection, issues were addressed at the liturgy meetings held at Marywood. Sister Carmelita Murphy commented that these meetings "allowed us to encounter one another at a depth of soul and scripture, growing the bonds of respect with each other."[16]

By 1987, the proclamation of the Scriptures at Eucharist came from *The Inclusive Lectionary* by Priests for Equality. In 1992, the liturgy team at Dominican Chapel/Marywood, Father Greg Heille, OP (Saint Albert the Great Central Province of Dominican Friars), and Michelle Rego-Reatini developed a psalter using the new psalm translations from ICEL (International Commission on English in the Liturgy). Michelle recalled:

> We were looking for an all-inclusive book, something that would contain the songs, psalms with inclusive language, and the prayers. ICEL had a new

---

15. Nancy A. Hardesty, *Inclusive Language in the Church* (Atlanta: John Knox Press, 1986), p. 15.
16. Conversation with S. Carmelita Murphy, April 7, 2012.

translation of the psalms, which hadn't been released yet. We begged them to allow us to pilot the new psalter translation. They gave us permission, and then I worked on the pointing [marking] of the psalms so they could be chanted. We also found hymns to use and got permission to change the language so that they, too, would be inclusive. I think of that psalter as my first child.[17]

Father Greg commented, "Michelle and I spent a couple of years really working on that spiral bound psalter. She was working on music and psalmody. I was working on prayers. That was a huge project, very demanding."[18]

It would have seemed to be a minor change in the prayer life of the congregation, yet all of these adaptations opened the members of the Congregation to a deeper awareness of who they were called to be — women of wholeness, healing, and hospitality: wholeness in their own preaching of the Gospel, healing in their ministries, and hospitality in their living. The Sisters began to see the truth in the statement that "To speak accurately of God and lovingly to our neighbor requires the use of inclusive language. Anything less is a rejection of God's revelation of God's selfhood and a withholding of God's gift to the needy, food for the hungry, and cure for the sick."[19] The use of inclusive language in the prayer life of the congregation, subtle though it was, transformed the Sisters into being more conscious of being true daughters after the heart of the Triune God and in the spirit of Dominic.

They were called to be women of wholeness, healing, and hospitality.

Although they could not have envisioned the results of what they wrote at the 1969 Chapter, the Sisters had, from the start, recognized the value of both personal and communal prayer and how both are instrumental in being open to God's revelation:

> We will strive then to remain open to all God's self-manifestations, realizing the value and the need for involvement in the liturgy, other forms of common prayer, community life, personal encounter with others, the world of human events, and reflection in solitude. The personality of each Sister, her life situations and vocational commitment will determine in broad outline

---

17. Michelle Rego, in a phone conversation on March 13, 2012.
18. Fr. Greg Heille, OP, in a conversation on October 14, 2011.
19. Hardesty, pp. 15-16.

the pattern of these events in the rhythm of her life. This rhythm makes up the context in which she responds to the initiative of the Holy Spirit in her life. In the most profound sense of the word, then, the style of her prayer is rooted in the depth of her person.[20]

> **The style of each Sister's prayer is rooted in the depth of her person.**

Liturgical Dance

With the invitation to develop a more personal relationship with God, Sisters embarked on the discovery of various prayer styles that touched their hearts, drawing them more deeply into an experience of intimacy in prayer. Among these prayer styles was liturgical dance. Liturgically and scripturally rooted in the Judeo-Christian tradition, dance was seen as an expression of joy, praise, thanksgiving, or even anguish that enhanced the worshiping community's prayer. But, as Catholic Christian liturgy was formalized in the sixteenth and seventeenth centuries, liturgical dance was all but lost. Gestures or movements were defined for the priests, but the congregation remained in a passive position.[21] However, the Second Vatican Council's document *Sacrosanctum Concilium* called for the renewal of the liturgy and for "full, active, and conscious participation" on the part of the faithful. Liturgical dance was one way that allowed Sisters to participate more fully in the liturgy.

> **The Second Vatican Council called for "full, active, and conscious participation" on the part of the faithful.**

Sister Rosemary O'Donnell described the significance of liturgical dance in her own prayer life:

> For me liturgical dance is a form of prayer. It is my preaching. It is a way to get in touch in a very physical sense with the feelings that are at the core of my being. Sometimes liturgical dance is more meaningful for me than oral prayer because through it I can communicate feelings that cannot be expressed in words. It brings me great joy to share it with others.[22]

---

20. *Religious Life: Lived Reality,* vol. 1 (1969), pp. 71-72.
21. Kathleen Kline-Chesson, "The Living Word: Dance as a Language of Faith," http://www.religion-online.org/showarticle.asp?title=1106 (accessed March 12, 2012).
22. S. Rosemary O'Donnell Oral History, May 16, 2011, Marywood Archives, Folder 2011.196, p. 9 (revised October, 2013).

Sister Mary Ann Barrett recalled that much of the liturgical dance occurred during the summer sessions of the AIRS program (Aquinas Institute of Religious Studies). The intent of dance was to include a lot of people, though only certain people did the dance. "Sometimes we ended up with the whole congregation doing gestures," she stated. "Liturgical dance was received well but wasn't real widespread in the congregation. I think, as with many things following Vatican Council II, we didn't do enough education as to why we were bringing dance in."[23]

Body movement has not been foreign to the Dominican Order as is evidenced by Saint Dominic's Nine Ways of Prayer — postures or positions in his prayer, which served his preaching of the Gospel. In his introduction to the little book *The Nine Ways of Prayer of St. Dominic,* Simon Tugwell, OP, states:

Liturgical dancers (left to right): Srs. Charlotte Mondragon, Rosemary O'Donnell, Connie Ankoviak, and Denise Solomon.

> In our own time, we seek to share the good news of Jesus Christ with those around us searching for justice, hungering for truth, yearning for peace, looking for forgiveness, and needing love. In this, St. Dominic is always ahead of us, the preacher of God's grace to the world. As we consider his ways of prayer, let us not forget that he did it all to preach the Reign of God and to move others to conversion of heart.[24]

Following the founder's example, sisters used liturgical dance as a means by which the good news was proclaimed with the potential of drawing others into a more intimate experience of God's love.

Liturgical dancers: Srs. Mary Ann Barrett (left) and Rosemary O'Donnell assist with the ritual of incensing.

---

23. Phone conversation with S. Mary Ann Barrett, March 12, 2012.
24. Simon Tugwell, OP, *The Nine Ways of Prayer of St. Dominic* (Dublin: Dominican Publications, 1978), p. 6.

Charismatic Renewal

St. Dominic's Ninth Way of Prayer: walk in solitude and union with God.

Though having little influence on the prayer life of the Congregation as a whole, another powerful experience for some of the members was the Charismatic Renewal. In convoking the Second Vatican Council, Pope John XXIII prayed:

> Divine Spirit, renew your wonders in this our age as in a new Pentecost and grant that your Church, praying perseveringly and insistently with one heart and mind together with Mary, the Mother of Jesus, and guided by blessed Peter, may increase the reign of the Divine Savior, the reign of truth and justice, the reign of love and peace. Amen.[25]

The Spirit clearly inspired the Council Fathers with their desire for *aggiornamento*, the term used in Vatican Council II to refer to bringing the Church up to date. With the Council documents soon translated into English, the English-speaking Catholic faithful were enjoying a taste of that same Spirit that had moved the bishops. With the belief that the outpouring of the gifts of the Spirit on the early church on Pentecost was not limited to that specific day in history, but that God continues to pour forth spiritual gifts on the church of today, the Charismatic Renewal began to sweep through the Catholic Church shortly after the close of the Second Vatican Council. Its initial introduction was experienced at Duquesne University in Pittsburgh, Pennsylvania:

God continues to pour forth spiritual gifts on the church of today.

> Shortly afterwards in the United States of America, in February 1967, a group of faculty and students from Duquesne University, Pittsburgh, Pennsylvania, gathered for a weekend retreat. This weekend is often referred to as the 'Duquesne weekend', and is considered as the beginning of the Charismatic Renewal in the Catholic Church. The retreat concentrated on the first four chapters of the Acts of the Apostles. And there was an expectation that the Holy Spirit would make His presence felt. They were not disappointed. All present experienced a deep work of God within their Spirits, and charismatic

---

25. Western Washington Catholic Charismatic Renewal, "Burning Bush Pentecost Novena," http://www.wwccr.org/pentecost/burning_bush.htm (accessed March 14, 2012).

gifts were manifested in the group. Once the 'Pentecostal movement' entered the Catholic Church it very quickly found a home there.[26]

Serving as novice director at the time, Sister Karen Thoreson was in a unique position to take advantage of all the opportunities afforded her for being updated in theology and Vatican Council II. She was able to share her wisdom with those in her charge at the time; however, on a personal level, she found the Charismatic Renewal to be among the most rewarding experiences.

> Prayer meetings were starting at Aquinas College. Msgr. Bukowski began the meetings. I was invited by one of our Sisters, but I hesitated because I thought it was a little suspect. You know, not everyone was accepting it. So I did not go. But that summer when I was in Chapter some of us really felt we needed the Holy Spirit. By that time, the prayer meetings had been moved down to Saint Mary's in the city, so some of us — Sister Eileen and her sister [Sister Gilbert Popp] and Sister Bridget Hall and myself — thought we would go down and get an infusion of the Holy Spirit. So we went to a prayer meeting. I was hooked on the first one, because I remember thinking, "This is just like the early Christians that you read in the Acts of the Apostles that Saint Luke writes about." The presence of God was so strong. I was drawn from the first time. So I became involved in that. That has been a lifesaver to me.[27]

For Sister Amata Fabbro, her experience of the Charismatic Renewal influenced her ministry of teaching Scripture at Aquinas College.

> When I was down studying at Notre Dame the last year there (the spring of 1967), the Catholic Charismatic Renewal had come on to the Notre Dame campus from Duquesne. We Sisters found out about it. I attended a couple of prayer meetings and I could see the value of it. I asked to be prayed over for an increase of the experience of the Holy Spirit. It was a magnificent experience. I think that that really helped me not only spiritually, but it also

---

26. Ian Petit, OSB, "The History of the Charismatic Renewal," http://www.dentoncatholic.org/history.html (accessed March 14, 2012).
27. S. Karen Thoreson, September 15, 2008, Marywood Archives, Folder 2009.0427, p. 18.

helped me in teaching Scripture. You come out of graduate school, and you are so filled with all these methodologies that you're almost forgetting the prophetic thrust of the whole Scriptures. That did so much for me, to use methodology in a very balanced way but to try to get people to see that the Scripture is the work of the Holy Spirit. When you respond to it, the Holy Spirit in you is responding to it.[28]

Annual Retreat

As Sisters were availing themselves more and more of educational and formational opportunities, they were also seeking other spiritual opportunities, specifically regarding their annual retreat. One of the enactments of the 1969 Chapter stated:

> That we manifest a concern for the Sisters' need for new approaches to retreat and periods of renewal, and that the individual Sister, taking into consideration both her own needs and those of the community, be free to make appropriate choices of time, place, and form.[29]

As opportunities for diverse retreat styles expanded, one group of Sisters, namely those in the ministry of housekeeping, had a dynamic advocate in Sister Bede Frahm. Addressing the discrepancy between the teaching/nursing Sisters and those in domestic service, Sister Bede presented a paper at one of the renewal Chapters requesting that the Sister housekeepers be allowed to make a real retreat. Though the housekeepers were able to attend the conferences of a retreat, it was expected that they still work in the kitchen after the conferences. Despite receiving some negative feedback for her initiative at the Chapter, Sister Bede succeeded in obtaining some level of equality for the Sister housekeepers.

The Sisters in food service got time off for retreat and they got one day a week off. The other thing was that those who wanted to had educational

---

28. S. Amata Fabbro, July 7, 2010, Oral History, Marywood Archives Folder 2011.019, p. 77.
29. *Religious Life: Lived Reality,* vol. 1 (1969), p. 73.

opportunities. Sisters Janet Marie Heitz, Dominica Nellett, and Nancy Coyne all got a certificate from Fontbonne College [in St. Louis]. They went to the certificate program so that they could be certified.[30]

Sister Bede soon made a name for herself in promoting spirituality for housekeepers not only in the Grand Rapids Congregation but nationally. Along with Brother Herman Zacarelli, CSC, and Fr. Ken Silvia, CSC, she gave workshops and retreats around the country, becoming one of the first Sisters in the Congregation to take on the preaching identity of the Order. Reflecting on one particular retreat in Santa Rosa, California, Sister Bede humbly recalled, "Ken had given a talk earlier in the morning and I followed him. When I got finished with my talk, the Sisters all followed me out and Ken joked, 'Yes, when you give a talk, all the Sisters follow you out and they want a copy of what you said. I give a talk and nobody cares what I said.'"[31]

Food Service Directors celebrate graduation from Fontbonne College in St. Louis, Missouri (left to right): Srs. Patricia Kennedy, Ann Terrence Wieber, Dolores Stein, Maxine Plamondon, Julia Nellett, Dominica Nellett, and Maureen Sheahan.

Dominican Identity

Sisters also found opportunities for retreat at locations other than the Motherhouse. Primary among these opportunities were the retreats offered by

---

30. S. Bede Frahm, January 31, 2011, Marywood Archives, Folder 2011.194, p. 29.
31. Frahm, p. 29.

the Parable Conference in Chicago, Illinois. According to the website on Dominican life:

> *Parable Conference* was born in 1976 out of dialogue and collaborative thinking from a group of U.S. Dominicans, women and men, who believed that the Order's preaching mission could best be carried forward by uniting their efforts to address the needs of the contemporary church and world. Following in the 800-year-old tradition and spirit of St. Dominic de Guzman, *Parable Conference* worked with the Dominican Family — Laity, Associates, Sisters, Nuns, Friars, and companions in mission — to preach the Gospel.[32]

The Parable model of retreat was a collaborative effort wherein the retreat team consisted of two Friars and two Sisters who would take turns preaching on the Scriptures of the day. Eucharist was celebrated daily and along with the praying of the Office these communal prayer times allowed for ample silence the rest of the day. The shared reflection among retreatants at evening prayer proved to be as inspiring as the preaching itself. Held at Motherhouses and retreat centers across the country, these retreats not only allowed Sisters the opportunity for quality preaching, they also helped to deepen the Congregation's identity within the Dominican Family.

Preaching

In addition to the Dominican Family identity deepening, Sisters were coming to a deeper understanding of their role in the Order of Preachers. Sister Gretchen Sills shared:

> Well, I never considered myself a preacher. Yes, we were teachers in the classroom and yet over the years, you gradually learned that even though you didn't call yourself a preacher, whenever you were in the classroom and you were helping these young people, whoever they were, you were really preaching the Gospel values.[33]

---

32. http://www.domlife.org/2008Stories/ParableClosure.html (accessed March 15, 2012).
33. S. Gretchen Sills, April 20, 2009, Marywood Archives, Folder 2009.0602, p. 75.

In 1975, the Dominican Leadership Conference (DLC) set up a commission to study the relationship of Dominican women to preaching. In its report to the DLC, the commission emphasized that though its task was primarily in regard to Dominican women, its study demonstrated that the issue of preaching was also for all baptized, non-ordained women and men.

Sr. Megan McElroy preaching the Word of God.

> This is not a Dominican issue but a question about the nature of Christian baptism and of being a Christian. Does not the gift of Christian faith include its proclamation? Is there not a universal evangelical charism latent in baptismal grace, which then must be related to the variety of ministries of the community, and to that community's order and leadership? . . . What is argued theologically for Dominican women in terms of preaching is argued *a fortiori* on behalf of other Christians who are not ordained priests or deacons yet endowed by nature, charism and preparation for this ministry.[34]

The issue of preaching was for all baptized, non-ordained women and men.

Using theological, historical, and ecclesiological hermeneutics (interpretations), the study determined that women had had a share in the preaching mission of the Church to varying degrees, though their voices were often silenced. Noting the contributions of women in society and the Church, especially in the twentieth century, and that "The approval towards the end of the nineteenth century[35] by the Master of Rome [reference to the Master General of the Dominican Order whose office is at Santa Sabina in Rome] of the Sisters of Third Order Congregations to use the designation 'O.P.' instead

Women had had a share in the preaching mission of the Church — though their voices were often silenced.

---

34. Dominican Leadership Conference, "Unless They Be Sent: A Theological Report on Dominican Women Preaching," November 1977, p. 2.
35. The actual date for the change from OSD to OP was 1927.

of 'O.S.D.' may have been a sign of a new event in the Dominican family,"[36] the commission acknowledged:

> We look to the Church to expand its understanding of the nature of preaching, to accept more deeply the baptismal priesthood of Christian men and women. Similarly, Dominicans can look to the members and leaders of the Order to reflect upon the possibility that the nature of the Dominican life is disclosing itself in new ways. The relationship of men and women in the Dominican family will not remain the same. There has come the collective call to Dominican women not only for ministry (for they have been *de facto* in the ministerial life of the church for a long time), but to preaching and to public confirmation of their ministry. [In] the Order of Dominic, the general mission of preaching has remained the same, but its realization in the members of the Dominican family is expanding because the social and psychological dimensions of our time encourage that alteration.
>
> We are at the edge now of a new work, one which will offer Dominican women the opportunity to exercise fully that charism which is the source and meaning of the Order's existence and its particular grace. The full flowering of the Dominican charism and its extension to all who have received the call to preach can express in a new way the saving action of the Word which has become Flesh for us, and who has already announced the Lord's Year of Favor.[37]

The commission concluded its report with a desired hope that the Church would

> ... grow in the Spirit by allowing more Christians to exercise that charism of speaking publicly in the community. Women, Dominican women as well as others, today find themselves called by nature and grace to preaching because of the liberating opportunities, which their society offers them and because of the inner dynamic of their own Religious communities. This is a good cause for the Dominican Family to support. The Christian

---

"We are at the edge of a new work, one which will offer Dominican women the opportunity to exercise fully that charism which is the source and meaning of the Order's existence and its particular grace." The Dominican Leadership Conference

"Today, Dominican women find themselves called by nature and grace to preaching." The Dominican Leadership Conference

---

36. DLC Proceedings, p. 8.
37. DLC.

women preaching is emerging both as a voice in the world and as a gift of the Church.[38]

With such encouragement from the DLC (Dominican Leadership Conference), Dominican Sisters began to lay claim more fully to the preaching charism of the Order. The Parable Conference retreats gave Sisters the opportunity to exercise the ministry of preaching in collaboration with the Friars at Motherhouses, retreat centers, and other ministerial locations.

For the Sisters in Grand Rapids, the Living the Word retreats, commonly referred to as the Constitution retreats, gave ample opportunity for many Sisters to engage actively in the preaching. Sister Teresa Houlihan recalled:

> The revised *Constitution and Statutes* were ready to send to Rome as the work of many committees, and all revisions and consultations had been completed. We, the Council, wanted the Congregation to "own these documents." Making a retreat based on the *Parable* model and our newly minted *Constitution and Statutes,* led by teams of our own women seemed to have merit.[39]

Sr. Carmelita Murphy, Co-Director of Parable Conference

Sister Carmelita Murphy recalled, "Inviting Sisters to preach was not casually done."[40] Sisters with a background in Scripture, theology, spiritual direction, and the capacity to preach were invited to be the retreat leaders. The first retreats were held in the summer of 1986, and the congregational mailing of August, 1986, reflected:

> A sentiment that describes something of the spirit of the two hundred twenty-eight women who participated [thus far] in the *Living the Word* (Constitution) Retreat is, "God is doing something new in our midst!" A particular joy for many was the preaching charism evident in the retreat team members and in the retreat participants. The preaching of our Sis-

"God is doing something new in our midst!"

---

38. DLC, p. 11.
39. S. Teresa Houlihan, e-mail, February 27, 2012.
40. Conversation with S. Carmelita Murphy, April 7, 2012.

ters was blessed and the daily faith sharing of the retreatants built up the community.[41]

In reflecting on her experience of the Constitution retreats, Sister Gretchen Sills stated, "I remember the Constitution retreat that we had with Phyllis Ohren and Suzanne Eichhorn. That was the best retreat! I had those tapes, and I would listen to them. I wore the tapes out listening to those afterwards because they were just exceptional on the vows."[42]

Sisters were encouraged to take homiletics courses wherever they were offered to hone their preaching skills. Several Sisters took advantage of the Preaching Certificate program that was offered at Aquinas Institute in St. Louis; and once the novitiate was relocated to St. Louis, several of the novices would take the Foundations of Preaching course also at Aquinas Institute. All returned from their experiences with a passion for the preaching mission of the Order. The Congregation, too, offered opportunities for Sisters to develop their preaching charism. In the fall of 1987, Sister Carmelita Murphy and Father Greg Heille, OP, offered an eight-week course on preaching at Aquinas College.[43] During the annual study days in 1995, a workshop was offered by Sister Cathy Hilkert, OP (Akron Dominicans, now Sisters of Peace), and Father Jude Siciliano, OP (St. Martin de Porres, Southern Province of Dominican Friars), entitled *Enkindled by the Word: Dominican Life Formed by the Word*. They encouraged Sisters to become so identified with being a preacher that when asked, "Who are you?" their automatic response would be, "Sister N., preacher."

Though many in the church hierarchy were reluctant to allow non-ordained women and men to preach, Bishop Ken Untener, Bishop of the Saginaw Diocese where many of the Sisters served, welcomed and encouraged the opportunity. Sister Mary Ellen McDonald served in the Saginaw Diocese for over twenty-four years in parishes where no priest was available to serve as pastor. In recalling her experience, she shared:

> Bishop Untener felt very strongly that the church should hear the voices of women. But he was also very firm on the need to be trained first and he

---

41. *News 'n Notes,* vol. 1, no. 8 (August 1986) Dominican Sisters, Grand Rapids.
42. S. Gretchen Sills, Oral History, Marywood Archives, p. 15.
43. Conversation with S. Carmelita Murphy, April 7, 2012.

offered workshops and classes in this area given by himself and by bringing in professors from seminaries, etc. Bishop Untener told us we were expected to preach at the weekend Masses. We shared this with the sacramental ministers (priests) who were assigned to preside at Mass and the sacraments.... Some would prefer a priest whether he had the gift of preaching or not. Many people (men and women) were very grateful and affirming for the voice of women at liturgies.[44]

> Some would prefer a priest whether he had the gift of preaching or not. Many people (men and women) were very grateful and affirming for the voice of women at liturgies.

* * *

As members of the Church responded to the call of Vatican II to be a pilgrim people on the path of holiness, the style, manner, and language of prayer changed for the Sisters as well as the laity generally. Less prescriptive, more personal, spoken in the mother tongue, prayer became a more intimate experience of God. The emotions of the individual were acknowledged through dance or styles such as that of the Charismatic movement. It was only a matter of time before the physical space of liturgy would be changed to reflect the newer forms of worship.

Sr. Lupe Silva proclaims the Word of God.

Sr. Barbara Hansen preaches the Word of God.

---

44. S. Mary Ellen McDonald, e-mail communication, March 19, 2012.

Dominicans at Prayer

*From the rising of the sun to its setting,
let the name of the Lord be praised.*

PSALM 113:3

RUMOR HAS IT that St. Dominic prayed so long and so loud well into the night that he sometimes frightened the brethren who were awakened by the loud sounds coming from the chapel. There is no doubt that prayer is an essential principle of the Dominican Order. From its foundation in the thirteenth century to its multitudinous manifestations throughout the world in subsequent times, prayer is at the core of Dominican life.

Prayer is at the core of Dominican life.

Over the centuries, Dominicans have stamped their prayer life with four particular emphases. First, Dominican prayer is *ecclesial*, which is to say, aligned with the official Church. Yet it is innovative in its ability to hold the tension between continuity with tradition and adaptation for the purpose of preaching the Gospel. Second, Dominicans at prayer are *incarnational*; they recognize the human body is not to be disregarded, but rather incorporated into daily prayer. Third, Dominican prayer is remarkably *cognizant of women's ways* of knowing and praying. Fourth, Dominicans at prayer have maintained a *loyalty* to Dominican feasts, saints, and special devotions such as the rosary and remembering the deceased members of the Order.

Dominicans at Prayer

Dominican Prayer Is Ecclesial, Yet Innovative

Dominic's early experience as a canon regular of the Cathedral of Osma in Spain was that of a monk in the late twelfth century. He prayed the Divine Office daily and spent a great deal of time in solitude and contemplation.[1] As an ordained priest he frequently celebrated the liturgy of Eucharist. Moreover, Dominic knew that the power of Scripture was a key to the truth of God's care for humanity, especially when preached well. It was his specific innovation and the specific charism of the Order he founded to preach the Gospel to all peoples, and to do that exceedingly well in both word and action, especially for those who had been led astray by the divisive heresies of his age. The signs of the times in the thirteenth century propelled Dominic to found a Religious Order marked by adaptation and flexibility to meet the needs of that day.

Holy Cross Convent in the city of Regensburg, Bavarian Region of Germany, is the foundation for twelve U.S. Congregations, including the Dominican Sisters ~ Grand Rapids, Michigan.

This spirit of adaptation for the sake of ministry was observed in the nineteenth century when the Sisters arrived in the United States from Bavaria where they had lived a cloistered monastic life. There they had followed the custom of their day in the recitation of the Divine Office, as did all nuns living an enclosed life of solitude, prayer, silence, and contemplation. However, those customs could not long persist given the transatlantic voyages to the mission territory of America in the nineteenth century.[2] For many groups of Dominican Sisters whose teaching and apostolic responsibilities were increasing, the lengthy time needed for the choral chanting of the Divine Office soon necessitated its replacement with the shorter prayer known as the Little Office of the Blessed Virgin Mary. For the Grand Rapids Dominicans this change took place in 1894, seventeen years after their arrival in Michigan from New York and two years after the legal incorporation as the Sisters of the Order of St. Dominic in Grand Rapids. In addition to the

---

1. See M. H. Vicaire, *Saint Dominic and His Times* (New York: McGraw-Hill, 1964), for details about Dominic's life. Chapter 3 describes the young Dominic: "Dominic always found both strength and joy in the recitation of the canonical office . . ." (p. 43).

2. N.B. Not all Congregations of Dominican Sisters derived from European foundations. Those founded in America, however, were influenced by the monastic customs of the European tradition.

shorter Office, the Sisters continued morning meditation in common as well as a number of devotional customs, such as specific prayers before meals, prayers for the dead, the daily recitation of the AA rosary, a monthly Sunday retreat day, and weekly Sunday processions.

About seven decades later, adaptation and flexibility were called for again, this time by the documents of Vatican Council II. Soon after its close, the Sisters met in Chapter, not to elect a Prioress and Council, but rather to deliberate on their lives together and begin the renewal mandated by that Council. As a result of this seminal Chapter in 1969, *Religious Life: A Lived Reality* was published. A shift is evident in the expression of prayer from one of recitation of prescribed prayers to be read, chanted, or recited from memory to that of a personal experience of God. As stated in the newly written document, "Prayer is a meeting with God, an experience of God."[3] The venue of prayer was expanded to explicitly include: "community life, personal encounter with others, the world of human events, and reflection in solitude." At the same time solidarity with the Church was guarded by the stated affirmation that "prayer life revolves around the Eucharist and the Divine Office."[4]

The Sisters, desiring to be faithful to the traditions of the Church and responding to the directives of Vatican Council II to return to the spirit of the founder and to read the signs of the times, realized a similar need to be innovative in their prayer life as increasingly diversified ministries proved to be a challenge to a common schedule of prayer.

The principles regarding prayer were affirmed and two more were added at the Sixteenth General Chapter in 1972. First, the concept of prayer as mission was emphasized. In the words of the proposal: "We live in a world of suffering people; we are faced with the issues of dehumanization and injustice. Therefore, our personal and community prayer are united with the pain and suffering of the Body of Christ."[5] The second principle treated the custom of remembering those who had died.

The following is taken from the proceedings of that Chapter:

> **"Prayer is a meeting with God, an experience of God."**
> *Religious Life: Lived Reality*

> **"Our personal and community prayer are united with the pain and suffering of the Body of Christ."**
> *Religious Life: Lived Reality*

---

3. *Religious Life: Lived Reality,* vol. 1, p. 71.
4. *Religious Life: Lived Reality,* vol. 1, p. 73.
5. *Religious Life: Lived Reality,* vol. 2, p. 7.

> Shared prayer and worship is (sic) an essential element of living corporately in that we become more like the first Christian community, a fervent, joyous community, united in heart and soul with the whole Christ, supporting each other daily in our common pilgrimage and in our various apostolates. Just as the individual sister must discover and develop her own best rhythm of prayer, so together the Sisters of each local community must search for and work out a program of prayer and worship best suited to their needs and the demands of their apostolate.[6]

Open to experimentation in prayer and schedule, the Sisters affirmed that "since prayer revolves around the Liturgy of Hours and the Liturgy of Eucharist, we encourage participation and creativity on the part of the individual members and local communities in planning meaningful liturgies which are in basic solidarity with the Church," and "that opportunities for varied experiences in contemporary forms of communal prayer be made available to the Sisters."[7]

Now these many years later, the Sisters celebrate their tradition of prayer with a renewed focus on its two communal and ecclesial anchors, the Liturgy of the Hours and the Liturgy of the Eucharist — both sources of growth for celebration, community, mission, and personal conversion. As in Dominic's day adaptation is needed for the sake of preaching the Gospel. Then and now, time and energy are limited commodities for everyone.

Dominic too recognized the need for economy of time and energy for his Friars. The story is told that he urged his men to pray "fortiter, frates" and to sing "breviter et succincte,"[8] which is to say: pray strongly, briskly and without a lot of additional words. He did not want them to be lingering so long at prayer that they did not get to the study and apostolic work which was the purpose of the Order. In like manner, Sisters in the twenty-first century began to experiment with modes, times, and manner of prayer which would suit their new ministries with varied schedules, evening meetings, travel, and demands on time and energy. Today Morning and Evening prayers are

---

6. *Religious Life: Lived Reality*, vol. 2, p. 4.
7. *Religious Life: Lived Reality*, vol. 2, pp. 4-5.
8. David F. Wright, OP, in *Dominicans at Prayer* (Dominican Liturgical Commission. Parable Conference for Dominican Life and Mission, 1983), p. 15.

chanted daily at the Motherhouse and in some form wherever groups of Sisters live. This prayer includes preaching or reflection on the Gospel prescribed for the day. The specifics of the prayers of the Office designated by the official Dominican Ordo are sent out each month for Sisters' use wherever they are living. Sisters living together schedule Morning and Evening Prayer at times that work for them in their daily lives. Some of the Sisters at the Motherhouse pray the Rosary together daily and it is always prayed communally as one of the rituals at the time of the death of a Sister.

Dominican Sisters have reclaimed their original charism to be preachers of the Gospel; to that end, they have reinvigorated their study and contemplation of Scripture, and many have relinquished some of the devotional practices of the past. And in their prayer, the Sisters continued the Dominican tradition of engaging the body, mind, and spirit through words, bowing, kneeling, processions, and gestures that served to involve the whole person, thus relating to the incarnational reality of the Christian mystery.

Dominic's Prayer Was Incarnational

Dominic involved his whole body in prayer.

No doubt, it was Dominic's study of the Gospel that informed his prayer life with the incarnational reality of the life and death of Jesus. And it was in appreciation of the Incarnation that Dominic involved his whole body in prayer. His successor Blessed Jordan of Saxony described nine postures or gestures Dominic used in his own prayer. These are known as Dominic's Nine Ways of Prayer.[9]

Through the centuries, Dominicans have developed customs that acknowledge the body in worship. Through their choir to choir recitation of the Office and processions, Dominicans recognize the incarnate reality of the other; through ritual gestures of bowing, genuflection, and prostration, Dominicans acknowledge their own incarnation. Once a part of daily prayer, these gestures are now used less often, yet have never entirely disappeared. A new way of recognizing the importance of the body in prayer is the Sisters' willingness to restore liturgical dance and gestures following the reforms of

---

9. John Vidmer, OP, *Praying with the Dominicans* (New York: Paulist Press, 2008). The nine ways of prayer are described on pp. 13-15.

Vatican II. Dominicans pray with their whole being, body and soul, mind and spirit.

During this post-Conciliar time, Sisters were experimenting with various forms of communal prayer, searching for the prayer times and forms that nourished the spirit within and expressed basic solidarity with the Church. These prayer forms included contemporary liturgical or even popular music, poetry, readings from diverse religious sources, as well as the use of psalms, other Scripture passages, and the inclusion of periods of quiet reflection and sharing. Sometimes these communal prayer forms were planned by committees, other times by individual Sisters. They varied in length, often taking longer than the traditional Office. In time the prayer became simpler. For some, traditional bodily rubrics gave way to sitting on floor cushions, listening to Scripture, sharing reflections on the readings, praying a psalm or two, praying aloud for personal or global needs using spontaneous rather than prescribed words.

Dominicans pray with their whole being, body and soul, mind and spirit.

The Welcome of Women

Perhaps it was the influence of his mother, Blessed Jane of Aza, renowned for her generosity and compassion, that led Dominic on the path of recognizing women's potential as powerful partners in prayer and providers of hospitality for the Holy Preaching charism of the Dominican Order. In fact the first organized group of what would become Dominicans was composed of women. In 1206, Bishop Diego and Dominic were instrumental in establishing a convent for women who desired to return to the Catholic faith, having relinquished the Catharist heresy. It was in response to their needs for a safe house that the first foundation was begun near Fanjeaux, France, at a crossroads known then and now as Notre Dame de Prouille.[10] Before his death, Dominic also established convents for Sisters in Madrid and in Rome.

Notre Dame de Prouille, thirteenth-century foundation of the Dominican Nuns in southern France

Further evidence for Dominic's regard for the Sisters is found in his response to the request of Diana d'Andalo of Bologna, Italy, for a convent for

---

10. Vicaire, p. 119.

Sisters. After consulting with the brethren and bringing the matter to prayer, he stated: "It is essential in every way, brethren, to build a house of sisters, even if for that it were necessary to cease constructing ours."[11] Perhaps it was his affirmation of women from the very beginning that gave the Sisters the confidence to pursue an inclusive use of language when that consciousness arose in the general culture of the country in the latter part of the twentieth century.

In the post-Conciliar years, Sisters became more conversant with Scripture, as well as the intentions and purpose of the foundation of the Order itself. Couple this with the rising consciousness of the systematic exclusion of women through the historical record of the centuries of Western civilization and it is no surprise that many women began to resist the use of exclusively male references to God or God's people. Many Sisters longed for prayers that were voiced in an authentic language recognizing the existence of women in the story of salvation, in the Scriptures, and in the Church today.

As women and men studied the Bible, they found women who were decisive and active. And they found that the words and actions of Jesus portrayed an inclusive attitude toward women. Far from passive acceptance, Mary questioned the angel in Luke 1:34 and sang a song of freedom from oppression in the Magnificat (Luke 1:46-55). Mary's cousin Elizabeth found her voice and spoke in contradiction to expectation, naming her son John (John the Baptist) rather than the expected naming after his father. In John's Gospel, readers found Jesus speaking in parables that referenced women's experience. Jesus' parables used images of women baking bread or sweeping the house to find a lost coin, or insisting on justice from the unjust judge — all evidence that Jesus noticed and validated the experience of women. The reality that Mary Magdalene, Joanna, and Mary the mother of James (Luke 24:10) were the first to tell the others about the Resurrection encouraged women to believe that they too could reflect on and share the Word of God with others.

In the United States, the signs of the times clearly indicated that women were becoming more conscious of fairness and the lack thereof in the cultural expectation for gender. It was becoming commonplace to see a woman doctor, lawyer, college professor, bus driver, or police officer. In 1972 Con-

---

11. Vicaire, p. 335.

gress passed Title IX, a law making it illegal to discriminate against girls in schools receiving federal monies. Linguists such as Robin Lakoff[12] began to bring attention to the ways that language usage denotes and reinforces, fairly or not, who has power and status.

The Council of Vatican II had invited experimentation to respond to the signs of the times. So it was that during Advent of 1985, members of the Congregation received an inclusive-language psalter for use in Liturgy of the Hours, accompanied by the following statement:

> We as church women are experiencing an important moment in the Church — a moment in which women and men together are joining in the effort to transform our attitudes regarding the value and personhood of women in the church and in society. This timely affirmation of the dignity of the human person is part of our ministry as women and men of the Order of Preachers.[13]

Meanwhile, a joint commission of the Catholic Bishops' Conference was working toward the publication of an inclusive language liturgical psalter. An interim text was available from the Carmelite Sisters of Indianapolis, Indiana. These Sisters granted permission for the Grand Rapids Dominican Sisters to reprint a limited edition of their copyrighted text. The Sisters used these books, often supplementing them with readings and hymns and Dominican resources at Marywood and in local houses.

The majority of Sisters welcomed the inclusive-language psalter and found praying it a joy and a source of hope for a more permanent volume and, perhaps even more so, for more changes in the official Church's approach to women. They were aware that liturgy shapes consciousness and belief, as the ancient principle, *lex orandi, lex credendi* states — "as we pray, so we believe."

Liturgy shapes consciousness and belief.

An interim innovation in the Liturgy of the Hours occurred in 1992 when, with the herculean effort of the Liturgy Team, a common prayer book of the Liturgy of Hours was produced which used (prior to official publication but with permission) the inclusive language psalter of the International

---

12. Robin Lakoff's work in linguistics brought attention to class, power, gender, and social justice as they intersect with language usage.

13. Letter to the Sisters from the Prioress S. Teresa Houlihan and Council, Advent 1985. Marywood Archives.

Commission on the Use of English in the Liturgy, along with certain Dominican additions.[14] Fr. Greg Heille and Michelle Rego-Reatini worked on its form, compilation, and publication. It was known as the Big Gray Book, and although it was beautifully written the binding was cumbersome to use.

The Big Gray Book was to be the source of common prayer for the next thirteen years; in the introduction the hopes of the writers are expressed:

The interim Office Book, also known as the Big Grey Book: lyrical in translation but a cumbersome binding

> There is perhaps no collection of religious poetry in human history that has had greater influence on worship and prayer than the Book of Psalms. To this end, we endeavor to create a book for Common Prayer that achieves this liturgical accessibility and beauty. It is hoped that this book will serve the needs of this Congregation and those associated with this Congregation as a worthy guide to "full, active participation" in the "Prayer of the Church with Christ."[15]

Given the size, weight, and cumbersome binding of the Big Gray Book, the Sisters hoped this was a temporary edition. They had been through multiple forms of the Liturgy of the Hours and by this time knew many of the things they desired to enhance their praying of the Divine Office.

The time had come for a more permanent solution, not only for the Sisters in Grand Rapids, but for other Dominican congregations of Women Religious in the country. Sister Jan Schlichting, from the Akron Dominican Sisters Congregation, who had completed her degree in liturgy at Notre Dame, called together a Steering Committee consisting of Sisters who were professionals and scholars in the areas of liturgy, theology, Scripture, music, and preaching. After the initial meeting, the desire and need for a common prayer book for Dominican women was clear.

The next step was to include more Congregations and to galvanize re-

---

14. This effort was simultaneous with that of the Dominican men of the St. Albert the Great Central Province. One of their members, Fr. Frank Quinn, OP, participated in the work of the ICEL, whose task, relative to the psalms and canticles, was to "unlock the meaning and power of the original Hebrew for worshippers." Grand Rapids Dominican Sisters, *Common Prayer Book* (1992), p. iii.

15. *Common Prayer Book,* p. iii and p. ii.

sources. In September 1999, the Steering Committee proposed asking Dominican Congregations to send two representatives to a colloquium on August 12 and 13, 2000. Desirable characteristics were that the prayer book be a single volume, inclusive yet consistent with the Church's prayer, easily held, portable for travel, beautiful in language and appearance, with Psalm settings that were easy to sing. They hoped it would reflect both a global perspective and Dominican values, and be paced to allow for contemplation and/or preaching.

The translators based their work on the ancient Greek or Hebrew forms, keeping in mind the literal meaning as well as seeking ways to elegantly express that meaning in contemporary English. Diverse biblical names for God are used throughout the prayer book. The rationale for this practice is explained in the preface of the book, which also captures the six-year process in the realization of the dream:

> *Dominican Praise* grew from a dream of Dominican Sisters from several congregations in the United States that women in the Order would have a book from which to pray that would be ecclesial, Dominican, and contemporary. Its language would be inclusive, and the book itself beautiful and portable. We envisioned a book that would strengthen our solidarity with one another in the Dominican Family, enabling us to pray in common. We imagined a book that would be a sacramental of our Dominican common life and charism.[16]

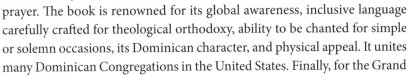

Dominican Praise: A Provisional Book of Prayer for Dominican Women © 2005 is currently used daily by Sisters and Associates and is revered for its beautiful translation and elegant binding.

Many Sisters reported that *Dominican Praise* returned them to praying the Liturgy of the Hours with the Church with greater zeal and on a more regular basis. Associates of the Dominican Sisters throughout the United States also use the book for daily prayer. The book is renowned for its global awareness, inclusive language carefully crafted for theological orthodoxy, ability to be chanted for simple or solemn occasions, its Dominican character, and physical appeal. It unites many Dominican Congregations in the United States. Finally, for the Grand

---

16. *Dominican Praise: A Provisional Book of Prayer for Dominican Women* (2005), p. xii.

Rapids Dominicans, this publication fulfills the need and desire expressed in their Constitution, promulgated in 1990, which states, "Through the Morning and Evening Prayer of the Church, we unite with the whole church in giving praise and thanks to God."[17]

Renewed Tradition of Dominican Prayer

After Vatican Council II, forms of communal devotional prayer, common when Latin was the language of liturgical prayer, waned as the richness of liturgical prayer in English began to take root in the consciousness of Women Religious. The rosary, often a communal prayer in the past, was retained more often as a private devotion. Sisters were encouraged to nurture their prayer life in ways that were fruitful to them as they listened to where the Spirit of God was leading them. There was a renewed awareness of the beauty of creation as a source of meditation and contemplation of the wonders of God. Vatican Council II affirmed the world as the context of the mystery of salvation, and writers began again to name creation, God's first revelation, as mystics had done in the thirteenth century. Awareness of the seasons of the year, always a part of the liturgical cycle, became more pronounced with the rotation of the chapel tapestries according to the liturgical cycles, and the revitalization of ancient practices such as the *O Antiphons.*

The initiation of the *O Antiphons* during the season of Advent reclaimed a traditional liturgical practice, both rich and ecumenical, in its call to deep scriptural and contemplative prayer. These candlelight ceremonies of Evening Prayer with preaching by a variety of Christian believers foster and deepen awareness of the gift for preaching that resides in the local and surrounding community and enhance the prayer of the community gathered. This prayer with preaching and songs of hope-filled prophecy nurtures a contemplative spirit and offers a welcome counterpoint to the frenzy of the prevailing, materialistic holiday culture of the pending Christmas celebrations.

Yet another evolution in prayer is the manner of remembering the deceased. The Office of the Dead and manner of funerals had been long influenced by the medieval emphasis on judgment and suffering, both in this

---

17. *Constitution & Statutes,* #9, p. 5.

> **Sisters felt a renewed awareness of the beauty of creation as a source of meditation and contemplation.**

life and for a time of purgation in the life hereafter. Prior to Vatican Council II, the Sisters had numerous ways of remembering the deceased in prayer. Members who died were entitled to a set of required prayers on their behalf. These included the celebration of Masses once a week and saying the Office of the Dead at the time of the death of a Sister and in general on a weekly basis. The parents and siblings of the Sisters were to be remembered in the Mass, Rosary, and Office.

The devotional practice of praying the Stations of the Cross had included remembering one of the deceased Sisters of the Congregation whose name was randomly drawn from a small wooden box prior to the devotee's walk around the chapel walls pausing at each depiction of a moment in the last hours of Christ before his death. When the theology of Vatican Council II brought a greater emphasis on the Resurrection of Christ and a redeemed humanity and gave less attention to purgatory, such devotions were bound to undergo a transformation.

> **Vatican Council II put more emphasis on the Resurrection of Christ and a redeemed humanity.**

Now a variety of ways to pray for the deceased members of the community was encouraged and the numbers mentality, i.e., quantity of Masses said, number of rosaries prayed, was to be avoided. Sisters were encouraged to plan their own funeral liturgy. No longer would the ancient hymn *Dies Irae (Day of Wrath)* be sung. Now the hymn was more likely to express a joyful flight on eagle's wings, borne on the breath of dawn.[18] It was to be a celebration of thanksgiving and belief in resurrection; it involved the Sister's family of origin where possible. Currently, the celebration of the Sister's life begins with the welcoming of her body and the procession to Chapel. The Office of the Dead is prayed in the morning of the next day and the remembering service in the context of evening prayer is held. During this service family and friends remember the Sister through storytelling about her life. The following day the Mass of Resurrection is celebrated. During this liturgy the Book of the Gospels is placed on the casket, reminding all that the Sister preached the Gospel with her entire life. As the liturgy concludes, the Sisters, family, and guests gather in the Chapel lobby and outside under the portico as they pray the final prayers of committal and farewell. As the hearse leaves Marywood for burial at Resurrection Cemetery, the *Salve Regina* is sung in

> **During a Sister's funeral liturgy, the Book of the Gospels is placed on the casket, reminding all that she preached the Gospel with her entire life.**

---

18. Michael Joncas, "On Eagle's Wings," is a commonly chosen hymn for funerals.

the manner of the ancient Gregorian chant. All present are then invited to dine together to continue the celebration of thanksgiving for the Sister's life.

The fullness of Dominican prayer is most evident during Congregational gatherings and festivities. Whether these are Area Meetings, Chapter and Assembly meetings, or the annual Dominican Days meetings in early August, the Congregation carefully plans its prayer time together. These prayers always include liturgical expression through the Liturgy of the Eucharist and the Liturgy of the Hours, often with preaching by a member of the Congregation. Years of training have borne fruit in the sound of many voices raised in joyous hymns of praise, whether in simple chant or four-part harmony. The importance of liturgical music and hymnody of excellent quality has been impressed on the hearts and souls of the members through the decades of work by skilled musicians and liturgists. Although other varied forms of prayer have broadened and further enriched the contemplative prayer of the congregation, liturgical prayer remains at its core. Finally, the full strength of identity of the Congregation becomes clearest when gathered in singing.

Jarek Kozal and Sr. Laurena Alflen lead the Sunday Assembly at the Easter Vigil in Dominican Chapel/Marywood.

Dominicans at Prayer

These occasions are marked by a joyous, prayerful energy unified in song while wondrous in diversity.

Overall, during these times of transition, the Sisters grew in their awareness that their relationship with God depended on personal prayer as well as communal prayer and that it was their responsibility to foster both. The commitment to prayer is clear in the Constitution of the Congregation:

> We are an active-contemplative community rooted in the spirituality of the Order of Preachers. Our Dominican tradition of prayer is twofold: liturgical and contemplative. The two primary expressions of our liturgical prayer are the Liturgy of the Eucharist and Liturgy of the Hours. These celebrations unite with the Church's mission to pray unceasingly.
>
> Our prayer life is nurtured and supported by Scripture, reflective reading, solitude and silence. Contemplation strengthens us for ministry, study and common life. We cherish those prayer forms honored by our Dominican heritage.[19]

In broad strokes, these are the marks of the prayer life of the Congregation that have developed over the decades following Vatican Council II, yet adhering to the basic foundational principle of the Dominican Order to "contemplate and to give to others the fruits of that contemplation." Contemplation as an essential starting point, the inevitability of change, justice as the constitutive element of the Gospel, the charism of preaching — all are recognized in the prayerfully wrought statement guiding the Sisters into the future: "Inflamed with contemplative love, we die and are reborn as we walk together preaching justice."[20]

> **The Sisters' relationship with God depended on personal prayer as well as communal prayer, and it was their responsibility to foster both.**

> **"Inflamed with contemplative love, we die and are reborn as we walk together preaching justice."** The Twenty-fourth General Chapter 2012

---

19. #12, pp. 4-5.
20. Direction Statement formulated and affirmed at Twenty-fourth General Chapter 2012.

New Places for Prayer: Chapels — Renovated, New, and Restored

As common prayer and ecclesial experience, liturgy flourishes in a climate of hospitality: a situation in which people are comfortable with one another, either knowing or being introduced to one another; a space in which people are seated together, with mobility, in view of one another as well as the focal points of the rite, involved as participants and not *as spectators.*[1]

PERHAPS THE MOST transformational event for the Congregation in light of the Second Vatican Council was the renovation of the chapel from 1983 to 1985. However, this was not the first attempt at a renovation. "At the time of the congregation's Centennial in 1977, the idea was pursued but insufficient funds prevented [the] undertaking of a major renovation."[2] The idea was reconsidered in 1980, and members of the Congregation were invited to a meeting to discuss plans that had been developed for a possible renovation. Sister Laurena Alflen recollected, "It was all planned how they were going to renovate the chapel, but the Sisters said 'No, we don't want this.'"[3] The Sisters were not ready for it and so the renovation plans were "deferred until further study and consultation could be made."[4]

The 1982 Chapter of Affairs recommended that there be a study regarding

---

1. *Environment and Art in Catholic Worship*, Bishops' Committee on the Liturgy, National Conference of Catholic Bishops, par. 11.

2. S. Aquinas Weber, letter of May 19, 1980 (from Renovation Plan, 1980-1981 box), Marywood Archives.

3. S. Laurena Alflen, January 14, 2010, Marywood Archives, 2010.0295. Revised October 21, 2013.

4. Leadership letter, June 16, 1980, Marywood Archives (Srs. Marjorie Vangsness, Elizabeth Eardley, Aquinas Weber).

the renovation of the Marywood Chapel. The Prioress and Council — Sisters Teresa Houlihan, Phyllis Ohren, and Patrice Konwinski — quickly set about the task and created a Committee on Chapel Renovation.

The Chapel at Marywood prior to the renovation in 1985

We were three people that first term. It was demanding. We thought even though we were looking already to the future and finances, that we wanted to establish spirituality and prayer and liturgy at the heart of what we thought we were, of what we thought who the Sisters are. We still have a great commitment to liturgical prayer. When we come together, we want to sing, we want to pray, we want to hear people preaching, and so we decided we would renovate the chapel.[5]

Adrian Dominican Sisters Barbara Chenicek and Rita Schiltz of INAI Studios in Adrian were hired as the designers of the space. With a combined background in painting, blacksmithing, textiles, pottery, and metalwork, the Sisters' design work was influenced by the 1977 document *Environment and Art in Catholic Worship* published by the United States Bishops' Committee on the Liturgy in 1977. In a letter to the Leadership Team, they explained their vision of design for liturgical space:

It is our experience that most architects work out from past patterns and models of church spaces they have seen, and what they believe "Chapel" is. We believe that the courageous commitment to renewal, to revitalizing space, demands a consideration of furthering the "frontier" of worship space. It is

---

5. S. Teresa Houlihan, Nov. 25, 2008, Oral History, Marywood Archives, p. 6 folder no. 2009.

an opportunity to make better space than we have ever known before; to further advance the experience of ourselves and the Church of our time into understanding and experiencing what it is that we enter into, when we pray.[6]

Education and formation of the Congregation in regards to their work were critical to the INAI artists. It was important for them and the Leadership Team that the Congregation take ownership of the chapel renewal and renovation. Sister Teresa Houlihan recalled the experience:

The Adrian Sisters prepared the Congregation very well — very, very well, right from the beginning. They came at least six times to meet with the whole Congregation. The first time they came they brought slides of their work: What holy spaces are meant to be; what holy spaces looked like in the time of monasticism, in the time of Regensburg, right down to what do they look like now.... everybody said, "Show us. Show us your plan!"[7]

With such enthusiasm, the renovation of the chapel quickly commenced. Prior to the demolition, however, the Congregation celebrated in prayer all that had been and all that would be in the chapel space. In her call to prayer at the ritual entitled "Prayer of Thanks for What Will Be" Sister Jean Milhaupt surfaced memories that the space had witnessed in its celebrations since its opening in 1922. In inviting the Congregation to offer thanks to God for their memories, she also encouraged them, "Let us look forward with expectant faith that the renewed sacred space will give us a 'renewed sense of being women of prayer, women of apostolic spirituality, women of the Gospel.'"[8]

One of the avenues that allowed the Sisters to take ownership of the chapel renovation was in participating in the creation of the seven seasonal tapestries that would hang in the chapel.

---

6. Barbara Chenicek, OP, and Rita Schiltz, OP, letter of August 21, 1982, Marywood Archives.

7. S. Teresa Houlihan, Nov. 25, 2008, Oral History, Marywood Archives, p. 28, folder no. 2009.

8. S. Jean Milhaupt, "Call to Prayer," "DCM — Long Range Planning — Community Chapel Renovation 1983-84," Marywood Archives.

On February 23, 1985, Sisters Barbara and Rita conducted a day-long Stitchery Workshop. The two design servants/masters presented an artistic and practical orientation to perhaps our largest-ever sewing project. Components of each tapestry were laid out. Only their designers and the keen of eye could imagine the finished products. Under the able supervision of Sisters Marge Stein and Aurora Valerio and six other Grand Rapids Dominicans, we continued through May 1985 to bring our individual gifts to this communal project to transform raw materials into seven finished appliqued liturgical tapestries.[9]

In reflecting on the experience, several Sisters shared their insights. Sister Jarrett DeWyse commented, "The energy was palpable. What a marvel this will be — bits and pieces of old vestments, new fabric and thread, one stitch looping over another, all becoming the amazing gift of Pentecost! As each season's tapestry appeared in the chapel, one or other felt the stitches and recalled creating this prayer cloth." Sister Jean Reimer reflected, "Stitching the tapestries seemed a wonderful way to 'take ownership' of the Chapel: even those of us with limited sewing skills could be part. I chose the 'sackcloth and ashes' of Lent. I still love it. It is richly somber-purple, tan, black and brown. A piece of humanity: glorious and not so glorious." Sister Emma Kulhanek added, "I remember spending time with our Sisters stitching the stitches, big or small, crooked or straight. It reminded me of the wonder of community — being together, diversified, accepting and open, just as the stitches were that we worked. I recall it every time I see it in the chapel."[10] It was not until hindsight that the Congregation was able to recognize that the sewing of the tapestries was "a hallmark moment of community building."[11]

> "Spending time with our Sisters, stitching the stitches, big or small, crooked or straight, reminded me of the wonder of community."
> Sister Emma Kulhanek

As the renovation continued, the Council — Sisters Teresa Houlihan, Patrice Konwinski, Carmelita Murphy, and Joan Thomas, elected in 1984 — began the search for a chaplain to serve the Congregation. Recognizing that the renovation was

Dominican Chapel/Marywood: tapestry for Lent

---

9. "Cloths of Heaven: The Liturgical Tapestries of Dominican Chapel/Marywood," *Dominican Futures*, vol. XVI, no. 1, (Winter 2007), p. 4.
10. "Cloths of Heaven," p. 5.
11. "Cloths of Heaven," p. 2.

a new moment in the Congregation's history, they evaluated the needs of the Congregation and campus in terms of ministry and spirituality and consulted with several priests in the area, both Dominican and diocesan, who had a solid understanding of liturgy. What became clear was that the new chapel would be an opportune time to introduce a new way of doing things.[12] Given the Congregation's strong liturgical background, it was also important that whoever was invited to serve would have an understanding of that history. Just having someone, anyone, fill the position would not do. The priests who were consulted also had a similar sense in this assessment.

Fr. Greg Heille, OP, celebrates Eucharist in Dominican Chapel/Marywood.

The search eventually led to the hiring of a liturgical team rather than a chaplain and music minister. As part of their discernment, Father Gregory Heille, OP from the St. Albert the Great Central Province of Dominican Friars, and Sister Virginia Smith from the Sinsinawa Dominicans, attended the tapestry workshop, which gave them an initial introduction to the Sisters, and they met with the Prioress and Council. Father Greg recalled his experience of coming to the decision to come to Grand Rapids: "It was just a moment of big possibility that no one was really quite imagining. They [Prioress and Council] were looking for a part-time chaplain and all of a sudden we were looking at a team of two full-time people and a new chapel full of possibility."[13] In a note she sent to Sister Carmelita shortly after the tapestry workshop, Sister Virginia shared her own enthusiasm:

12. Research Notes, "Gregory Heille, OP, Job Applicant Process, 1985," from File Marywood Archives.
13. Fr. Gregory Heille, OP, in an interview held on October 14, 2011.

Greg and I NEVER stopped talking all the way home! We both laughed right out loud several times when I found myself talking about next year in terms of "when," NOT "if"!!! . . . In my more sane moments, I am even more overwhelmed to think that your Congregation is willing to entrust so much responsibility in that extraordinary worship space to me. Do you honestly believe that I can be stretched enough to develop the superb liturgy which that space deserves?[14]

Sister Virginia's comments reflected the respect she and Fr. Greg had for the Congregation's liturgical history. Father Greg commented:

Sr. Virginia Smith, OP (Sinsinawa), the first liturgist-organist at the renovated Dominican Chapel/Marywood

We were very inspired, very inspired by the liturgical history of the Congregation with Dom Virgil Michel. . . . I had studied at St. John's, Collegeville, and so I was very moved. We all were. We would tell the stories about Virgil Michel, and that inspired us. We didn't think we were *beginning* a tradition; we were very aware that we were *continuing* one.[15]

The chapel renovation was completed by its targeted date of June 30, 1985. Bishop Joseph Breitenbeck celebrated a Rite of Blessing on July 28, which was followed by Mass with Father Greg Heille, presiding. Several Sisters were in attendance then, but the first Congregational celebration in the new chapel

---

14. S. Virginia Smith, OP, in a note to S. Carmelita Murphy dated February 24, 1985. Marywood Archives, Box AR23. Box 2.
15. Fr. Greg Heille, OP, interview on October 14, 2011.

was held during Saint Dominic's Day Weekend, August 3-4, 1985. Sister Teresa Houlihan recollected, "It was the centerpiece of the weekend: a great gathering, so many Sisters, wonderful music (both song and instruments), participation in the ministries and as a member of the assembly, I recall the great joy and enthusiasm for all we, as a Congregation, had brought to completion."[16]

With the opening of Dominican Chapel/Marywood, the transformative impact on the Congregation was only beginning. Early on, there was a sense that not only was the space itself being changed, so was the "lived reality" of the Sisters. The chapel's renovation became a symbol of the continued renewal happening within the Congregation. In an interview with *The Grand Rapids Press*, Sister Teresa Houlihan stated, "Our intention is to welcome persons here, to accommodate them, to be more open. We feel it's time we served the church of Grand Rapids in a new way.... With this chapel, we are inviting the public in, in a whole new way. We are telling the people we are here."[17] Sister Carmelita Murphy affirmed the same thought: "The renovation of the chapel was a symbolic movement from the monastic to apostolic lifestyle. We threw open the doors to the public and welcomed the laity into one of the most intimate

Fr. Greg Heille baptizes Max Maodush-Pitzer at Dominican Chapel/Marywood.

"The renovation of the chapel was a symbolic movement from the monastic to the apostolic life. We wanted to place the heart of our life into the heart of the city." Sister Carmelita Murphy

16. S. Teresa Houlihan, e-mail correspondence, February 27, 2012.
17. Chris Meehan, "A New Moment: Renovated Chapel at Marywood Viewed As a Symbol of Renewal," *The Grand Rapids Press,* September 21, 1985.

New Places for Prayer

Dominican Chapel/Marywood Sunday Assembly Choir

expressions of our life. We wanted to place the heart of our life into the heart of the city."[18]

Their comments mirrored what had been one of the early goals for the renovation stated by Sisters Rita Schiltz and Barbara Chenicek: "The Chapel is *the* center of your Motherhouse space. It will reflect what you are; will draw others to see and experience that."[19] Just as the Second Vatican Council had thrown open the windows of the Church to encounter the world, so the Congregation was throwing open the doors of its most sacred space for others to encounter God.

Once the doors were opened, it did not take long for the neighboring community to discover Dominican Chapel/Marywood. The Congregation made a concerted effort to communicate that the public was welcome. Mass times and other events were published in *The Grand Rapids Press* and the diocesan newspapers. A Sunday Assembly of Sisters and laity soon evolved. Father Greg recalled, "I think a big part of the success of the Sunday assembly was Virginia Smith, who as an excellent musician, went to work very

---

18. Conversation with S. Carmelita Murphy, April 7, 2012.
19. In a letter to the Prioress and Council and the Liturgy Planning Committee, March 28, 1983, Marywood Archives, p. 4, part IV.

Instrumentalists at Dominican Chapel/Marywood Sunday Assembly celebration of Eucharist (left to right): Martha Lesinski, Sr. Mary Navarre, Kim Buchan, Fr. Don Heydens, Sr. Julia Mohr, Susan Engbers

quickly on a choir and that very quickly started drawing lay participation."[20] Though at times it was difficult for some of the Sisters to accept the more social atmosphere in the chapel before Mass was to begin, it became evident that Dominican Chapel/Marywood was a place of refuge for people who needed a place of worship where they felt included and welcomed. Michelle Rego-Reatini commented:

> The Chapel was a place for lay folks who felt dis-enfranchised. . . . There were several married (ex-) priests, people who were gay or lesbian, single people who didn't fit in any particular place, mis-fit Catholics who had felt isolated from the Church. The chapel was a haven for folks who wanted to worship in the Catholic tradition and needed a place where they could evolve and not be "schismatic."[21]

20. Fr. Gregory Heille, OP, interview on October 14, 2011.
21. Michelle Rego-Reatini, in a phone interview on March 14, 2012.

Dominican Chapel/Marywood became a venue where those who felt marginalized in both Church and society encountered the healing presence of Christ in the hospitality and openness of the Sisters.

The opening of Dominican Chapel/Marywood inaugurated *The Year of the Liturgy*, a year of prayer, study, and preaching, which was a collaborative effort between the Grand Rapids Dominican Sisters and the Grand Rapids Diocesan Office of Worship. This collaborative venture was also the impetus for other ecumenical efforts with neighboring faith communities and organizations. The opportunities reflected well the invitation spoken of in the brochure given to guests of Dominican Chapel/Marywood: "a space open to all in quest of peace, a place where God is home."[22] *The Year of the Liturgy* featured such speakers as Mark Searle, Director of the Liturgical Studies Program and faculty member at the University of Notre Dame, and Albert Moraczewski, OP, of the Pope John XXIII Medical-Moral Research and Education Center in Houston, Texas; events such as *A Celebration of Christian Unity Week* and *Gospelfest* in Celebration of Black History Month; and Solemn Evening Prayer celebrations with a variety of preachers from the Congregation and from the ecumenical community.

Dominican Chapel/Marywood open house, 1985

The liturgy team of Father Greg Heille and Sister Virginia Smith made it a point to become actively involved in not only Diocesan events but also in interfaith opportunities and the ecumenical efforts of the Grand Rapids Area Center for Ecumenism (GRACE). Father Greg related:

---

22. *News 'n Notes*, January, 1986, Office of Life Development, Dominican Chapel/Marywood, Marywood Archives.

Marywood was very involved in the activities of GRACE. We also did an annual Thanksgiving service with the Reformed Church next door and the [Greek] Orthodox Church across the street and the Temple [Congregation Ahavas Israel] on Michigan (Street). We had good relationships with Rabbi Albert Lewis at the Temple [Emanuel] on Fulton (Street) and with the pastor of the Lutheran Church on Robinson Road. So there was the neighborhood ecumenism and the GRACE ecumenism. We also created speaking events. John Pawlikowski, OSM, the Holocaust scholar from Chicago, came and dialogued with Rabbi Lewis, things like that.[23]

In 1990 Sister Virginia Smith made the decision to return to parish ministry in Wisconsin, and Michelle Rego-Reatini was hired to fill her position on the liturgy team. Though she was the first non-Woman Religious to hold the position at Marywood, the Sisters were gracious and accommodating. Of her ministry, Father Greg said, "Michelle's huge contribution was musical. It was building on the work that Ginny had done with the choir. We had worked really hard in the Ginny days to acquire the hand bells. Michelle just ran with it, and Michelle worked very hard with me on music, so I was singing more."[24]

Having served nine years with the community, Father Greg decided to leave Dominican Chapel/Marywood in 1994 and return to parish ministry. Father Joseph Vest, a diocesan priest from the Louisville Archdiocese in Kentucky, took over the ministry. After one year, Father Joe discerned he was called back to Louisville as a parish priest, and Michelle Rego-Reatini left the position to raise her son.

With the liturgy team positions open and the very real possibility that there would be no full-time priest to serve the Congregation, the Council — Sisters Barbara Hansen, Ann Walters, Dolorita Martinez, and Lisa Marie Lazio, elected in 1994 — discerned the possibility of creating the position of Coordinator of Liturgical Life. They invited twenty to twenty-five Sisters with experience in pastoral ministry and parish administration to participate in a discernment weekend. What surfaced in reality was the ministry of Co-Directors for Pastoral Life for the Congregation. Sister Diane Zerfas

---

23. Fr. Gregory Heille, OP, interview on October 14, 2011.
24. Fr. Gregory Heille, OP, interview on October 14, 2011.

and Father Paul Colloton, OP, served as the first team.[25] The primary focus of their ministry was the liturgical leadership and pastoral care for the entire campus. However, the ministry was also innovative in that it was a model of collaborative leadership. The experience in the past had been that the priest presided at the sacraments while the woman on the team served in the role of musician. The new style of ministry offered an experience of what collaborative ministry in this role could be. Sister Diane shared:

> The model of ministry we offered gave hope to people about the shared ministry of balancing the masculine and the feminine. . . . The dynamics of the team, I think, emphasized the value of collaboration, the richness that develops when you have the group planning the liturgies (prayers, music, and ritual).[26]

"Our model of ministry gave hope to people about the shared ministry of balancing the masculine and the feminine."
Sister Diane Zerfas

In reflecting on some of the challenges regarding the new style of ministry, Sister Diane commented that the biggest difficulty was that there was little to no precedent for what they were doing, so they often felt like pioneers. Currently, there is no permanent ordained chaplain on the campus. Sister Janet Brown, who is appointed the Director of Liturgical Life, coordinates the services of a rotation of retired priests to celebrate the weekday and Sunday Masses.

The innovations at Dominican Chapel/Marywood harken back many decades to the work of Sisters Estelle Hackett and Jane Marie Murray in the early days of the liturgical renewal in the 1920s and '30s wherein the emphasis on teaching liturgy

---

25. The second team was S. Carmelita Switzer and Fr. Robert Kelly, OP, a Dominican Friar of the Central Province.

26. Phone conversation with S. Diane Zerfas, April 19, 2012.

(Left to right) Associate David Lincoln, Sr. Janet Brown, and Msgr. Gus Ancona assist with the lighting of the Paschal candle for the Easter Vigil.

was participation rather than passive watching. Then as now, liturgy became the "work of the people" as its etymology denotes.²⁷ Sister Diane emphasized how nearly sixty years later, the liturgical ministry of the Congregation continued to teach so that the ritual might come alive in the people. The new model of ministry was a means of continued transformation, for "it took our love of liturgy and made liturgy a part of life."²⁸

Chapel of the Word at the Marywood Health Center

Dominican Chapel/Marywood is not the only formal worship space on campus. With the construction of the Marywood Health Center completed in 2005, a new, beautiful place for worship was created by Sisters Barbara Chenicek, OP, and Rita Schiltz, OP. Unencumbered by preexisting architectural challenges, the two Sister/designers created a new space for worship with tall windows encompassing a view of soaring trees and wetlands — a constant reminder of God's exquisite Creation. Again, every detail was taken into consideration for the Sisters and future visitors including an adjustable ambo for those proclaiming the word from a wheelchair and a clear Plexiglas railing to accommodate the view of those hearing Mass from the balcony. Dominican traditions are evident in the art work which reflects God's Word spoken to us through Creation, through traditions of the Church, and through human interaction, for example, the Annunciation. A stunning wall sculpture depicting the names of the great cloud of witnesses of Dominican women and men graces the south wall. It is aptly named the Chapel of the Word.

The third chapel on Campus is a restored space in the newly renovated

The tourist goes through the land, while the land goes through the pilgrim.

27. From Latin *liturgia*, from ancient Greek λειτουργία, from λειτ-, from λαός ("people") + ουργός, from ἔργον ("work"), the public work of the people done on behalf of the people.
28. S. Diane Zerfas, phone conversation, April 19, 2012.

Aquinata Hall, a long-term, assisted living community. The lovely stained-glass windows were designed by Sister Blanche Steves in 1967 and are as relevant today as they were on the day they were installed. They depict in symbol and word the always timely message of the Beatitudes.

Conclusion

It is said that the tourist and the pilgrim travel the same road; however, the tourist goes through the land while the land goes through the pilgrim.[29] To be the Pilgrim People of God is to be a people on the move, allowing the "land," the life of God, to go through us and to create us into a people after the heart of God. It is the journey of transformation. To be on pilgrimage is to have one's heart and eyes focused on the destination who is God, while being open to the terrain that shapes and molds the traveler.

Since the Second Vatican Council, the experience of the Dominican Sisters of Grand Rapids has demonstrated how they have faith-

Sr. Marie Benedict O'Toole sits in front of the stained glass windows in the Chapel at Aquinata Hall.

---

29. Peter J. Miano, "Pilgrimage or Tourism," *The Society for Biblical Studies Newsletter*, 30 September 2009, http://www.sbsedu.org/L3_e_newsletter30.9.09PilgrimageTourismB.htm (accessed April 14, 2012).

fully embarked on the journey of pilgrimage, of transformation. The prayer life of the Congregation has marked the terrain of the Sisters, both communally and individually. It is what gives life to the other dimensions of being Dominican. Faithfulness to the journey in the midst of the chaos and calm of the life of the Congregation, the Church, and the world over the years has proven to be a witness that continues to provide courage, confidence, and strength for those facing concerns of the day. Responding to the whispering and blowing of the Holy Spirit, the Dominican Sisters of Grand Rapids continue to grow ever more in the holiness to which all are called.

PART II

Study: Essential to Dominican Life

Dominican women and men claim the special place of study in their lives as an essential element since the days of their thirteenth-century founder, St. Dominic, who sent the first brothers, also known as Friars, to the universities advocating for study even if it meant dispensation from community prayer and other monastic practices. In the next century, the most famous Dominican of the Middle Ages and perhaps of all time, Thomas Aquinas, reinforced the importance of the life of study by his commitment to the pursuit of God through both faith and reason.

Where Saint Benedict claimed the motto "Prayer and Work," Dominic, by contrast, promoted the idea that study is a labor in love. That study, however, was never for its own sake but rather it was to be a transformative experience for the head and the heart emboldening Dominicans to preach the truth of God's Word to the whole world. And the truth of God's Word is the truth of God's love for that world. Dominicans study, not to be great intellectuals, but to be preachers of God's truth in love to the world.

In the following chapters, the reader will learn how the Sisters responded both communally and individually to the call of Vatican Council II to study Sacred Scripture, the traditions of their founder, and the signs of the times in order to be faithful daughters of the Church and faithful to the legacy of study as daughters of St. Dominic.

In the chapter "Study Transforms the Community," the story is told of the leadership of the prioresses and their councils. They offered opportunities and encouraged the Sisters to engage in programs and conferences to study liturgy, theology, preparation for ministry, and the writings of leading voices of Vatican Council II such as Cardinal L. J. Suenens and his groundbreaking work, *The Nun in the World*.[1] What followed was a plethora of topics, issues, and direct experiences, including the deep analysis of the documents of Vatican Council II, the emerging understandings in human psychology, etiquette for modern times, contemplative prayer, canon law, and global politics, including liberation theology. Collaboration became the "coin of the realm" as Dominican Sisters across the country shared resources, travel, and expertise. Workshops and committees on current issues kept the Sisters learning, growing and changing to meet the challenges of the new day.

Initial formation and theological and ministerial preparation are the topics of the third and fourth chapters in Part II. Formation in the newcomer's identity as a Dominican Woman Religious is described as it changed through the decades culminating in the existing practice of a collaborative Dominican novitiate, wherein the individual woman learns how to begin her road toward full Dominican life as a member of a specific Congregation as well as a member of the broader national and international family of Dominicans. Ministerial preparation includes both the field of theology as well as other fields of study such as the humanities, sciences, medicine and health care as well as the economics of household management and nutrition.

In the last analysis, the Sisters know that it is not so important what they actually do each day — preparing meals, teaching theology, serving as midwife, praying for peace — but who they are in their relationship to God and each other in truth and in the light of God's Word shining through the Gospel of Jesus. It is for this that the Sisters pray and study each day — an inseparable union intrinsic to their lives as Dominican women in this time as it was 800 years ago when the Dominican story began.

---

1. Leon Joseph Cardinal Suenens, *The Nun in the World: Religious and the Apostolate* (The Newman Press, 1963). Cardinal Suenens challenged apostolic women religious to be open to the changes in the world and to adapt their way of life to serve fearlessly in the modern world.

Study Transforms the Community

Study is an essential component of our Dominican life and mission. It informs our ministry, enriches our common life and is integral to our prayer. We commit ourselves to formal and informal study in order to bring careful consideration to decisions concerning our life and mission.

CONSTITUTION & STATUTES, #17

THE YOUNG SISTER carefully tied an apron around her waist, grabbed a dust mop, and made her way down the hall of the House of Studies. It was a subterfuge on her part. Her destiny was the in-house library — not a cleaning detail. But this was Saturday morning when cleaning had top priority no matter how many papers were due on Monday. Even in the 1960s there was some ambivalence among the Sisters on the importance of study over the maxim that "cleanliness is next to Godliness." Even though Dominicans hold study as a principal feature of the order, for the Sisters, manual labor had replaced that principle in the Middle Ages when education for women beyond the literacy needed to read the Divine Office was seldom pursued. This was true from the earliest years of the Order: "They [the nuns] spin and weave it [the wool] at all the hours when they are not engaged at the Divine Office, and they do so according to ancient custom and the formal order of our father St. Dominic, who willed this so as to drive away idleness, the mother of all vices."[1]

In America, prior to Vatican Council II, Sisters studied for their academic degrees. They also studied approved books on spirituality and theology such

---

1. M. H. Vicaire, *Saint Dominic and His Times* (New York: McGraw-Hill, 1964), p. 129.

STUDY

Young Sisters studying for their bachelor's degrees lived at the House of Studies on Aquinas College Campus.

as Thomas Aquinas's *Summa Theologica*. During meals an appointed lector read from approved books such as the lives of the saints, and once each week the Rule of St. Augustine was read during dinner. Silence was maintained throughout the meals and there was no expectation or opportunity for discussions. Novels, nonfiction, biographies, newspapers, magazines, television, and radio were not available to the Sisters in their formative years during their postulancy and novitiate. The Superior regulated the use of television on the missions. News broadcasts were usually allowed as was access to a newspaper. The convent was considered a stable and sacred place apart from the secular world which was a place of materialism and restlessness in opposition to the "more austere, but happier way of life"[2] found in the

---

2. This phrase taken from the Rule of St. Augustine was often quoted by Sisters after a period of celebration such as Christmas or Easter when the rules for silence and abstinence were relaxed for up to three days.

peaceable monastic way. Most convents and monasteries, influenced by the Rule of St. Benedict, embraced the motto *ora et labora* (prayer and work) in one fashion or another. For Dominicans, the *labora* meant to study; this was always true for the men of the Order, and was becoming more true for the women as they became teachers, nurses, and social workers in America.

The Dominican Penchant for Study

As soon as the Dominican Order formed in southern France in the early years of the thirteenth century, the privileged place of study held sway in the daily life of the Friars. Houses for the men were established in cities like Paris and Bologna where great universities existed. The unusual practice of dispensation was quickly put in place because Dominic and his successors recognized the heavy burden of keeping the rules of the traditional monastic life while at the same time engaging in the itinerant life and assiduous study necessary for preaching the Gospel. The principle of dispensation gave the local Superior the authority to dispense anyone from anything that would "interfere with study, preaching or the good of souls."[3] From its beginning, then, Dominican life was itinerant (on the move, not stable) and geared for "the sake of preaching and the salvation of souls . . . primarily and passionately directed to the goal of being useful to the souls of our neighbour."[4] The overall trajectory throughout the centuries was one of movement away from enclosed monasticism to active apostolic ministry.

Some of this spirit of "on the move" had been dimmed, although never entirely extinguished, in the centuries that followed the foundation of the Order. For women, particularly, the rule of enclosure prohibited movement. Once a convent of Sisters was established, the inhabitants had little opportunity to travel except as missionaries to establish a new convent with the same rules of enclosure. For many Sisters, study was diverted to the pursuit of perfection through attention to minutiae. The degree to which study was focused on details can only seem strange to us today.

An example of this attention to minutiae can be observed in the com-

---

3. Simon Tugwell, OP, *The Nine Ways of Prayer of St. Dominic* (Dublin: Dominican Publications, 1978), p. 47.
4. Tugwell, p. 47.

ments made at a conference held in 1952 for the novice directors of Dominican Sisters' Congregations in the United States. At the conference the speaker reminded the gathered novice directors of the need for "uniformity of Constitutions, uniformity of ceremonials and rituals, uniformity of the habit (clothing), and uniformity in the recitation of the office (official prayer of the Church)."[5] Unity of mind and heart was thought to be realized through uniformity in all aspects of daily life.

After the lecture on ceremonials and rituals, the listeners at the conference asked questions about the number of candles to be used and whether or not the Sisters ought to face the altar when they bowed their heads at the name of Jesus, or maintain the choir to choir position during the head bow.[6]

With the promulgation of the documents of Vatican Council II, this emphasis shifted from one of focus on the perfection of non-essentials to the cultivation of the deepest of Dominican values. By returning to the sources of their lives — Scripture and the Dominican traditions — and by attending to the signs of the times, it became clear that the Sisters' lives were not to be about obsession with perfection, but rather about living life in search of truth as Dominic had done, preaching and teaching the Word of God all along the way.

Dominican Sisters had no hesitancy to immerse themselves in the arduous study and discussions called for by the Council Fathers. Three documents and an official letter were particularly instrumental in the renewal of Religious Life. These were *Lumen Gentium, Gaudium et Spes, Perfectae Caritatis,* and the *moto proprio, Ecclesiae Sanctae* (a special letter written by/approved by a Pope), known as the report of the *Post-Conciliar Commission for Religious.* Together these four texts provided the guidelines for the renewal of Religious Life called for by Vatican Council II. They would each become objects of much study for the Sisters.

> The Sisters' lives were not about obsession with perfection, but rather about living life in search of truth as Dominic had done.

The Local Scene and the Discipline of Study

All over the world, Women and Men Religious took the mandate of Vatican Council II to heart and began to study the documents. Now the story turns

---

5. Proceedings from the conference, Marywood Archives Box, 28.1.
6. Marywood Archives.

to the Grand Rapids Dominicans specifically, and the ways and means this group sought to implement the documents of Vatican Council II and the post-conciliar instructions.

A period of transformation in both daily life and work began. It was characterized by diversity, creativity, social consciousness, and unity of purpose rather than uniformity of manner. The times were unsettling for some, yet rewarding for others.

The ground for this renewal had been well prepared through four happenstances. There may have been other precursors, but these four stand out as specific to the Grand Rapids Dominicans: the liturgical renewal of the late 1920s and early '30s; the study of theology during summer schools, first in Grand Rapids, then at St. Paul Seminary in Saginaw; book discussions on Cardinal Suenens's groundbreaking work, *The Nun in the World*; and the giftedness of elected leaders. All of these set the stage for the intense communal study that began the renewal of the Congregation.

Sr. Jane Marie Murray receives the Alleluia Award; Msgr. Joseph E. Shaw is with her.

The Liturgical Movement and the Writings of Murray and Hackett

A pre–Vatican Council II development in religious education came about in the Grand Rapids Congregation as the result of the enthusiasm of two sisters, Sisters Jane Marie Murray and Estelle Hackett, in the liturgical reform movement headquartered in Collegeville, Minnesota. These two Sisters with the help of a team of Sisters wrote a series of forward-thinking textbooks called the *Christ Life Series,* published by the Macmillan Company in 1935. Unlike the Baltimore Catechism, which was the mainstay of Catholic religious education for decades, these textbooks called for much more involvement on the part of both teacher and students. Rather than memorizing the dogmas and doctrines of the Church, as was the method with the Baltimore Catechism, the *Christ Life Series* had the goal of not only accruing the knowledge of the faith but also of living the faith in a way that affected daily life. This was a method of putting theory into practice, or of *praxis,* long before the concept was developed in the pedagogy of the educational establishment in the decades that followed. And it was a precursor to the reform of the liturgy that came about as a result of the Vatican Council II document *Sacrosanctum Concilium/Constitution on the Sacred Liturgy,* which aimed to achieve greater participation on the part of the laity.

It is no surprise then that meaningful liturgical celebrations have been and continue to be a source of spiritual strength and hope for the Dominican Sisters and Associates[7] as well as a number of Catholics in the environs of Grand Rapids who celebrate Sunday Eucharist at Marywood.

> **Meaningful liturgical celebrations of Sunday Eucharist at Marywood are a source of spiritual strength and hope.**

The Ongoing Formation of Sisters through Study of Theology

Prior to Vatican Council II, Sisters in the United States had begun to upgrade their own academic preparation through the Sister Formation Conference. While sympathetic and supportive of the Conference, the Grand Rapids Dominicans had their own version of higher education for new members through both Aquinas College and a summer school program in theology at St. Paul Seminary in Saginaw, Michigan, with credit from Aquinas College.[8]

Sisters who attended the summer school for theology both in Grand Rapids and at St. Paul Seminary remember studying the *Summa Theologica* of St. Thomas Aquinas until just before the time of Vatican Council II. Then, as one sister recalled, in addition to the *Summa,* they were assigned texts by theologians such as Edward Schillebeeckx, OP, Ladislas Orsy, SJ, John Courtney Murray, SJ, and Karl Rahner, SJ. The priests teaching at the seminary sensed something important had happened at Vatican Council II.

> We were in theology (St. Paul's Seminary, Saginaw Summer Institute). I had graduated with a bachelor's in '62. Then we went off to summer school for the Theology Institute. And in '65, the Vatican Council closed. On graduation day or our last day there the Dominican Fathers (I can't remember which

---

7. Associates are non-vowed women and men connected to the Congregation. See Glossary for fuller definition.
8. Marywood Archives, Box 28.1.

Professors and Sister students at St. Paul Seminary Institute of Theological Study in Saginaw, Michigan

one) said, "I think this might turn out to have been an historic Council. We really should have you filled in on it before you leave this theology program. So tomorrow we will have a two hour lecture/explanation of the Vatican Council before you finish." And so we did.[9]

> "I think Vatican Council II might turn out to have been historic."
> A Dominican Father

The schedule of course offerings at the Institute of Sacred Theology in Saginaw expanded considerably in the summers that followed the Council. They now included Old Testament, Religious Education, Living Faith, Christian Freedom, the Church, Sociology and Anthropology in Religious Education, Role of Arts in Religious Education, and Christ in the Gospels. Where once the only text required was the *Summa Theologica,* the primary texts required in 1968 were the Bible and the Documents of Vatican Council II.[10]

The long-studied *Summa,* the masterpiece of St. Thomas Aquinas in the thirteenth century, with its exhaustive compendium of medieval philosophy, science, and theology, no longer held the primary place in the curriculum — to the delight of some[11] and the dismay of others.

---

9. S. Nancy Malburg, Oral History, July 29, 2009, Marywood Archives.
10. As found on a 1968 brochure advertising the program. Marywood Archives, Box 28.1.
11. In table conversation April 3, 2013, Sister Angelina Abeyta recalled her study of the *Summa* and wondering at the time how God could be so complicated.

STUDY

Cardinal Suenens' *The Nun in the World*

Before the close of Vatican Council II, a group of Sisters teaching at Aquinas College had begun to study the book by Cardinal Suenens, *The Nun in the World*. One of those Sisters recalls the occasion of how and why this study happened the way it did as well as the ramifications.

Sister Marjorie Vangsness, the Superior at the college convent, recalls the event as if it were yesterday although it was 1963:

> All of us read it [Cardinal Suenens's book, *The Nun in the World*] and were impressed by it. I wished we could do something with it. That was before the days of faith sharing and group meetings. Shaking in my boots, I proposed to the Sisters that we meet together to discuss this article. I further proposed that we draw a name from a hat as to which one of us would lead the discussion. The suggestion was accepted and one Sister's name was drawn. Since Sister Bertrand was very hard of hearing, we proposed having the meeting in the fireplace room down on the lower level of Holmdene where we lived. There the twenty-eight of us would be closer together, and all could hear. As we went down the stairs the Sister who was to lead was weeping. I said, "Sister, you don't have to do this if you prefer not to." "No, no," she said, "I will do it." And she did and did it very well. We had agreed that I would call time at the end of an hour, so the discussion would not go on forever.
>
> We surprised ourselves. We had a very good discussion and when the hour was up; all agreed that we should do this weekly.[12]

There followed years of weekly discussions. Sister Marjorie noted that two Sisters who chose not to participate set chairs near to the discussion group so that they could hear what went on. She also noted that in the months following the weekly discussion, Sisters seemed to be freer to bring up any topic to talk about among themselves with greater freedom. She also noted that Sisters began to be more verbal at faculty meetings at the college. Where once there was an unspoken rule that Sisters would say very little and always defer to the Superior and never publicly disagree with one another,

---

12. S. Marjorie Vangsness, "Memories of My Years in Office." Unpublished, Marywood Archives.

now they could stand and express an opinion with courtesy and respect even though another Sister might disagree.

Foresight and Courage in Leadership: Mother Victor Flannery and Sister Aquinas Weber

In 1964 in her sixteenth year of leadership Mother Victor wrote to the Sisters:

> The rapid changes and continued progress of our times will take extreme poverty of spirit not to cling too much to the past. The present is our challenge and we must meet it as Dominic would were he here today! In short, Sisters, what you and I must do today to be witnesses to Christ in the world is: Find Dominic's tune for this nuclear space age; find what our witness needs to be and then adapt and translate Dominic's tune to these needs.[13]

"Find Dominic's tune for this nuclear space age." Mother Victor

Before she left office two years later, Mother Victor, embracing the spirit of collegiality that must have seemed foreign to one who had lived most of her life in a time and in an institution which was strictly hierarchical, asked the Sisters to submit suggestions for the revision of the Congregational Constitution. In the past, Sisters had been asked to submit proposals and concerns for General Chapters; this was an entirely new idea. The effect was electric. Some ninety percent of the Sisters responded with ideas and almost all Sisters felt ownership in the decades-long quest that lay ahead — the revision of the *Constitution and Statutes* in keeping with the spirit of Vatican Council II.

The successor to Mother Victor was chosen in 1966. Sister Aquinas Weber had been marked for leadership from an early age and was currently serving as superior (head) of the House of Studies for young Sisters newly professed and furthering their studies at Aquinas College before being sent out to the missions. Having entered in 1944 from the small village of Hannah, in northern Michigan, Sister Aquinas[14] could not have fully known what lay ahead of her and the Congregation, yet she sensed change as she assumed her role as Prioress of the Congregation.

---

13. Mother Victor Flannery, Circular Letter, 1964, October Feast of SS. Simon and Jude, n.p.
14. After one year as Prioress, Sister Aquinas signed her letters as Sister rather than Mother.

In her opening address to the first Chapter of Affairs (1969)[15] Sister Aquinas accurately read both the spirit of the times and the spirit of the Congregation:

Dominican Sisters House of Studies, a residence for Sisters on Aquinas College Campus

> The winds of modern change have been swirling around us and at some points have left many people breathless, sometimes anxious, sometimes apprehensive. But it must be remembered that the winds of change that have been blowing have not been generated by men, but by the Holy Spirit.
>
> For the past two years we have been preparing for this day and through pre-Chapter preparations we have expressed our ideas and views in an intelligent and open manner. The materials and proposals drawn up by the various commissions and houses constitute a call to action; otherwise they are merely words on a printed page.[16]

Conscious of the seriousness of the task ahead, Sister Aquinas further stated:

> All of us realize that the renewal of a Religious Community is serious and perilous work — one which involves much faith, hope, and trust, but one which is not without its risks. While the Church enjoys a divine guarantee of indefectibility, a religious order does not have such assurance. . . . We are mindful that first and foremost the starting point for renewal must be the Gospel. The charism of the founder also enters into the works of renewal —

---

15. The term given to a Chapter called to address the business of the Congregation, but not to elect new leadership.
16. *Religious Life: Lived Reality* (1969), p. iv.

a charism which must be measured against the Gospel before it can serve as a criterion of renewal. . . . current practices of the Congregation must be judged and remodeled against Gospel values and the truly evangelical insights of the founder.[17]

Sr. Aquinas Weber, Prioress, 1966-72

Clearly, Sister Aquinas had studied the documents of Vatican Council II, especially the one related specifically to Religious Life, *Perfectae Caritatis.* She would now, along with her Council, guide the membership through the study and period of experimentation that would follow. Her hand was a steady one on the wheel of the ship that would now navigate unknown waters. With the Gospel in one hand and the traditions of the Dominican Order and the daily newspaper in the other hand, Sister Aquinas guided the Congregation through the storms of change with resolve and calm. If she was anxious, it never showed. Gospel values and the insights of our founder would be her guide. And she did not falter.

Prepared through the liturgical renewal begun in the late 1920s and promoted through the Sisters who wrote the *Christ Life Series,* attuned to theology through the summer schools at St. Paul's Seminary, guided by the foresight of two prioresses bridging the Vatican Council II years — the Sisters began what would be decades of intense study and experimentation.

---

17. *Religious Life: Lived Reality,* pp. iv, v.

Into a Period of Intense Study and Personal Renewal

Our Dominican vocation calls us individually and communally to a life-long commitment to disciplined and faithful study.
CONSTITUTION & STATUTES, #19

THERE MIGHT HAVE been a loud crashing sound, or bells, whistles, or announcements of one kind or another when the decade known as the Sixties came into time's relentless chronology. But there was not much sound at all to mark this momentous decade; and there was little sound at all when the Bishops of the Roman Catholic Church went home from the meeting of Vatican Council II; it was quiet when Pope Paul VI published a *moto proprio (Ecclesiae Sanctae)* to aid Women and Men Religious in implementing the Vatican Council II document specific to Religious Life, *Perfectae Caritatis*. The silence was deafening; yet much would change and quickly.

It is difficult to find a copy of the 1966 paperback book edited by Walter M. Abbott and translated by Joseph Gallagher containing the sixteen documents of Vatican Council II. If the searcher is lucky enough to find a copy of the book owned by a Sister, chances are that it will show the signs of much use. The brittle and yellowed pages will be underlined and dog-eared. It will be evident that this is a book that has been studied over and over again. Three individual sections will be found to be more worn than others. These are *Lumen Gentium, Gaudium et Spes,* and *Perfectae Caritatis*. Why these three?

Into a Period of Intense Study and Personal Renewal

Lumen Gentium, also known as the *Dogmatic Constitution on the Church,* made the remarkable statement that all are called to holiness by reason of their Baptism. The pursuit of holiness was no longer reserved to the ordained or those who took vows in Religious Life. The distinction was not lost on Sisters who had worked hand in hand with the laity and knew firsthand of their generosity and goodness. They knew very well the self-sacrifice and holiness of women and men who parented the children they taught. Most Sisters had no difficulty claiming this new notion of the laity as "priestly people." Many Sisters held no regret for losing a special status as uniquely called to holiness through their vows. Most Sisters gladly relinquished the metaphor of their status as the *Sponsa Christi* or "bride of Christ" for a more contemporary one of a pilgrim people on their journey with so many others toward the building up of the kingdom of God. For most, this new teaching resonated with personal lived experience.

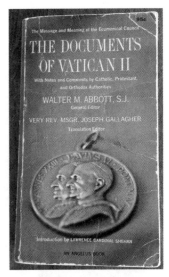

Documents of Vatican II, edited by Walter M. Abbott, SJ, 1966

The second well-thumbed document is *Gaudium et Spes,* also known as the *Pastoral Constitution on the Church in the Modern World.* One need not go beyond the first sentence to recognize the pastoral tone of this last document to be promulgated by the Council. It states:

> The joys and the hopes, the griefs and the anxieties of the men [sic] of this age, especially those who are poor or in any way afflicted, these are the joys and hopes, the griefs and anxieties of the followers of Christ.[1]

"The joys and hopes, the griefs and the anxieties of this age are those of the followers of Christ."
Gaudiam et Spes

The split between the sacred and secular, the dualism between daily life and religion was diminished, if not obliterated, in this remarkable document. And the Sisters who had come from and worked with families of ordinary Catholics and non-Catholics alike in schools, hospitals, and social service identified with this statement and could only nod a heartfelt, "Yes! This sounds right to us."

The third document that was well-studied by Women Religious is known

---

1. Documents of Vatican II retrieved from Vatican website: http://www.vatican.va/archive/hist_councils/ii_vatican_council/.

as *Perfectae Caritatis* or the *Decree on the Renewal of Religious Life*. This document called for Religious to renew by adapting to modern conditions, i.e., *aggiornamento*, while also remaining faithful to the purpose and insights of both Sacred Scripture and their founders, i.e., *ressourcement* — a return to the sources. Furthermore, and this notion was revolutionary, they were to accomplish this renewal in collaboration with all members of their congregations and/or institutes. This notion of both collegiality and subsidiarity was distinctly modern. This renewal involving all the members would happen through General Chapters and Chapters of Affairs (called for business, not elections).

Meetings became a constant reality (left to right): Srs. Marybride Ryan, Barbara Hansen, and Sandra Delgado

This intense study would need to take place during the summer months when teaching Sisters (the majority of members) were not required to be in school. Thus began a series of summer institutes, workshops, presentations, seminars, and, in some cases, graduate education.

What was it like for those in the process of this re-education? Some describe the times as an unfolding of a beautiful flower, of joy in the anticipation of what could happen, of hope in the promise of what could come.

For others it was all happening too fast; there was fear of what might be lost and fear of a capitulation to the modern era which was viewed by some as more psychology than theology. One sister reflected back to 1970 when she was participating in a summer program at Aquinas College designed for updating the Sisters. She recalls:

The modern era was viewed as more psychology than theology.

> I remember as it was going on, I could tell that what we were learning and hearing was getting scarier. I could tell Sister L. was afraid, "Oh, oh. We're going too far." But we needed that. It was really a push forward. People were speaking future-wise of the growth, of the true message of Vatican Council II, of renewal of us. I felt as though it was very challenging. I think it was

four weeks but maybe it was only two. It had a wide range of speakers and some very fine ones that made you stop and evaluate, "What is this Religious Life about?" . . . It was a wonderful time but you also didn't quite know what was happening. It was challenging.[2]

In the years between 1969 and 1979 the community held ten Chapter sessions and sponsored innumerable workshops, seminars, institutes, presentations, and studies, too many for detailed listing here. The following paragraphs describe a few of these with comments from those who participated at the time.

Chapter of Affairs from June 20 to July 25, 1969

A harbinger of change to come occurred prior to the first post-Conciliar Chapter of Affairs held in 1969. Sister Aquinas enlisted a facilitator, Brother William Quinn, FSC, who offered a four-day pre-Chapter workshop for delegates in May of that year. It was the beginning of the era known for its use of newsprint and group process. Brother Quinn engaged the delegates in small group brainstorming on futuristic speculation about the world, the church, and the community. Using poster-sized newsprint pages, small groups listed their vision of the three arenas from three different time spans — ten years ago, the present, and ten years into the future. The results were electrifying for the participants. In basic principles the groups were very much in agreement; differences, where they existed, were in minor affairs. Without negating the old definition and purpose of Religious Life, "to save our own souls and the souls of others," the delegates articulated a contemporary definition of Religious Life based on their own experiences of living it. "Religious life is a loving community of free consecrated persons sharing their lives, their worship, their service and their celibacy."[3]

Thus galvanized and hopeful, the delegates were ready for the first of ten sessions of Chapter in the decade that followed. At the close of the first

---

2. S. Jean Marie Birkman, Oral History, January 2011, Marywood Archives.
3. Group Dynamics Workshop for Chapter Delegates at House of Studies May 8-11, 1969, with Bro. William Quinn, FSC, and Bro. Richard Neville, FSC, Marywood Archives, Box 28.1.

STUDY

More meetings (left to right): Srs. Eileen Popp, Aurora Valerio, and Ann Porter

session, the delegates published the remarkable document known as *Religious Life: Lived Reality*. The title is significant as it marks the shift from the notion of Religious Life as the pursuit of perfection, immutable throughout the centuries, to a dynamic living of life in the here and now — God's Word revealed in Scripture, the great tradition of the Church in one hand and the needs and reality of contemporary life in the other hand.

Study and More Study

Sensing that change was in the air and dedicated to the discipline of study, the Congregation continued to offer workshops immediately following Vatican Council II with its call for *aggiornamento,* i.e., "bringing up to date."

Vatican Council II closed on December 8, 1965. August 1-3 of the next year, 1966, the Congregation sponsored a workshop for the Sisters. "Fulfillment of Feminine Personality in the Religious Life" was offered by doctor and psychologist Robert McAllister, PhD, MD. The insights of modern psychology are evident in the notes taken by Sr. Thomas Marie McGee, one of the participants. Thus began the renewal that recognized and adapted to the modern world and its acknowledgment of the needs of every human for a balanced life. In her notes, we observe the shifts by what is said, left unsaid, and by what Sister Thomas Marie chose to note:

> . . . need continuing affection of her family and friends outside the community. She should maintain it by visiting them or have them visit her. She should maintain it by letters and phone calls.

> ... within community she needs the affection of new friends ... the individual will like some better than others ... and will want to form close ties with a few ... the relationship should not be maligned by suggestions that there is something sordid in liking one person more than others. ...
>
> Personality adaptation is highly individualized. Religious Life, on the other hand, stresses conformity to seek submission of self, suppression of individuality. But a young woman can separate herself from physical presence of family and friends, but not psychologically from influences. Fulfillment of personality and living the life of a religious are not incompatible.[4]

It was not only the depth and complexity of the inner life that called for updating at this stage of renewal. Many Sisters had entered shortly after or even prior to graduation from high school; they had never lived on their own or navigated the public sphere without the supervision of parent or superior. Everyday events such as eating out at a restaurant, calling a cab, negotiating public transportation were simply not in the life experience of many. Sensing the need for a gentle guide book along the lines of Emily Post or Amy Vanderbilt, Jeanne Marie Lortie, OSB, penned a small but valuable booklet aptly entitled *Gracious Living* in which she discusses the "social amenities that must be met in our world today."[5]

> Today Sisters are constantly on the go, either alone or with others. They are attending conventions, conferences, workshops and lectures throughout this country and abroad.... The manners of a Religious should have three qualities: dignity, humility, and gentleness.[6]

The booklet contains tips for traveling by train, plane, or ship; for staying in a hotel, eating in a restaurant, or attending the theater. There are instructions on the art of conversation — on what topics to avoid, e.g., avoid pontificating, don't be a "killjoy," avoid sarcasm, don't interrupt others, and so forth.

---

4. Notes from the conference, Marywood Archives, Box 28.1.
5. Letter from S. Lortie to S. Aquinas, Marywood Archives, Box 28.1.
6. S. Jeanne Marie Lortie, OSB, *Gracious Living* illustrated by S. M. Constance Hickok, OSB, photography by S. Noemi Weygant, OSB (Duluth, MN: Priory Press, 1970).

Rules of etiquette around eating are listed with a light touch of humor. She states:

> Eating is not a pretty performance at best, but eat one must, so every effort should be made to do so in as polite and unobtrusive a way as possible. Table rules are given to ensure against our doing anything displeasing to others.[7]

To smooth the way when eating what she terms "awkward" foods, twenty-eight food items are listed with tips for the proper way to eat them. Everything from apples and bananas to spaghetti and spare ribs are listed. About the spare ribs, it is written in upper case letters: DO NOT LICK FINGERS.[8]

Concerned about the reality of Sisters evermore in the public eye, Sister Aquinas contacted a woman by the name of Anne Culkin, who offered a course of personality development for Women Religious. Ms. Culkin's course came with the promise of lectures on a pleasing personality, good grooming, posture, sitting, walking, and elimination of disturbing mannerisms. There were lessons on table etiquette and restaurant eating; consideration of others, what pleases, what detracts, true femininity, purpose, role and nature of women, voice diction and conversational techniques, ending with "What the lay person still looks for in its Sisterhood."[9]

If some Sisters felt they had unwittingly found themselves in a finishing school for the debutante, they made little fuss about it and endured the lessons with good humor and patient endurance.

The changes to come would go far deeper than table manners. In 1966 a Mental Health Workshop was sponsored for all Sisters. It was held at Aquinas College Wege Center and included several prominent speakers — usually priests who were themselves struggling with the new ways of world and Church.

To be pleasing to others was a deeply held conviction of the proper role of women, pleasing in both manners and interior motivation. In the aforementioned workshop on the "Fulfillment of the Feminine Personality in the Religious Life," Dr. McAllister said, "The woman's need to accomplish takes

---

7. Lortie, pages unnumbered.
8. Lortie, pages unnumbered.
9. Marywood Archives, Box 28.1.

Into a Period of Intense Study and Personal Renewal

And more meetings (left to right): Srs. Joyce Ann Hertzig, Ellen Mary Lopez, and Marie Elegia Timm

a special form which is characteristic of her sex. She has the need to be of service to others and the need to surrender."[10]

At the same time, McAllister encouraged a broadening of the world view and experience of the service-oriented women in apostolic religious life:

> Yes, I might be so bold as to suggest that religious have hobbies. That they be encouraged to read widely, to watch a little more TV at times; to learn about and argue politics, to become familiar with the theater, the arts, perhaps to get interested in some community affairs. It seems to me that, unless she lives in a contemplative order, the time has passed when Sister can be sheltered from the world. I think the world needs her to feel her compassion, and I think she needs the world to be touched by the pain that is there.[11]

> "I think the world needs Sister to feel her compassion, and I think she needs the world to be touched by the pain that is there."
> Robert J. McAllister

In the same workshop, the danger of too much "world" is recognized. Fr. Dominic Rover cautioned the Sisters to remember the Scripture passage that states:

---

10. Marywood Archives, Box 28.1.
11. "Fulfillment of the Feminine Personality in the Religious Life" by Robert J. McAllister, PhD, MD, p. 5, Marywood Archives.

Make your home in me, and I make mine in you. I am the vine, you are branches. He (the one) who remains in me bears fruit, but cut off from me you can do nothing. As the Father has loved me so I loved you. Dwell in me, abide in me, remain in me, make your home in me.[12]

Contemplative Prayer 1967

The struggle to understand and reconcile the tension between sacred/secular, Church/world, Religious/Laity continued in the topics and discussions of the late sixties. In a winter seminar, Father Thomas Dubay, SM, taught that the contemplative life was primary; that contemplative meant "clinging to God with mind and heart." He taught that this deep communion with God led to love of neighbor. He cautioned, however, of the danger of taking this love of neighbor too far. "Avoid undue familiarity with others." Fr. Dubay endorsed balance between familiarity with the *outside* and the safety of the *inside*.[13]

Summer 1967

Ten Sisters attended a workshop at Rosary College (now Dominican University) in River Forest, Illinois, on the topic of "Renewal through General Chapter." The participants ranged in age from 40 to 76 years old. They were among the leaders and potential leaders of the Congregation.[14] Each participant had the responsibility of summarizing one of the talks at the seminar; thus all members of the Congregation benefitted to some degree from the knowledge of the presenters by reading the summaries.

The titles of the presentations (all by men, save one) are laced with Vatican Council II ideas and reflect an attempt to adhere to the teachings of that Council:

---

12. Rev. Dominic Rover, OP, spoke on "Theology and Psychiatry and Religious Life as a Unitive Life," Marywood Archives.
13. Marywood Archives, Box. 28.1.
14. Among the participants and their approximate age at the time of the conference were: Srs. Aline Needham (66), James Rau (58), Bede Frahm (52).

Into a Period of Intense Study and Personal Renewal

"The Dignity of the Human Person," by Bishop Joseph Breitenbeck; "The Spirituality of Religious According to Vatican Council II" by Rev. Ernest Larkin, OMC; "General Trends and Innovations in Religious Government" by Ladislas Orsy, SJ; "Purpose of the General Chapter" by Rev. Edward J. Stokes, SJ; "Power of Experimentation" by Rev. Paul Boyle, CP; "Bureaucracy vs. Community" by Rev. Richard Schoenherr; "Formation Reassessment" by Mother Angelita Myerscough PB, PhD; "Theology of Community Life" by Fr. Aloysius Mehr, OSC; "History of Religious Government" by Rev. Stafford Poole, CM.

And still more meetings (left to right): Srs. Lenora Carmody, Patrice Konwinski, and Therese Rodríguez

1967 Canon Law Workshop

In addition to renewal through General and Extraordinary Chapters, the new laws for Religious as written in the revised Code of Canon Law required careful study and deep understanding. To that end Kevin O'Rourke, OP, announced an institute for Religious on the renewal mandated by Vatican Council II. The dates were set for June 5, 6 & 7, 1967. Penciled at the top of his letter to Sister Aquinas are words written in her handwriting: "Reserve 10 places for us."

From that institute and the publication on the renewal that followed, the Sisters began to understand and internalize the changes that would renew their lives together. Some of the key points of the revised laws for Religious are summarized here.[15]

Where in the past religious congregations waited for regulations to be handed down from the Vatican office for religious, the new norm recognizing the principle of subsidiarity established by Vatican Council II states "The chief role in renewing and adapting religious life belongs to the institute itself, especially through the general chapter."

While recognizing the earlier benefits of centralized authority, the principle of subsidiarity as expressed by Vatican Council II is based on the realization that women religious have "come of age," are highly educated and

---

15. Kevin O'Rourke, OP, *New Laws for Religious* (Cross and Crown reprint, 1967).

> "The chief role in renewing and adapting religious life belongs to the institute itself, especially through the general chapter."
> Kevin O'Rourke, OP

able to assume responsibility for their governance — always, of course, in accord with the Church's own approbation.

General Chapters are to be the vehicle of renewal in religious congregations. Each Congregation was to hold a chapter within the next two or three years to begin the process of renewal. If an ordinary chapter was not scheduled already, an extraordinary one was to be held. Furthermore, the extraordinary chapter may be held open for up to one year to provide opportunity for delegates and Sisters to study and experiment before making decisions.[16]

The changes would require a long period of experimentation regarding every aspect of community life — not contrary to the essentials. In the past Religious Life was seen as stable, with little change in structure and practice for hundreds of years. Now it was believed that ongoing growth and development required continual renewal to meet the needs of the people and to stay in touch with the needs of contemporary times.

In the past the Major Superior was the primary and only real authority in a given Congregation. Vatican Council II reinforced the role of the General Chapter as the highest legislative body of a Congregation. The Major Superior and her Council were to carry out the directives of the General Chapter, but not view their authority as above it. This decentralization of authority from the Major Superior and her Council to the General Chapter was accompanied by a specific directive in *Perfectae Caritatis* — return to the sources of Christian life and to the original inspiration behind a given community.

Vowed Religious interpreted this directive as an injunction to return to Holy Scripture and to the writings by or about their founder. Catholics in general were not inclined to study Scripture before the middle of the twentieth century when such

Yet more meetings (left to right): Srs. Chris Herald, Margaret Hillary, and Kathi Sleziak

16. O'Rourke, p. 3.

Into a Period of Intense Study and Personal Renewal

study was encouraged with the publication of the papal encyclical *Divino Afflante Spiritu* in 1943. This encyclical encouraged the study of the original languages of the Bible in order to gain a deeper and fuller understanding of the meaning of the sacred texts. Gradually the study of Scripture became incorporated into the culture of Catholic studies. Prior to this encyclical only the Latin version known as the Vulgate was deemed appropriate for Catholics to read, and interpretations of the Bible were left to priests and bishops. Studying or reading the Bible prior to this period was decidedly a Protestant thing to do. Now, however, Sisters began to study Scripture. One Sister remembers the resistance to those first efforts:

Return to the sources of Christian life and to the original inspiration behind a given community.

> I remember coming back [from a conference] excited about it. "Let's meet on Saturday evenings in the house and we can talk about the coming readings for Sunday." That was frowned upon by some saying, "We shouldn't be talking Scripture. We'll end up doing like the Protestants and just making private interpretations." But for the most part, the Sisters really enjoyed it when we got together.... We really had some good discussions just as preparation. That was a good pulling together of community.[17]

Scripture scholarship gradually picked up in speed and depth over the next decades.

Another directive from the document on the renewal for Religious Life propelled the vowed religious into the times in which she lived, "an adjustment of the community to the changed conditions of the times."[18] Vowed religious read this injunction as a call to read the signs of the times and to make changes accordingly. They also recognized that in order to adapt to contemporary times, rules and constitutions would need to be rewritten. Many items were obsolete and no longer relevant to life as it was being lived.

Preliminary to the rewriting, a group of the Sisters listed all the rules and regulations on the left side of a piece of paper, and on the right side, listed the actuality of life as it was lived in terms of the left side. The evidence was obvious — the two sides held little in common. One rather humorous example may suffice:

---

17. S. Jean Marie Birkman, Oral History, January 2011, Marywood Archives.
18. *Perfectae Caritatis*, #2.

In the Rule of St. Augustine which was publicly read every week, there is a sentence that states unequivocally: "The Sisters shall not go to the baths fewer than two at a time." In the fifth century when all baths were in public pools, such a tenet was necessary for safety's sake, but in twentieth-century America, it was a source of hilarity for newcomers. Yet other aspects of the Rule of St. Augustine are as relevant today as then, e.g., "When you pray to God in psalms and hymns, think over in your hearts the words that come from your lips."

Knowing that the task of re-writing rules and constitutions would not be easy, canonists advised the Sisters to refrain from abdicating the responsibility to those outside the Congregation — something all too tempting to women in particular who had been trained to trust the authority of priests and superiors rather than their own expertise and experience. Kevin O'Rourke advised:

> Rewriting the constitutions of a community will not be an easy task. We know, at present, the elements of our constitutions that should be eliminated, but do we know what new statutes should be added? . . . but in spite of all obstacles, we must not abdicate our responsibility. We should not ask persons outside the community to write our constitutions. We shall need to consult them, of course, but, for the most part, we should entrust this work to the members of our own community, involving as many of them as possible. The finished product will then be their work, not someone else's and as such, will be a much more powerful instrument of renewal.[19]

> "We must not abdicate our responsibility. We should not ask persons outside the community to write our constitutions."
> Kevin O'Rourke

Borrowing from the wisdom and experience of others had been a time-honored tradition for the Congregation. For a time, the Congregation used the Constitution of the Sinsinawa Dominicans.[20] The Sinsinawa Dominicans, in turn, had borrowed their Constitution from the Dominican Sisters in Stone, England.[21]

But this time would be different. This renewal would require the Sisters

---

19. O'Rourke, p. 11.
20. S. Schwind, *Period Pieces*, p. 213.
21. S. Mary Paschala O'Connor, *Five Decades: History of the Congregation of the Most Holy Rosary, Sinsinawa, Wisconsin 1849-1899* (Sinsinawa, WI: The Sinsinawa Press, 1954), pp. 84, 207, 241-42.

to plumb the depths of their own experience, conviction, and study to write a new Constitution for the years ahead.

But renewal this time would be different.

Summer of 1968 Institute for Renewal and Christian Leadership

Wasting no time in providing an opportunity to Sisters to learn about the pending renewal, Sister Aquinas planned an institute for the summer of 1968 using the facilities of Aquinas College.

The planning for the institute began in the spring of 1967. The eventual agenda listed ten topics and ten speakers, among them four women and six men. This recognition of women as experts was new in itself, as was the depth and breadth of the program. The hope had been for about 100 participants and the final count neared that goal with 98 Religious from all over the country attending; approximately one-third were from the Grand Rapids Dominican Congregation.

It was for this institute that the Baroness Catherine de Hueck Doherty hurtled into the sphere of the Grand Rapids Dominicans and left her mark. The proverbial "force to be reckoned with," she was an unrelenting advocate for social justice and ministry to the poor. She challenged the Sisters to go out into the "highways and byways," to really live poverty, and to be of service first and foremost. Sister Aquinas had asked her for a list of books for the Sisters to read in preparation for her presentation. In her reply she stated:

> But you have me across a barrel, Mother, if you'll excuse my putting it so plainly and a little vulgarly. The topic you have listed, "Formation of Community" . . . and believe it or not, I have no bibliography! Oh. I could list a number of books, but all that I usually have to say comes from my heart. I have tried to think of books that influenced me and I come always back to the Bible, especially the New Testament.[22]

The Baroness was uncompromising in her focus and compelling in her personal story of survival of the 1917 Russian revolution, and the link be-

---

22. Doherty in letter to S. Aquinas, April 18, 1968, Marywood Archives, Box 28.1.

tween her foundational community in Combermere, Ontario, and the Grand Rapids Dominicans continued for decades.

While the Baroness's topic was the Formation of Community, other topics during the five-week institute included: Group Dynamics, the Psychology of Woman, Theology of Religious Life, Current Trends in Theology, Today's Liturgy, the Living Community, Principles of Management and Business, the Renewed Religious, and a rather unusual topic for the times in the context of such an institute — Film.

Sister Ann Frederick Heiskel, the Audio-Visual Coordinator at Aquinas College, along with Fr. Donald Lozier, OP, offered the following films with discussion afterwards: *Sunday Lark; Roadsigns on a Merry-Go-Round; The Church in the World; The Medium is the Message* (a book by Marshall McLuhan); *12-12-42; Mark Twain; The Film as Art; Sundays and Cybele*. The titles of the chosen films are perhaps not so remarkable as is the fact that the medium of film itself was offered as a sanctioned means of learning — something that had been considered purely entertainment, perhaps frivolously so, now became a reputable medium of knowledge.

It had only been two years since the Sisters had heard from Dr. McAllister: "The woman's need to accomplish takes a special form which is characteristic of her sex. She has the need to be of service to others and the need to surrender." Now at this 1968 Institute of Renewal they would hear Sister Constance Davis, SND, clinical psychologist from the Archdiocese of Detroit, who recommended several authors for the participants to study before coming to the conference. Among them were Betty Friedan, *The Feminine Mystique;* Margaret Mead, *Male and Female;* Clara Thompson, "Some effects of the derogatory attitude towards female sexuality" in *Psychiatry,* 1950, 13:349-54. Although the actual content of Sister Davis's lectures is not available in the Marywood Archives, these readings and others recommended by her strongly challenged societal notions that a woman's fulfillment was found in a life of service and surrender.[23]

Also enlisted as speakers at the institute were Fathers Gerard Austin, OP, Philip Hanley, OP, and Edward J. Stokes, SJ. Equally notable were experts who declined the invitation to participate in the institute usually due to prior

---

23. Letter to S. Aquinas from S. Mary Constance Davis, SND, dated March 22, 1968, Marywood Archives, Box 28.1.

commitments. Some of these were: Rev. John L. McKenzie, SJ, from Notre Dame; Bernard Haring, Union Theological Seminary, NY; Sr. Marie Augusta Neal, SND, from Emmanuel College in Boston; Rev. Paul Boyle, CP; Rev. Thomas Dubay, SM, from Notre Dame Seminary, New Orleans; Ladislas M. Orsy, SJ; Fr. J. M. Tillard, OP.[24]

In the decades that followed, Sisters continued to attend workshops, institutes, seminars, and lectures on Religious Life and their place in it.

The Nineteen Seventies

In the 1970s the issue of possible "retirement," i.e., leaving compensated ministry, for large numbers of Sisters emerged. A program called *Focus on Your Future* began in the summer of 1970 and sought to encourage Sisters at or beyond retirement age to think about that pending event in a positive light. The notion promoted was that although a specific ministry, e.g., teaching, might be ending, there was great need for Sisters to serve in other ministries such as visiting the sick or tutoring. Also the idea of leisure activities was introduced as a positive opportunity to develop and enjoy hobbies or interests not attended to in the past. Sisters were aging along with their cohorts in the rest of the country; life expectancy was increasing steadily for both groups.

Programs for the elderly continued throughout the 1970s with *Enkindling Life* for Sisters in the pre-retirement and retirement years. It is notable that all of the programs for the pre-retirement and retirement years were organized and led by the Sisters themselves rather than outside experts. The trend to recognize and accept the "in house" expertise was becoming more evident.

Life-long learning programs for retirees called *Focus on the Present* were offered during this decade also. Bishop Thomas Gumbleton of Detroit spoke on Bread for the World and Maggie Kuhn, the founder of the Gray Panthers, spoke on the rights of the senior citizen. Through opportunities such as these, Sisters in all age cohorts became increasingly aware of the insights first articulated in the 1960s in the civil rights movement. All persons have a basic human right to have access to food, shelter, health care, and respect.

---

24. Marywood Archives Box, 28.1

The Sisters were increasingly ready to become more involved than ever before to take action on behalf of justice.

Contemplation Demands Action

The world's problems were up for discussion, and the discussion was expanding towards systems thinking rather than specific problems with singular solutions. An example of this level of analysis can be found in the relooking at Scripture. The teachings of Jesus could be and had been misused to justify oppression and mollify the oppressed, e.g., "Slaves, obey your masters" (Col. 3:22). When taken as a whole, however, the Gospel is a text of liberation and empowerment. The Gospel is clearly Good News for the people. The Sisters were challenged by two such systems thinkers in the 1970s, Gerald Mische and Fr. Gustavo Gutiérrez, a priest from Peru.

> When taken as a whole, the Gospel is a text of liberation and empowerment.

A Seminar on World Order was offered in the summer of 1978. It was sponsored by the Aquinas Institute of Religious Studies (AIRS). About 250 persons attended, most of them Grand Rapids Dominicans. The featured speaker, Gerald Mische, was from the World Law Fund and he proposed a planetary system of government. He was eager to propel the Sisters beyond their immediate neighborhoods. Fr. Philip Hanley, OP, director of AIRS, introduced him. This was in the midst of the Cold War when nuclear attack was on the minds of many and feared by all. The "rules of war" were being disregarded by the United States and other countries. In his introduction to Mische, Hanley called for the audience to think in terms of world view, world order, and world justice. Although the concept of a single world order never took hold, other than through the existing institutions such as the United Nations, Mische's list of issues is as relevant today as it was in the 1970s. He named the following: Peace, Ecology, Technology, Drug Abuse, "1984," Prison Reform, Poverty, Women's Rights, International Development, Urban Decay, Education, Care for the Elderly, Medical and Health Care, and Religious/Human Values. He saw Women Religious as valuable links into the networks of education and health care.[25] His thinking was too much of a threat to too many in the country and the idea of a world order faded; the

---

25. Marywood Archives, Box 28.1.

power of Women Religious to have an effect on the politics of the world, however, was not to be dimmed.

Sisters became aware of both the possibility and responsibility of having their voices heard at the national and international levels. Eventually, Sisters joined together to achieve status as a non-governmental organization (NGO) at the United Nations in New York City. First, Sister Carol Zinn, Sister of Saint Joseph Federation, and Sister Eileen Gannon, Dominican Sister from the Sparkhill Dominicans, worked in this capacity on behalf of the Dominican Leadership Conference. Later, Sister Lucianne Siers from the Dominican Sisters ~ Grand Rapids served as the director of the Partnership for Global Justice, a coalition with NGO status, joining the efforts of over 100 Congregations, groups, and individuals grounded in Gospel values working to encourage advocacy, education, and participation at the United Nations. The organization provided workshops on global citizenship for a just world.[26]

Yet still more meetings (left to right, facing camera): Srs. Marie Bernarde Salazar, Teresa Houlihan, and Carmelita Switzer

The second systems analyst to influence the community was a South American priest. Liberation Theology has been a contentious concept in the church; Gustavo Gutiérrez, OP, is regarded as the founder of the movement. A priest from Lima, Peru (he joined the Dominican Order in 1999), Gutiérrez wrote the foundational text on the movement in 1971. At this writing he holds the John Cardinal O'Hara Professorship of Theology at the University of Notre Dame. Although the movement has been co-opted by Marxist militants to justify violence, it was and is in its pure form an attractive hermeneutic (method of interpreting) of Scripture for those whose hearts are moved with compassion for the endless suffering of persons living in abject poverty with little hope for a future. Many of the Sisters resonated with this theology through their own prayer and experience.

---

26. For more information: http://www.partnershipforglobaljustice.com/.

STUDY

> **The United States was not always flawless in its relationship with the dictators in South America.**

One Sister recalls learning to question her own country's policies in Latin America. She came to realize that the United States was not always flawless in its relationships with the dictators there. Gutiérrez was not a proponent of violence, but did agree that some confrontation may be necessary to advocate for the people who were unfairly oppressed by government structures, structures that were often supported by the Church hierarchy. Sister Mary Ellen McDonald recalls a conversation with missionaries and other pastoral people with Gutiérrez at Notre Dame:

> At first they thought I was from the CIA, then they opened up and shared the pain of the mission and then I came back and knew we needed to change; our country was not always doing what we should be doing. The missionaries supported the people; they were there to free the people to use their own gifts. I changed from a "do-gooder" to a companion on the journey of mutuality. I'm convinced that Liberation Theology is a good solid theology. We need to go there; some people twist it to their advantage to support violence. But they end up being oppressive and keep people poor.[27]

In the 1970s the suffering of persons both far and near continued to be a cause of concern for Sisters and a frequent topic for study and action. Community Concern Days were sponsored by the Global Concerns Committee on topics such as global perspective, survival of the neighborhood, an inner-city view, and rural environments.

As well, workshops continued in the 1970s to promote the growth, development, and fullness of life for Sisters of whatever age. For three summers beginning in 1977, a program named *In Pilgrimage* was held for Sisters according to their age cohort: summer of 1977, for those who were between 35-45 years of age; the next summer, 1978, for those who were between the ages of 46-79; the third and last summer for the younger set, those under 36 years of age. Topics included human psychology, Scripture, theology of Church and Religious Life, call and mission, prayer and spirituality, Dominican presence in the modern world. The program ended with a directed retreat for the participants.

Toward the end of the decade in the fall of 1978, the Prioress, Sister Mar-

---

27. S. Mary Ellen McDonald in conversation with the general editor in 2012.

Into a Period of Intense Study and Personal Renewal

jorie Vangsness, summarized where the Sisters found themselves a little over ten years beyond the close of Vatican Council II. In her introduction to the Mission Institute featuring Sister Ann Willits, OP (from the Sinsinawa Congregation), Sister Marjorie noted that Religious Life was in a period of transition. The old image was no longer accurate, and a firm new image has not yet emerged. She faced the fact head-on as she reminded the Sisters that the options were extinction, minimal survival, or revitalization.

> We cannot downplay the past, we live because of it, but neither can we afford to be mired in it. Each of us needs to work at loving others to new life. We have to give each other the environment and the freedom to grow. We must encourage each other to take true responsibility for our own lives and for what flows from them. We are called to follow Jesus Christ and the vision He gives us in the Gospel.[28]

"Each of us needs to work at loving others to new life."
Sister Marjorie Vangsness.

The Nineteen Eighties

Ongoing programs of personal and communal development expanded in the 1980s. Collaboration became a preferred and privileged mode of operation. Collaboration extended first to other Dominicans, both male and female, and was particularly successful in the development and expansion of the Parable Conference, which functioned from 1977 to 2007. The work of this Conference is described in the chapter "Concentric Circles." A brief history and purpose of it is given here.

The Parable Conference was originally founded by the Sinsinawa Dominicans and the Saint Albert the Great Central Province of Dominican men, each of whom contributed seed money in the amounts of $7,500 for a total of $15,000. It was designed to be a unique place of collaborative ministry where the entire Dominican family (Friars, Laity, Nuns, and Sisters) could meet, study, reflect, and grow in the call to the Holy Preaching. The most dynamic collaboration was between the active Apostolic Women's Congregations and the Friars (men); the laity and nuns (cloistered women) were

---

28. S. Marjorie Vangsness, Marywood Archives, Box 28.1.

STUDY

occasionally active in the enterprise and the Associate members began to be more present in the later years.

Parable hosted major conferences on Dominican life and mission, particularly on matters of peace and justice. Albert Nolan, OP (South Africa), and Mary O'Driscoll, OP (Ireland), were featured speakers at these events. Parable offered pilgrimages such as the *Lands of Dominic* and Central America study tours; retreats entitled "Encounter with the Word"; conferences on Dominican Life and Mission; and informal gatherings for discussions on contemporary issues and the Dominican response. Two Dominican Sisters and two Friars worked together on most retreats and programs, offering a model of collaboration at its best.

Through the offerings of the Parable Conference over one thousand Dominicans traveled and learned about the foundation of the Order through lectures and a tour of significant Dominican sites in Spain, France, and Italy. Nearly one hundred Grand Rapids Dominicans enjoyed this remarkable experience, known as the *Lands of Dominic*.

Lands of Dominic in Europe (left to right): Srs. Mary Catherine Brechting, Genevieve Montreuil, Kateri Schrems, Mary Navarre, and Robert Ann Erno

A virtual experience of the *Lands of Dominic* began in 2006 for those not able to travel to Europe. The retreat experience offered a vicarious trip using slides, lectures, and discussions to simulate the actual event.[29]

An enduring feature from the *Lands of Dominic* pilgrimages and other offerings of the Parable Conference was the universal conviction among Dominican Congregations of women that they held much in common. As the various American Congregations told their stories of foundation on the bus trips between sites, the realization of the commonalities was stunning. In the fall of 2012, when the first Dominican Sisters Conference was held near Chicago, many of the Dominicans who gathered recalled meeting others on that trip of long ago. "We were together on the *Lands of Dominic*" was a common call that immediately conjured memories of joy, laughter, and camaraderie.

In the 1980s too, Central Committees expanded at the invitations of the two prioresses of that decade, Sisters Teresa Houlihan and Carmelita Murphy. The Continuing Life Development Committee began in 1985; Wholistic

---

29. All references to the Parable Conference are found in AR 7.1, Marywood Archives.

Into a Period of Intense Study and Personal Renewal

Living Committee and Option for Justice Committee began in 1986. Other committees such as Care of Earth and groups like Promoters of Justice began to meet and study issues prior to taking action. The call to serve in the modern world with all its diversity of problems and injustices was sounded again and again.

In June 1986 a seminar was held entitled "Justice Shall Come!" with Edward van Merrienboer, OP, the appointed Justice Promoter of the Dominican Order at the international level. The seminar examined the Dominican approach to justice as:

the invitation to look at the destiny of the world unflinchingly, to analyze the problems to be solved vigorously, to grapple with misery in its causes in order to make possible a universal upward movement of humanity.[30]

Srs. Rosemary O'Donnell (standing) and Katrina Hartman study the issues of the day.

The conference topics were outward looking, e.g., United States Bishops' Pastoral Letter on the Economy, Farmworkers Movements, Capital Punishment, Women and Peacemaking, and Hispanic Experience in the Church.

In the 1980s for the first time, uncomfortable topics such as addiction, trauma, and sexual abuse were brought out into the open among the Sisters. To be fully functioning people, the Sisters needed to pursue wholeness in their own lives and healing from their own wounds of the past. The study continued with little left unexamined. The Jungian con-

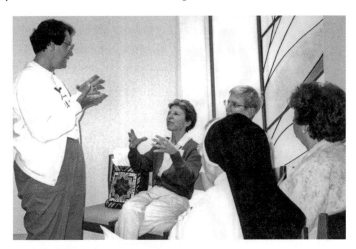

Sr. Edith Schnell (standing), and (left to right) Srs. Mary Kay Oosdyke, Jarrett DeWyse, Irene McDonnell, and an unidentified Sister (foreground) engage in group discussion.

---

30. Vincent Cosmao, OP, *Changing the World* (Orbis Books, 1984).

STUDY

cept "wounded healer" was a newly coined term that informed minister and ministry alike and was popularized by a book of the same name written by Fr. Henri J. M. Nouwen. It was the hope that participants would come to understand themselves better as well as the persons with whom they lived and ministered.

The Nineteen Nineties

In 1991 there were seventeen workshops attended by 200 Grand Rapids Dominicans and 75 others; over 100 Sisters used education/life development funds for the 1990-91 Summer Institutes. The studying continued. In 1991 a Summer Institute featured a potpourri of topics such as Scripture, Enneagram, Spanish language and culture, addiction, compulsion, caregiving, aging, music, and centering prayer.

The compassion of Jesus was felt in the hearts of the Sisters.

The study, pondering, living, thinking, and praying of the Sisters revealed a world with many needs and peoples in great anguish. The compassion of Jesus was felt in the hearts of the Sisters who realized that they would need to focus their direction, for the needs were overwhelming in magnitude and complexity.

To that end, at the General Assembly in 1992, the Sisters agreed on four Direction Statements to guide decision making and ministry in the years ahead. Two years later at the General Chapter of 1994, additional statements of commitment were added to the original group. The Direction Statements continue to guide the members of the Congregation in decision making about ministries. In summary, these state the Sisters' commitment to care for all Creation, to advocate for women and children in need, and to stand with and for the

(Left to right) Srs. Carmelita Murphy, an unidentified Sister, Tereska Wozniak, Ardeth Platte, and Joanne Davey engage in spirited debate on the Direction Statements.

Into a Period of Intense Study and Personal Renewal

materially poor. The Sisters are also committed to building community with each other and to collaboration in ministries that effect systemic change.

Communal study continued into 1993 with the offerings of the Summer Institute which included a wide variety of issues and events, but now each was related in one way or another to the Direction Statements:

New Mexico Tour; Enneagram; Relationships; Assertiveness Training; Your Money/Your Mission; Aesthetic Hunger; Honoring the Nurturing Role of Beauty in Our Lives; Prayer with Image and Song; Beginning Spanish; Medical Ethics; Music for a Summer's Eve; Scripture: Stories of God; Awareness through Movement; Women, Money & Spirituality; First Aid; Preaching Workshop; Art Therapy; Tai-Chi.

The 1990s continued to unfold with workshops associated with anti-racism, retreats on ecumenism, personal prayer, and poverty. The newly incorporated apostolate known as Dominican Center/Marywood began in 1993 and became a center for spirituality and conferencing that continues to serve the Dominican Sisters as well as the larger civic community. The founding and growth of Dominican Center will receive fuller treatment in a subsequent chapter.

In Retrospect

Looking back on these years one sees several waves unfolding from then until now. The first was a time of deconstruction of what had been, e.g., the emphasis on details, perfectionism, docility, excessive compliance, the letter of the law, practices that were foreign or Medieval and therefore mostly meaningless to contemporary life. While

Srs. Joan Thomas and Emilia Atencio exchange greetings at a meeting.

STUDY

it might seem a relief to be free of these restrictions, it was at the same time a letting go of that sense of serenity and stability that one felt in being a small, yet vital part of a grand enterprise of saving one's own soul and those of the people one served. It meant relinquishing the consolation of being a special and privileged people who had only to follow the rules and obey superiors, and the "hundredfold" would be theirs in Heaven.

The next wave was a time of reconstruction — if not that, what? This was a period of intense study and experimentation. What is essential? What would happen if . . . ? What are the essentials without which the Congregation would cease to exist? What are the authentic values of the evangelical counsels? Is a recognizable outward sign necessary to witness to the vowed life of a Woman Religious?

The third phase, of internalization of values, is happening now. A new founding began with the Chapter of 2012. The Sisters asked: Who are we? We are Dominicans and thus committed to a contemplative life, energized and informed by Scripture and the signs of the times in which we live. We are Dominicans and so we are active as well as contemplative. We are baptized Catholic Christians and so we know about death and rebirth and we choose to walk with and speak out on behalf of all who suffer injustice. As Dominican Sisters ~ Grand Rapids, we are women who can, with full heart, proclaim, "Inflamed with contemplative love, we die and are reborn, as we walk together preaching justice."[31]

Through years of study the transformation of the community took place, a transformation that carries forward the voice of Vatican Council II, that promotes and upholds the role of the laity, the rising up of social consciousness, and the preaching of the Gospel of Jesus. Vatican Council II principles of inclusiveness, collegiality, and subsidiarity are now ingrained in the lives and hearts of the Sisters. There is no turning back.

There is no turning back.

---

31. Proclamation from General Chapter 2012.

Formation — Becoming a Sister

Instruct the wise, and they become wiser;
teach the just, and they advance in learning.
PROVERBS 9:9[1]

Formed by the Word

How does a woman become a Woman Religious? Any baptized, Catholic woman who is a free agent may seek to become a Religious, but no one is born to it, and only a few are called. To become a member of a group, be it a school, a church, a business, or a branch of the military, a person may expect a period of orientation to learn the customs of the group and to see if it is a good match. Prior to marriage, the customs of this culture call for a period of dating or "going with" before the couple makes a permanent commitment to each other. The same is true for joining a Religious Congregation. The word used to describe this period of orientation or "going with" is *Formation,* and in this case it is a prolonged period stretching five to eight years.

A woman who enters Religious Life begins this period known as Formation to discern if this is the life for her, and if so, how to identify this way of life as her own, to become a Sister at the core of her being. On the other hand, the Congregation also discerns if the congruence between the individual and

---

1. *New American Bible,* revised edition (NABRE) released March 9, 2011.

the group is a sound one. The word *formation* itself is a problem. One may ask, "Formed to be what, to do what?" Each of us is formed in our mother's womb, as is written in Psalm 139:13: "You formed my inmost being; you knit me in my mother's womb."[2] The word *formed* comes from an old French word meaning to mold, model, or shape. For lack of a better word, that is the word that is used for this crucial beginning to life as a Sister.

In this chapter the topic of formation in the life of a Sister is addressed as experienced during and after the Second Vatican Council when many external customs changed almost overnight. The next chapter will address the topic of theological and professional preparation as Sisters heeded the call of Popes, Vatican Council II, their own leaders, and their dreams to become more fully prepared and certified for the ministries in which they were already or would become engaged.

Formation practices for the neophyte to Religious Life had not changed in the many centuries leading up to Vatican Council II. These practices included a name change,[3] uniform clothing, separation from family and friends, limited communication — to name but a few. All converged to form the newcomer's identity as *Sister/Nun,* as Woman Religious. Visually, this change was easier to see before the renewal of Vatican Council II when uniformity in dress, mannerisms, and decorum was valued as a sign of unity. In many cases, they even had very similar handwriting.

During and after renewal most visual symbols were dropped; alternatives needed to be discovered to aid the novice in forming her identity as a Sister. Outward signs were few and far between.

In the pre-Conciliar days of formation the stages toward full membership were: aspirant (for those of high school age at Marywood Academy), postulant, novice, first profession, and final profession. The rules were straightforward, unchanging, and clear. Everyone knew what was expected. Few questions were asked because the answers were clear ahead of time. With the renewal many questions were asked and traditions were challenged.

> **With few physical cues to distinguish one sister from another, young children could be confused. When five foot Sister Elaine replaced the much taller Sister Eileen, a first grader greeted her with an astonished, "Sister, you shrunk!"**

> **During and after renewal most visual symbols were dropped; alternatives needed to be discovered to aid the novice in forming her identity as a Sister. Outward signs were few and far between.**

2. NABRE.

3. At reception, a formal ritual at which time the woman received the habit and the official status of "novice," she also received a religious name chosen for her; it was customary to drop the use of the surname except for legal purposes, e.g., driver's license, passport.

The Vows

Where once the definition of the evangelical counsel of obedience was clear, i.e., unquestioning and quick compliance with authority, now a new concept of obedience was taking root. Although still expected to be obedient to lawful authority within the context of her community, the individual Sister may never abdicate her responsibility to her personal conscience. Now the concept of obedience is enlarged based on the Latin origin of the word itself: *obedire*, "pay attention to, give ear, to listen." The concept of blind obedience as a positive attribute of adults was deeply challenged by the political and geopolitical events of World War II. Along with this awakening in the consciousness of the culture was the notion among thoughtful people that one should not only question authority before obeying, but one ought to speak up to authority when faced with unjust or harmful practices of that authority. Religious obedience to Superiors was not immune from these considerations. Heartfelt obedience to the community meant participation in new government structures, listening not only to lawful authority, but to one another and making decisions based on the common good of all.

> Heartfelt obedience to the community meant listening to one another and making decisions based on the common good of all.

Poverty was challenged as a good in itself. Real poverty is an evil to be alleviated. The need to live simply that others might simply live became more relevant than the custom of asking permission to use things. Evangelical poverty came to mean depending on one another, sharing resources, freeing oneself from useless clutter to be unencumbered for the itinerancy demanded of the life of a Woman Religious. The Sisters no longer engage in the rather arcane practice of using the "our" pronoun for everything from toothbrushes to computers. At the same time, Sisters do not purchase or own houses, cars, bank accounts, appliances, or other large items.

> The need to live simply that others might live became more relevant than the custom of asking permission to use things.

While it continues to mean refraining from those expressions of intimacy particular to marriage, chastity has become framed in the idea of a generous, altruistic love and openness to others; a pursuit of right relationship with all creation. Refraining from an exclusive love of one partner, the Woman Religious is freer in time and energy to love inclusively, even to love the unlovely, or those most rejected or isolated in prisons and on death row.

> The Woman Religious is freer in time and energy to love inclusively, even to love the unlovely, or those most rejected or isolated.

STUDY

The Renewal Period

While initial formation changed dramatically, the fundamentals remained the same. The challenge came in discerning what was fundamental and what was non-essential. Nomenclature signaled subtle shifts in meaning of terms not considered fundamental.

Terms to describe the steps on the path to full incorporation as a Woman Religious were among the first things to change. *Postulant,* a word from the Latin meaning "to ask," became *Associate,* which then changed to the term *Candidate;* the term *Novice* stayed the same and *Young Professed* became those in *Initial Commitment* because youth no longer accurately described the group.

Although the names changed, the purpose did not. The Candidate period remains one of assessment for both the woman and the Congregation. During these months, the Candidate becomes better acquainted with the Congregation and vice versa. She studies the specific Congregation of the Dominicans in Grand Rapids as well as the history of the international Dominican Order. She prays with the Sisters, lives with them, studies the *Rule* and the *Constitution and Statutes,* and meets with an appointed director to continue the mutual discernment. When the Candidate feels ready to take the next step (not less than six months nor more than two years), she writes a letter of request to the Prioress for admission into the Novitiate.

In the parlance of Religious Life and by the Code of Canon Law, the novitiate year is a period of at minimum twelve months wherein the individual is freed from the tasks of ordinary life to deepen her spirituality and discern her compatibility with the new life she is about to undertake. It is also a trial period wherein the Congregation determines the suitability of the Candidate to this new way of life. At her reception into the Novitiate the woman receives the right to use the title Sister and also claims a special title such as "of the Holy Spirit" or "of the Mother of God." At this point the woman was (in the past) given a religious name chosen for her by the Prioress. With Vatican Council II's renewed emphasis on the centrality of the sacrament of Baptism, Sisters were given the option to return to their Baptismal name.[4] Since that

---

4. "The baptized, by regeneration and the anointing of the Holy Spirit, are consecrated as

time, all newcomers have chosen to retain the names given to them at Baptism, and as of 2014, eighty percent of the Sisters living had chosen to return to their Baptismal names.

The Novitiate period is composed of two parts, a canonical year and an apostolic year. As the name suggests, the canonical year is a legally prescribed time of intense spiritual introspection with extended periods for prayer, study, and reflection. During this year, ministry is minimal and processed through the lens of theological reflection. On the other hand, during the apostolic year of the Novitiate, the Sister lives and works as a member of the Congregation. She participates in all meetings and enjoys both the privileges and responsibilities of membership.

For most of the Dominican Congregations of Sisters in the United States, including the Grand Rapids Dominican Sisters, the canonical year is now held in St. Louis, Missouri, at the Collaborative Dominican Novitiate with formal study at the nearby Aquinas Institute, a fully accredited graduate school and seminary sponsored by the Dominican Order.

The Collaborative Dominican Novitiate began in 1988 to provide an enriched program for participating Congregations and to introduce the Novice to the larger Dominican family of Sisters from other Congregations as well as the Brothers who are a part of the International Order of Dominicans. It also provides the opportunity for a supportive peer group when numbers in individual Congregations are few. It is designed to comply with the Canonical requirements for a twelve-month Novitiate. The legitimacy for the Collaborative Dominican Novitiate in St. Louis was affirmed by the appropriate Vatican authority on August 8, 1991.[5]

Although many fears and hesitations were voiced as the collaborative venture began, it has been and continues to be a rich and varied experience of the Dominican family in the United States. Some of the fears voiced at the outset were:

---

a spiritual house and a holy priesthood, in order that through all those works which are those of the Christian man [sic] they may offer spiritual sacrifices and proclaim the power of Him who has called them out of darkness into His marvelous light." http://www.vatican.va/archive/hist_councils/ii_vatican_council/documents/vat-ii_const_19641121_lumen-gentium_en.html #10.

5. Rev. Joseph A. Galante, Undersecretary of the Congregazione per Gli Istituti Di Vita Consacrata E Le Società Di Vita Apostolica, Marywood Archives, 28.2.

Can the novice start something at the CDN (Collaborative Dominican Novitiate) and then not fit in at home or might she decide to transfer to another Dominican Congregation that she likes better?

Might the Novices want to form community among themselves — a new Dominican community?

The Novices experience a year of living common life with a clear Dominican identity. How will they fit into a community of women who are renewed but more generic in their identity?

In the words of one founding member: "Isn't this frightening? What is being lost, dying, being born? What is the future?"[6]

To the credit of the original Congregations, the vision of the Collaborative Dominican Novitiate was realized and none of the fears materialized. Novices feel stronger attachments to their home Congregation than ever. Although some discern that Religious Life is not for them (which is one of the purposes of the novitiate year), no Novice ever transferred to another Dominican Congregation as a result of her experience in this novitiate. Although deep and lasting friendships are formed, the Novices have never moved toward the formation of their own separate congregation.

Now in its twenty-fifth year (2013), the Collaborative Dominican Novitiate continues to offer an outstanding program of formation and education. It provides the newcomer a unique opportunity to deepen her spiritual life with the help of skilled directors and in the company of her peers. Through this time set apart she comes to understand the meaning of the evangelical counsels of voluntary poverty, consecrated chastity, and prophetic obedience. Above all, it is a time in which she can deepen self-knowledge and further discern her vocation to Religious Life.

The Apostolic Novitiate is a year for the woman to experience ministry as "Sister." It may occur either before or after her Canonical Novitiate period. The Apostolic Novice may be in full-time ministry and study or a combination of part-time in each. Her ministry is located on a site determined in

---

6. Collaborative Dominican Novitiate, Marywood Archives, Box 28.2.

collaboration with her director. She meets with the novice director regularly to continue discernment and integration. Again when the woman feels ready for the next step she writes a letter of intent to the Prioress. At this time another evaluation of the woman takes place which consists of communal evaluation by the local community, the formation director, and the woman's personal evaluation. The Prioress and Council interview the woman and make their decision after reflection, prayer, and dialogue.

The temporary profession period is a time for the woman to integrate all aspects of her call to Dominican life. The woman meets with a mentoring team of three or four Sisters who assist her in her continuing discernment toward final profession. She also meets with the formation director periodically. As the period of temporary vows ends (from three to six years), the woman may ask to renew her vows, request to make final vows, or leave the community. As in the period prior to first profession, the woman herself, her mentoring team, community, and director join in a formal assessment to discern her suitability for final, i.e., permanent vows.

The process is long and deliberate with due regard every step of the way for the freedom of the woman to make the choice carefully and without any coercion which would invalidate her final vows.

Among Grand Rapids Dominicans, the transition from pre– to post–Vatican Council II formation pro-

Sr. Chela Gonzalez (right) makes profession of vows to Prioress Nathalie Meyer, April 28, 2012.

grams was complicated by an untimely death. In April 1965, the novice directress Sister Cecile Byrne died at the age of fifty-eight after a brief illness. Sister Cecile was regarded as a strong and imposing woman well educated and prepared for the task at hand. She was a self-assured woman who directed the novices with confidence and a no-nonsense approach.

After months of interim directors, Sister Karen Thoreson was appointed the Director of Novices.[7] Her preparation for the new role consisted of one summer session at an institute that touched on Scripture, Vatican Council II, and psychology. Sister Karen reflected on her experience:

> The most challenging thing was that I was supposed to train them (the novices) in the traditions of the community. What were the traditions? I'd go to somebody in leadership, and in the beginning I got straight forward answers. Pretty soon, I didn't get answers. . . . That was the most challenging. In many things, there were no fast rules, because some people were doing something and some people were doing something else (staying with the old).[8]

Whereas previous entering classes were largely young women in their late teenage years, such was no longer the case. The class entering in the fall of 1968 consisted of six women — five of whom were in their mid to late twenties and only one a recent high school graduate. Most had careers already in place; one, born in Peru, struggled with both language and culture. Of those six, two remain. One of those who remained reflected that it seemed as if both the candidates and the Congregation were searching during her novitiate period. Ambiguity and confusion described the days of her formation, and only later through programs after final profession, along with life experience of living in community and mentoring by more seasoned Sisters, did she acquire the understanding of what it meant to be Dominican.

One of the former customs of the probationary period concerned the manner of a postulant's or novice's departure from the life. There was a sense of shame or failure connected with a decision to return to the secular world. In the experience of those who stayed, it was an unsettling event. The pos-

---

7. Note another change in terminology. S. Cecile had been the Mistress of Novices; her successor would be known as the Director of Novices.

8. S. Karen Thoreson, OP, Oral History, 2008, Marywood Archives, Folder 2009.0427, p. 17.

Formation — Becoming a Sister

tulant or novice who decided to make the choice to leave or was told to leave simply disappeared. No comments were made, no questions were asked. She was there one day and gone the next.

Those who left, either through their own choice or those of their superiors, relate their experience of departure from the convent to the outside world. They describe being led into a small room where they found the clothes they were wearing when they entered. They put these clothes on and left the building. A parent, relative, or friend waited to take them home; all future contact was severed. Some felt anger, shame, loss, grief. Those who stayed felt many of the same emotions, but no one said anything until one day in the spring of 1968. This group had been teenagers during the Civil Rights movement and had learned about the power of a cohesive group to make changes. As a group they approached their superior and said, "No, we don't want this." And so it was that a ceremony of farewell was begun for postulants or novices who were leaving. The stunning reality is not that the custom changed, but that the initiative for the change came from the candidates/novices, and their superiors listened to them. This would have been unheard of in the days prior to Vatican Council II and the cultural changes of the 1960s.

Former member Ann Banner Hayward enjoys a reunion with Sr. Geneva Marie Schaub.

Currently, former members have been invited to visit and reconnect with the Congregation in whatever way is comfortable for them. With the aid of technology, former and current members are often in touch with one another, asking for prayers and communicating on matters of mutual interest.

Theological and Professional Study

The truth we seek is found in all reality. Our study is not confined to any one discipline, but leads us to attend with reverence to the manifestations of God's presence in the whole of Creation.

CONSTITUTION AND STATUTES, #18

THE SAYING THAT "the cake is baked by age forty" has not been true about the Sisters in the Catholic Church, and nowhere is that more evident than in the renewal period that followed Vatican Council II. Sisters well past the age of forty continued to prepare themselves for new ministries as well as to deepen their competence and update their knowledge in traditional ones.

Ministry preparation widened and broadened in both the fields related to religion as well as in traditional areas of study for teaching, nursing, and social work. As new ministry opportunities opened, Sisters prepared for them by going back to school for the appropriate degrees. Those Sisters not needing academic degrees pursued certifications or did whatever it took to update their skills and knowledge for ministry. Gradually, it became an expectation that a Sister would have the training she needed before starting a ministry and would not be expected to learn it as she was engaging in it.

Before Vatican Council II, ministerial preparation was predominantly of the apprentice variety. A young woman was usually sent out to teach prior to finishing her undergraduate degree. Where possible, she would be assigned to a school where a seasoned teacher served as a mentor. Housekeepers too would often be sent to a convent where a more experienced cook would teach her the intricacies of the task, although many housekeepers began in smaller missions where the individual was left to improvise or lean on the teachings of her own mother's ways of the culinary arts.

A former novice director recalls the motivation for further education:

> As we looked at the world around us, we saw new places where our gifts, talents, and treasures could (and perhaps should) be used. As we reflected back over our history, of what led us to become teachers, administrators, builders of schools and hospitals, guardians of orphans, we recognized that the needs of the people had changed and that we were being called to respond to these new needs. Yet, in order to respond fully and appropriately, we needed to return to the classrooms, not as teachers but as students. . . . This is much the same as what Saint Dominic did for the friars — he sent them to University *before* sending them out to preach. Indeed, we were returning to the roots of our founder![1]

> "We needed to return to the classrooms, not as teachers but as students!"
> Sister Mary Donnelly

Aquinas Institute of Religious Studies (AIRS) Program

Begun in the summer of 1952 as an initiative of the Grand Rapids Dominicans to continue the education of their Sisters in theology, Sacred Scripture, canon law, and ascetical and spiritual theology, the program was initially known as the Institute for the Spiritual Formation of Sisters. The original purpose was to better prepare Sisters as Catholic educators[2] and to expand their vision of Religious Life. Taking six credits each summer for four summers, the Sisters earned a Certificate in Theology at the completion of the program.

With expansion of the curriculum in 1958 and again in 1964, the program expanded to six summers and the degree upon completion was a Master of Arts in Religious Education. As the program grew in numbers and inclusion

---

1. S. Mary Donnelly, unpublished reflections 2012.
2. Although Catholic Sisters were responsible for most of the teaching of religion in elementary and secondary schools, the study of theology itself was closed to them, save one school at St. Mary's College, Notre Dame, where S. Madeleva Wolff, CSC, established the School of Sacred Theology, which was open to women, in 1944.

of students beyond the Sisters themselves, the summer school moved its location several times — from Marywood to Grand Rapids Catholic Central to St. Andrew's Cathedral parish hall in Grand Rapids to Saint Paul Seminary in Saginaw and finally to Aquinas College in Grand Rapids where it concluded operations in 1983.

While the secluded physical arrangements at Saint Paul Seminary, Saginaw, were conducive to developing a spirit of community among faculty and students, other circumstances, such as inadequate library facilities, lack of exposure to other scholastic disciplines, and insufficient contact with society in general, led the faculty to engage in a three-year self-study of curriculum, accreditation, and location. Two results came out of this 1966 self-study. First, move the Institute to Aquinas College and second, develop a new thrust to the curriculum which recognized the needs of lay women and men as well as vowed religious and clergy. The new program, broader in scope and design, not only offered courses for Religious, it was now open to lay women, lay men, and clergy. With the change of location and curriculum the Institute changed its name to the Aquinas Institute for Religious Studies (AIRS). The Institute sought and received renewed accreditation from the North Central Association of Colleges and Secondary Schools.

The Institute had an integrated approach, providing not only a first-rate education for those who taught religion, but also an opportunity for the individual to live in community with faculty and peers sharing daily prayer, especially the Eucharist. The genius of having faculty and students residing in the same residence hall, sharing meals, prayer, liturgy, and fun together resulted in a much fuller learning experience. Informal conversation among faculty and students outside of the classroom lent itself to fuller and deeper integration of the material presented. This approach to education, having adults study, live, pray, and play together created an electric spark of learning. This spark ignited the excitement of new learning as mature minds grappled with philosophical and religious problems and ideas.

In the thirty-one years of the AIRS program 618 people received either a Master's degree and/or a Certificate in Theology. Among the Grand Rapids Dominican Sisters, 204 earned a Master of Arts in Religious Studies and 111 Sisters earned a Certificate in Theology. Among those who were not members of the Grand Rapids Dominicans, 165 Women Religious, and 138 priests, brothers, lay women, and lay men received either a Master of Arts in Religious Studies or a Certificate in Theology.

The AIRS program broadened the students' understanding of theology, liturgy, the world, and themselves. According to Sister Joan Thomas, who served as administrative assistant from 1972-1981 and director from 1982-1983, "Our Sisters had the dream and the foresight to provide the setting and the challenge for minds to meet, for faith to be shared, and for lives to touch one another."[3] The program's emphasis on community, study, and communal prayer was thoroughly Dominican. A spirit of inclusivity and hospitality was evident in all aspects of the program, which led to a deeper appreciation and understanding, not only of the material presented, but of those with whom one shared learning and living. The program was far from being an exclusive enclave of like-minded people, for the long-term director of the AIRS program, Fr. Philip Hanley, OP, often included an atheist or agnostic individual among the instructors, proclaiming that Catholicism must hold its own in the "marketplace of ideas." And it did; and the faith life of the participants grew stronger with each summer's passing days. At a time when there were few opportunities for education of this type, the AIRS program was truly unique. It is evident that the Institute fulfilled its purpose of educating those who would teach religion, as well as deepening the personal faith life of its participants.

> Fr. Philip Hanley, OP, often included an atheist or agnostic individual among the AIRS instructors, proclaiming that Catholicism must hold its own in the "marketplace of ideas."

Theology in Other Colleges and Universities

While many Sisters sought a degree or certificate through the AIRS program, others found religious studies further afield.

Approximately twenty-five Sisters completed a graduate-level degree in a religion-related field in colleges and universities across the United States from Boston College and Providence College in the East to Holy Names College in Oakland, California, in the West. Several attended Creighton University in Omaha, University of Notre Dame in Indiana, the University of St. Thomas in Houston; Marygrove College, Detroit; Mundelein, Loyola, and Catholic Theological Union in Chicago; St. John Seminary, Plymouth,

---

3. S. Joan Thomas in conversation 2013.

Michigan; St. Mary of the Woods, Indiana; Loyola, New Orleans; Washington Theological Union and Western Theological Seminary, Holland, as well as others.

Two Sisters studied theology abroad at the University of Louvain in Belgium for one semester in 1971. This opportunity was made available by the Bishop of the Diocese of Grand Rapids, Joseph Breitenbeck. Concerned about losing Sisters to other states with the pending defeat of Proposal C, which would have provided public funds for the financially strapped parochial schools, the Bishop offered a semester of study at Louvain in exchange for a promise on the part of the Sisters to remain in the Diocese in the area of adult education for at least four years upon their return.

One of those Sisters, Jarrett DeWyse, remembers it well:

> Our studies were in English since the Flemish School of Theology had an English speaking sector to accommodate the American Seminary located in Louvain. Along with our classes, we visited many of the catechetical centers in Europe, gleaning the latest in theological thought and process. Upon returning to Grand Rapids, we served in the Diocesan Office of Religious Education for four years, setting up five week series of classes in parish centers around the diocese, using the Catholic paper as the content and employing adult education processes. We also did facilitator training of lay directors of parish education, Sisters and clergy from the area as well as teaching in the program ourselves. Since much of the development of Vatican Council II theology was just making its way to the parishes, it was a fruitful endeavor for the adult church as they engaged in understanding and assimilation of the ideas about the church as "the people of God." Topics in the series included The Church, Justice in the Modern World, Scripture Study, Morality, and Sacraments.[4]

Bishop Breitenbeck had caught the spirit of collegiality promoted by Vatican Council II and his confidence in and support of the Dominican Sisters was a boost of morale, not only for the two who went to Louvain, but for all those who did not go, who knew that the Bishop of the Diocese of Grand

---

4. S. Jarrett DeWyse in an e-mail to the general editor on April 21, 2013.

Rapids was willing to financially support the education of adults and wanted Sisters to be part of that new endeavor.

For other Sisters, the place of study was often determined by the geographical region where a Sister lived or by the financial aid available. The presence of other Sisters in the area for supportive community was another consideration. The variety of schools and colleges brought a diversity of approaches. Then as now, there was and is a rich spectrum of thought and positions on matters of theology/religion — all of which make for lively dinner conversations.

Not everyone understood the zeal of the Sisters in their pursuit of degrees in the sacred arts. One Sister recalls the following incident as she completed her doctoral studies at Catholic University of America in Washington, DC.

Sr. Barbara Reid, teacher and preacher

> ... one of our Dominican Brothers could not imagine what a woman would do with a degree in Scripture. It happened when I was in doctoral studies at Catholic University and living at the Dominican House of Studies. One of our Dominican Brothers from the House of Studies happened to meet another of our Sisters at a meeting. In the course of their conversation, he waxed eloquent about what a model student I was, practically living in the library, studying morning, noon, and night. Then he asked, "But what will she ever do with a doctorate in Scripture?"[5]

This Sister has dedicated her entire professional life to bringing Biblical scholarship in an accessible format to preachers, teachers, and catechists. The question has been answered in a way that this Dominican Brother could never have imagined.[6]

---

5. S. Barbara Reid, in e-mail April 2013.

6. S. Barbara has received numerous awards and published several hundred articles and book reviews. Her most recent books are: *Abiding Word* (3 vols., 2011, 2012, 2013), *Taking Up the Cross: New Testament Interpretations through Latina and Feminist Eyes* (2007) [Spanish translation: *Reconsiderar La Cruz* (2009)], the *Parables for Preachers* series (1999-2001), *A Retreat with St. Luke* (2000), and *Choosing the Better Part? Women in the Gospel of Luke* (1996). She is currently writing *Sophia's Table: An Introduction to Feminist Biblical Interpretation*, and is general editor for the 60 volumes of the *Wisdom Commentary Series*, forthcoming from Liturgical Press. She holds a doctoral degree in Scripture with a specialization in New Testament from Catholic University of America. Currently, she is a full professor, Vice President and

STUDY

Mission to Hungary with Srs. Juliana (left) and Elizabeth Barilla (second from left). Sr. Lucianne Siers (center) facilitated the mission through the auspices of the United States Conference of Catholic Bishops. This family offered hospitality to the Sisters in Hungary.

Sr. Mary Catherine Brechting teaching mathematics at Aquinas College

> Dangerous geographical regions were not a deterrent to the Sisters' work.

Of the twenty-five Sisters who completed graduate degrees in a field related to religion, several became pastoral administrators, often in remote parishes where no ordained priest was available. Others became hospital chaplains and hospice workers accompanying people in their most vulnerable moments in life and in death. Some worked for the evangelization of persons overlooked because of language barriers, poverty, or cultural differences. Still others administered religious education programs in parishes in the United States as well as in distant lands such as Eastern Europe after the fall of the Iron Curtain. Dangerous geographical regions were not a deterrent as several Sisters served or currently work in perilous regions of the world such as Honduras and Guatemala. Still others served in campus ministry at universities and colleges, as spiritual directors and in centers for retreats and spirituality.

Although many of these Sisters are now retired from compensated ministry, most felt it part of their ministry to train lay women and men to con-

---

Academic Dean at Catholic Theological Union in Chicago. She has served on the executive committee and the editorial board as well as book review editor for the *Catholic Biblical Quarterly* and was elected Vice President (and President-elect) of the Catholic Biblical Association in 2013. She also served as president of the Chicago Society of Biblical Research in 2000-2001.

Theological and Professional Study

tinue in the ministry. All continue to serve in some capacity as companions, listeners, tutors, wise and thoughtful women who share their lives, offer their prayers, and continue to be seekers in that sacred science known as theology and defined as "faith seeking understanding."

Secular Arts and Sciences

In his address to Sisters in 1951, Pius XII supported and encouraged sound professional preparation of all teaching Sisters.

> This presupposes that your teaching Sisters are masters of the subjects they expound. See to it, therefore, that they are well trained and that their education corresponds in quality and academic degrees to that demanded by the State. Be generous in giving them all they need, especially where books are concerned, so that they may continue their studies and thus offer young people a rich and solid harvest of knowledge. This is in keeping with the Catholic idea which gratefully welcomes all that is naturally good, beautiful and true, because it is an image of the Divine goodness and beauty and truth.[7]

This idea that teaching Sisters be well prepared in both methods and content was bolstered in the United States by the Sister Formation Conference, which grew out of a meeting of a small committee at the National Catholic Educational Association in 1952. It began with a presentation by Sister Mary Emil Penet, IHM, of Monroe, Michigan, who not only described the struggle to both form young Sisters in Religious Life *and*

7. Pius XII, Counsel to Teaching Sisters, paragraph 18, 1951, found on Vatican website.

Sr. Donna Jean Thelen with her students

prepare them to be professional teachers at the same time, but also presented an organized plan to solve the problem. Her presentation received a standing and prolonged ovation by the Sisters present, although not by the clergy who clearly saw the financial implications for the plan. Thus papal encouragement to have professionally prepared Sisters in the classroom corresponded with the Sisters' own felt need to send Sisters out to teach who were fully prepared to do so.

These forces coalesced to launch a nation-wide effort to prepare teaching Sisters with undergraduate degrees and certifications *before* entering the classroom. Although this effort was met with resistance from pastors and school superintendents who had grown to depend on large groups of Sisters ever ready to head the classrooms of parish schools for minimal salaries,[8] the times and the needs for greater education for the sake of the mission were overwhelming.

Sr. Ann Michael Farnsworth teaching at Marywood

Yet another reality supported the decision to educate Sisters before sending them out to teach. Changes in the certification requirements by states made it impractical to send Sisters out to teach prior to receiving their degrees and teaching certificates. A practice known as the "twenty year plan" had been in place for many years. In some cases, a newly professed Sister began teaching with few if any college credits, then took many years of summer school to finish her bachelor's degree. It took both courage and resolve to forfeit compensated ministry for full-time study. This decision was a risky

---

8. From 1940 to 1953 the cost of living had increased 93% while Sister salaries had increased 25%. In general Sisters were paid half the salary of Religious Brothers who in turn were paid half the salaries of their lay counterparts. See Karen M. Kennelly, CSJ, *The Religious Formation Conference, 1954-2004* (2009), pp. 9-10.

one: to decrease the number of stipends, small as they were, that the Congregation received, while at the same time, to increase the amount of money that the Congregation was spending on education for teaching Sisters.

Although states had increased the demands for teacher certification, it took an international crisis for the country to intervene at the federal level and fund education. In 1956 the Russian premier, Nikita Khrushchev, made a threatening statement to western ambassadors. His statement was translated: "We will bury you." One year later, in 1957 the Russians launched Sputnik and the Space Race was begun. The United States government became alarmed over the Soviet Union's aggressive posturing and its presence in space. Why were the schools in the United States not producing scientists comparable to the Russians? The National Defense Education Act (1958) led to resurgence in science and mathematics education, now viewed as essential to the defense of the country. *What Ivan Knows That Johnny Doesn't,* the title of a book comparing Soviet and American textbooks, reflected the fear that American schools were inferior to those in the Soviet Union. This was viewed as a dangerous situation as the Cold War escalated.

Some Sisters took advantage of the National Defense Education Act grants, studying mathematics, chemistry, biology, and other sciences. Frugal in living, vowed to hold all things in common, Sisters almost always were able to apply one grant to two individuals. So it was that Sisters received master's level and doctoral degrees through federal grants in the sciences and returned to teach and lead science and mathematics departments in high schools and colleges.

Humanities, Sciences, and Health Care

America in the mid-twentieth century began to move to the suburbs of major cities. Several reasons are given for this movement, e.g., post–World War II baby boom, influx of African Americans recruited from southern states to work in foundries producing automobiles in larger northern cities, crowded conditions in urban areas, and aggressive advertising for suburban living. Whatever the reasons, America was on the move. New schools were built and public schools were non-sectarian, no longer holding an anti-Catholic bias as had been true in the late nineteenth, early twentieth centuries. As

In the mid-twentieth century, America was on the move.

mentioned earlier, teacher certification demands became more stringent; education became more expensive; and the cost of living increased, making it impossible for Congregations of Sisters to live on the meager stipend that was customary in the parochial school system.

After Vatican Council II, parents felt less compelled to send their children to Catholic schools with their rising tuition costs.[9] The once-hoped-for public funding for non-public schools by way of Proposal C failed to pass in Michigan. Some schools engaged in mergers with neighboring parishes, but many closed and began catechetical programs to prepare children for the sacraments and to continue their religious education. Many parishes could not afford a full-scale operation of a separate school and religious education for both children and adults.

Sisters began to look for compensated ministry where it was available and in arenas that were compatible with the mission of the Congregation. That often meant returning to graduate school for a degree in religious education, the humanities, or sciences. Over one hundred Sisters received graduate-level degrees between the years 1966 and 2000; of these, eighteen were at the doctoral level. All of these Sisters are living as of this writing. Although most are well into their retirement years, they continue to serve as teachers, mentors, auxiliary staff in administrative positions, and in pastoral care.

Between 1966 and 2000, many Sisters received degrees in non-theological fields. In 1967, three Sisters received master's degrees related to teaching; the next two years saw thirteen master's level and/or doctoral degrees in fields of study ranging from library science and mathematics to biology, music, chemistry, philosophy, and administration.

While some funding for education of the Sisters beyond their bachelor's degree came from federal grants and scholarships, much came from the operational expenses of the Congregation. In 1969, as the availability of specific grants declined, a board was formed to advise the Prioress and her Council regarding Sisters' requests to study full time.

In the next two years, 1970-72, thirty-four graduate-level degrees were

---

9. The Council of Baltimore (1844) exhorted Bishops to establish Catholic schools in every parish and mandated that parents send their children to them. This was not reaffirmed by Vatican Council II.

earned in education, chemistry, physics, philosophy, psychology, the classics, and social work. The Sisters had clearly begun to prepare for work outside the traditional fields of elementary and secondary school teaching. In the next decade an average of five or six Sisters completed a graduate-level degree in a field of study other than religion each year.

Sisters attended colleges and universities that were both Catholic and non-Catholic, private and state land-grant types. A listing of some, not all, includes: University of Notre Dame, University of Oklahoma, Eastern Michigan University, Central Michigan University, University of Michigan, Michigan State University, University of New Mexico, Wayne State University, Western Michigan University, Ohio State University, Boston College, Boston University, University of Illinois, Rosary College (now Dominican University) in River Forest, Illinois; University of Detroit, Catholic University of America, Xavier University in Chicago, Creighton University, Bowling Green University, Ferris State University, Loyola University of Chicago, University of Wisconsin, Emory University, Purdue University, Mundelein, Regis University in Denver, University of Arizona, Washington Theological Union, and Laval University in Quebec, Canada.

Ministry in Medicine

Although nurses had been members of the Congregation since the 1930s, the numbers were initially few and the work confined to the care of the Sisters in their senior years. The value of the salaries of nursing Sisters was soon realized and the numbers thereby increased both for the ministry itself and as a means of subsidizing the ministry of education in parishes unable to pay a living wage to the teaching Sisters.

In 1952 Mother Victor wrote to the Sisters about the decision to serve in a hospital in California. In addition to the desire for each Sister nurse to "serve in the field for which she was prepared," Mother Victor freely acknowledged a practical reason for this decision: "Since each Sister assigned is to receive a salary the Community has nothing to lose and much to gain that will be added to our rapidly depleting coffers."[10]

10. Mona Schwind, *Period Pieces*, p. 271.

Sister nurses' salaries were five times that of teachers and these Sisters clearly subsidized the ministry of education. Sometimes this was at the cost of exhaustion from long hours, double shifts, and little time for recreation or respite. Although a few Sisters who had their RN degrees were sent to study for their master's degree at Catholic University, most were not expected to go beyond what was needed to work in hospitals for the salaries that could underwrite the ministries of the Congregation.

Nurses needed certification to work in hospitals. Uncertified aides might assist in the Sisters' own infirmary and often did, but hospitals, whether Catholic or not, could not hire a nurse without credentials.

Food Service Ministry

Housekeepers, as they were known, were often overworked and under-appreciated. While teaching Sisters had at least a break in the intensity of their jobs over holidays and summers, the housekeeping Sister continued the relentless tasks of meal preparation, laundry, and cleaning — on occasion assisted by the younger Sisters in the house. Unlike the customs of the old country in Europe, there was no official lower status for the housekeeping or extern Sister marked by a different habit or privileges; yet there was a feeling among many of a second-class status. As teaching and nursing Sisters left the convent for enrichment classes or a weekend workshop to upgrade their skills, the housekeeper often stayed home. That changed with the inimitable Sister Bede Frahm, born in South Dakota, a convert to Catholicism and a woman with a dream — to deepen the spirituality of those who were, by choice, chance, or appointment, in the role of "homemaker" for the Sisters.

Sister Bede Frahm was a woman with a dream to deepen the spirituality of those who were in the role of "homemaker" for the Sisters.

Sister Bede was missioned at St. Stephen's Parish, Grand Rapids, from 1955 to 1960. She had earned a Bachelor's degree from Fontbonne College, majoring in Home Economics with a double minor in Science and Philosophy. One day she asked Sister Agnes Leo Hauser, the Councilor in charge of education, "What if I asked the Sisters if they would like to come together and we would have a conversation about our work?" Sister Agnes Leo said, "That's wonderful." So Sister Bede sent out penny postcards inviting the Sister Housekeepers to come together. About seventy-five Sisters who were in housekeeping continued to meet and learn about nutrition and kitchen equipment; more importantly they began to think of themselves as having worth and competence.

Soon after, Sister Agnes Leo invited Sister Bede to attend a conference at Fontbonne College in St. Louis. It was a conference hosted by Brother Herman Zacarelli, CSC. Sister Bede recalls that first meeting:

> It was two like spirits meeting the same day. From then on we carried on a conversation. He was concerned about education. I was concerned about spiritual development. So I planned a retreat for our food service people. I asked him to get me a priest. He sent me Father Ken Silvia, CSC. . . . Ken was just a newly ordained priest and he has a charisma about him. I fell in love with the guy. He was that sensitive to people, to the housekeepers. He worked with Herman and I worked with him giving retreats for ten years. That began the conversation between Herman and me. I was the one who asked him to add the spiritual dimension to his workshops.[11]

Sr. Bede Frahm, innovator for education and development of food service sisters

The threesome formed a team who constituted the Food Research Center, which gave retreats for food service personnel in service to the Church. Sister Bede gave conferences on spirituality; Fr. Ken added the sacramental and theological dimension, and Brother Herman focused on the practical matters.

Sister housekeepers became known as Food Service Directors. They began to think of themselves as accomplished professionals entitled to time off, retreats, vacations, and ongoing education just like the rest of the Sisters. Sister Maxine reflected on her experience:

> After Fontbonne, we got to the point of asking for one day off each week and time off in the summer to study. We had more

---

11. S. Bede Frahm, Oral History, Marywood Archives, Folder 2011.194, p. 25.

Sr. Janet Marie Heitz in food service ministry

confidence and enjoyed more camaraderie with one another. It took me eighteen years, but I did get my degree.[12]

In the latter decades, women entering the Congregation have come fully prepared professionally with academic degrees and certification in teaching, nursing, occupational therapy, law, accounting, and other fields of study.

Conclusion

Much like the cleric in Chaucer's *Canterbury Tales* about whom it is said, "Gladly would he learn, and gladly teach," the Dominican Sisters continue to both learn and teach whether in a classroom, a hospital room, a kitchen, or parish center well into their 70s, 80s and 90s. As one Sister in her late 90s recently said, "I can't hear and I can't see, but otherwise I am in good health." This Sister is current in political issues, writes and calls her congressional representatives regularly, and responded to the crisis of the attack on the World Trade Center by resolving to read the Koran for better understanding of Muslims. Through vision blurred with macular degeneration and hearing aids turned to their highest level, this Sister continues to study, listen, converse, and teach us how to age with dignity and grace. On the Marywood campus, her numbers are legion.

A life of study and education leads to a questioning mind and independent thinking.

A life of study and education leads to a questioning mind and independent thinking. Until the twentieth century, most women in Western civilizations were not allowed to avail themselves of university education, and although the Catholic Church and Women Religious in particular did much to promote the education of girls and women, it was not until the 1950s that women were allowed to study theology. It was sincerely believed that women were too fragile to endure the rigors required by those who chose to pursue the "life of the mind." In parts of the world today, women's education is minimal if it exists at all, and some oppressive regimes forbid the education of women entirely,[13] an injustice which Dominicans everywhere in the world work to mitigate.

12. S. Maxine Plamondon, phone conversation with the general editor, May 7, 2013.
13. A fifteen-year-old Pakistani girl, Malala Yousufzai, was shot in the head at point-blank

Theological and Professional Study

Women Religious working with, in, and for the Catholic Church have stood their ground on the education of women through centuries. In the early years, the education and study of Women Religious was in a semi-monastic structure and was often imaged with the metaphor of *sponsa Christi*, the "bride of Christ." Protected by enclosure, habit, and custom, Sisters continued to be educated and to teach and serve others. After Vatican Council II, education and study continued but now in the company of ordinary people living their daily lives in all of their glory and grittiness. Like their pre–Vatican Council II counterparts, the Sisters live the evangelical counsels newly interpreted, but fundamentally the same. Out of action determined through contemplative prayer and study, supporting each other in community, serving the needs of the poor in fact and in spirit, the Sisters are more likely to resonate with the metaphor *filia justítia*, daughter of justice — with and for Christ and in the church Catholic.

The Sisters resonate with the metaphor *filia justitia*, daughter of justice — with and for Christ and in the church Catholic.

---

range for the crime of advocating for education for girls in 2012. She has become a symbol of the resistance of efforts to deny education to women by groups such as the Taliban.

PART III

Common Life: Essential to Dominican Life

COMMON LIFE IS one of the essential elements of living Dominican Religious Life. In the pre-conciliar era, common life meant doing almost everything together. With their communities founded in the medieval cloistered lifestyle, Women Religious lived — often quite happily — in a world marked by uniformity and commonality where most everything was spiritualized and daily events were often interpreted toward transcendence, e.g., the morning bell awakening the convent inhabitants was the "voice of God" calling one to rise. Even with the numerous restrictions to personal decision making, many women matured into fully functioning and happy adults. Others maintained a sweet and childlike dependence. Still others did not flourish under the system and were clearly unhappy individuals, but reluctant for a variety of reasons to break their vows and leave Religious Life. As the cloistered walls were breached with the arrival of the modern age as well as the impetus of Vatican Council II, and the rising consciousness of peoples everywhere, the world of the Woman Religious changed as well.

Like nearly every other aspect of Religious Life, the structures and daily reality of living common life have changed dramatically in the post-conciliar years. The following three essays describe some of these changes. Most members are convinced that the new ways of living community are in the best interest of the community, but some do not think so; nevertheless, a veritable tidal wave of change in common life occurred. Traditional large group living in a hierarchically structured configuration has been almost entirely abandoned over the past five decades.

> **One reality remains unchanged: the attitude of deep concern and care for one another and commitment to preaching the Gospel.**

In spite of the hardships, the awkward moments, the misunderstandings, one reality that remains unchanged is the attitude of deep concern and care for one another and the commitment to be about the ministry of "preaching" the good news of the Gospel to all people by whatever means possible and available. The shift has been one from living *in* community to living community. Sisters are *for* each other, even though they may not live with each other sharing the domestic tasks of everyday life.

The first two essays shed some light on both the means of and the reasons for the changes. In the first essay, the way that life was organized to foster community in the past is compared to the way it is organized now. This essay describes the changes in governance, work, housing, gathering times, committees, and other ways that Sisters come together to pray, to work, and to enjoy the companionship of one another.

In the second essay in this section, the actual practice of living together with all of its joys and difficulties is described. The change from uniformity in most things to unity in spirit is seen as the shifts occurred in the details of life from clothing to the daily schedule for praying, eating, sleeping, and working. The shift in authority to a more collegial form of shared responsibility among interdependent adults is also described.

In the third essay the many ways that life has expanded to include more people since Vatican Council II is described. Some of these people were former members while others are women and men who share a love for Dominican life, but are not called to a vowed expression of it. They are members of the phenomenon widespread among congregations of Women Religious throughout the nation known as Associate Life.

Yet another way in which the circle of community has expanded is through intentional and frequent collaboration with other Dominican Sisters both in this country and throughout the world. The Dominican Leadership Conference, regional alliances, e.g., Dominican Alliance[1] (Midwest/South), Dominican Federation of Sisters and Associates,[2] Parable Conference, Col-

---

1. Through the auspices of the Dominican Alliance, Sisters Kate Okolocha and Roseline Elemowu from St. Catherine of Siena in Nigeria live at Marywood and study for their degrees at Aquinas College.

2. The Dominican Sisters Conference (DSC) was formed in 2010 by joining the Dominican Leadership Conference and the Federation of Dominican Sisters USA. Its mission is to unite "the sisters and associates of the U.S. Dominican Congregations in their mission to preach

Common Life

laborative Dominican Novitiate, Dominican Justice Promoters, Dominican Institute for the Arts, and the Dominican Volunteers USA are all organized ways in which the Dominican gifts of prayer, study, common life, and service continue to flourish through collaboration. On the international level 151 Congregations of Dominican Apostolic Sisters from 110 countries joined together in 1995 for closer collaboration. Known as the Dominican Sisters International, the Sisters support one another in fostering a more compassionate world order through peace and justice. All of these groups are among the ways that the Dominican Sisters ~ Grand Rapids have extended the concept of common life to be ever-more inclusive.

---

the Gospel of Jesus, standing as a clear voice for truth, justice and peace" (e-mail from S. Pat Farrell, President of DSC, Jan. 16, 2014).

Life in Common — Structures That Hold Us Together

The common life, by enriching our prayer, ministry and study, forwards our Dominican mission of proclaiming the Gospel.
CONSTITUTION & STATUTES #25, P. 8

Speak of nothing as your own, but consider all things as community property. Your superior shall distribute food and clothing according to the needs of each, not in equal measure to all, for all do not have the same physical strength.
RULE OF ST. AUGUSTINE, USED WITH PERMISSION FROM
S. BARBARA BEYENKA, OP, SINSINAWA, APRIL 4, 1996

COMMON LIFE: IT is not exactly like a family, or the military, or a medieval court. It is not a company or business, college residence hall, sorority, or sports team. As it exists today, there are no models for common life as most Women Religious live it. It is new territory. What was in the past no longer is; the change has been swift and nearly complete. The Sisters do indeed love and care for one another. Yet, except in a few cases, they do not live in the traditionally structured convent of four to twelve members with a superior to oversee their lives together. Once it was the case that every aspect of life was regulated by rules interpreted and enforced by the local superior. That was the structure that held common life for many decades. Now the personal responsibility of the individual Sister is the norm for decision making in matters involving everyday life. Few Sisters live in the traditional convent configuration anymore, and those who do structure a collegial form of governance.

Structures are a necessity; without some underlying structure, neither house nor bird nest, neither body nor building could withstand the slightest breeze. So it is that structures held and now hold life in common for Sisters. Specific structures of governance and daily living continue to give shape and strength to the Sisters' way of life, even though the nature of the structures has changed.

General Chapters

In the pre-Conciliar era, General Chapters[1] were held every six years to elect a Prioress and her Council and to review the life of the Congregation. Proposals were submitted ahead of time and the Chapter sessions were held in secret. Much like the election of a pope, the delegates were sworn to secrecy and sequestered from any contact with others during the Chapter. No outsider was allowed in the Chapter room, not even Sisters who were not delegates. One-half of the delegates were from appointed Superiors and the other half were elected from those Sisters who had taken permanent vows. Until the Acts of Chapter were promulgated following the Chapter itself, no one other than the delegates knew what was happening.

The transition began in 1966 when Mother Victor Flannery, the Prioress for eighteen years, sensed the momentous changes that were about to transpire as she stepped away from her long tenure (1948-1966) as the Major Superior of the Congregation:

> We are assembled here today to take the steps preliminary to the election of a Prioress General. This group is assuming a tremendous task in a time when the whole Church seems to be in a state of flux and turmoil. . . . The matters to be treated as well as the time it is being held give great importance to this Chapter. We must proceed slowly. Not all the *new* is good nor is all the *old* — bad. It will take much prayer, prudence and working

---

1. Chapter is the name given to periodic official meetings in monasteries and religious houses to manage governance.

together for a common goal to have these days — when completed, ratified in heaven.[2]

The changes began immediately. Wider participation and greater transparency by way of daily briefings to all the Sisters marked the beginning weeks of this Fifteenth General Chapter. Two Sisters who were not delegates were brought in to assist with secretarial duties. A committee was established to sort through and categorize the 900 proposals that had been submitted. These were forwarded to fourteen committees to be discussed and acted upon by larger community participation. The opening windows of Vatican Council II had opened the way for greater participation, less secrecy, and higher levels of ownership.

Very quickly other changes took place. Practices from the medieval period, e.g., the age-old custom of kneeling to ask permission of a Superior fell by the wayside, as did the prostration known as the *venia*, which was an act of humility for infractions of the rule such as making a loud noise, coming late to prayers or meals, or dropping a dish in the refectory — a medieval monastic term for dining room.

Home visits, once restricted to every three years and always requiring a companion, were left up to the discretion of the Sister herself. Those whose homes were located overseas or at a great distance were encouraged to visit every three years.

The Chapter recessed with the election of Sister Aquinas Weber as the Prioress General of the Congregation. For the first time in living memory, the Chapter itself did not close, but remained open to reconvene the next summer for a second session — such was the immensity of the work to be done in response to the promulgations of Vatican Council II. And this Chapter was followed just two years later by a Chapter of Affairs in 1969 to continue the work begun in the Fifteenth General Chapter. For the first time, seculars, as they were known, were allowed to enter the Chapter room. Mr. Arthur Woodhouse, President of the Aquinas College Board of Trustees, Mr. John O'Connor, Director of Business and Finance at Aquinas College, and Dr. Norbert Hruby, President of Aquinas College, were invited to give an

---

2. Address at the opening of the Fifteenth General Chapter, 1966, Marywood Archives, File Drawer 01641.

accounting of the health and well-being of the college. This was a momentous occasion, marking a change in attitude and ownership for the college founded by the Sisters.

The Sixteenth General Chapter convened in 1972, electing Sister Norbert (Marjorie) Vangsness as Prioress. In her opening address, she called for trust in God and one another as the Sisters continued the journey begun just six years previously:

> The Lord has brought us this far through steps we cannot understand — we must put our trust in Him and go on from here. . . . Vatican Council II and *Ecclesiae Sanctae*³ gave us a leap forward into a different world. We cannot turn back. . . . Given then our common goal of showing forth to the world the God whose immense love we enjoy, we must provide effective means for the interplay of freedom and plurality in non-essentials along with the necessary tools for exercising responsibility and accountability for the quality of our life. This is no easy task, but it is an exciting one that should call forth all the creativity with which God has endowed us and which He expects us to put to good use.⁴

"The Lord has brought us this far through steps we cannot understand."
Sister Norbert (Marjorie) Vangsness

Since Sister Marjorie's term in office, there have been six Prioresses, each in turn helping set the direction of the Congregation "in keeping with the Gospel, the charism of Saint Dominic and the needs of the times," as stated in the *Constitution and Statutes*. They are: Sisters Teresa Houlihan (1980-1988); Carmelita Murphy (1988-1994); Barbara Hansen (1994-2000); Maribeth Holst (2000-2006); Nathalie Meyer (2006-2012); and Maureen Geary (2012-2018).

Governance between Chapters

Although Chapter is the highest level of authority when it is in session, surpassing that of the Prioress, the times between Chapters affect the lives

---

3. *Ecclesiae Sanctae* was an apostolic letter issued after the close of the Council giving directions for the adaptation and renewal of Religious Life.

4. S. Norbert Vangsness, Prioress, in *Religious Life: Lived Reality*, vol. 2 (1972), pp. viii, ix. Marywood Archives.

COMMON LIFE

of the Sisters on a daily basis. Prior to Vatican Council II, the Prioress as the Major Superior and the local Superiors were the sources of authority for all decisions great and small. With the principles of subsidiarity established by Vatican Council II, that changed.[5]

In the Dominican Order, governance is representative and participatory — and always for the common good. Building on this ancient tradition, the Congregation recognized the responsibility of the individual Sister to achieve the goals of the Congregation as never before. These ideals, laudable in theory, often fell short in the practice of the daily living in the post-Conciliar period. Sisters, who had been trained since childhood in the virtues of obedience and compliance, were not always prepared to handle the new freedoms and responsibilities with the adult maturation hoped for in the expression of the ideal.

These ideals, laudable in theory, often fell short in the practice of daily living.

For the first time, Sisters were given an amount of money monthly to be used for personal needs such as clothing, toiletries, entertainment, and so forth. The amount began with $10.00 and soon increased to $30.00 per month. Although a few women had earned money prior to entering Religious Life, many had come directly from high school and homes where they often simply asked their parents for what they needed. The custom of asking the superior for what was needed was not a big leap. Going to a store and purchasing items with one's own money was a large step and a new experience for many. Not surprisingly, there was a learning curve on the use of money as well as the cost of items.

Thrift shops and second-hand stores, combined with total inexperience in sizes and style, had some humorous results. A petite Sister relates:

> Honestly, when I first went to the store to buy something, I looked at the rack of clothes and I thought, "Size 12 looks good." Now, if you know me — but I bought it and I wore it. I thought people looked at me strangely. I went home and my sister said, "Oh my! You look like you just came off the boat!" because it was so big. But I had no idea.
>
> So my sister took me in hand and I got the size that should belong to me. All those things, I think, were very good for us because they wised you up.

---

5. Subsidiarity, a principle of Catholic social teaching, holds that human affairs are best handled at the lowest possible level, closest to the affected persons.

Life in Common

I don't believe that you went through what we went through: trying to find out what colors matched, "how do you wear your hair?" and "what do you do?" I enjoyed the whole process, a growth process.[6]

By 1972, the stresses of adaptation began to be felt. In her opening address at the Sixteenth General Chapter, Sister Mary Aquinas Weber summed up the situation:

I am aware of polarization amongst our members because of change in life styles, which include our manner of prayer, new works, types of government which involve principles of collegiality and subsidiarity, freedom in choice of dress, the use of a personal allowance, a change in our approach to formation and retreats — to mention only a few. It appears that the traditionally uniform manner of approach to the above has for the most part slipped from the scene of American Religious Life. Uniformity among us is surely not a primary value, but a strong sense of unity based upon mutual trust is essential if we are to realize our corporate and individual potential.[7]

> "Uniformity among us is surely not a primary value, but a strong sense of unity based upon mutual trust is essential."
> Sister Aquinas Weber

It took a great deal of mutual trust for the next big step toward practicing the principles of collegiality and subsidiarity called for by Vatican Council II.

For the first time in its history, the members of the Congregation were asked their preferences for place and type of ministry. Prior to this, the custom had been that the Sisters received their appointments on the Feast Day of the Assumption of the Blessed Virgin Mary, August 15th, and all were ready to move to a new assignment or remain at the former one. Many Sisters recall the tension and excitement as they gathered in chapel to receive the envelope that held the assignment determining the fate of their living and working for the next year.

Now Sisters apply for openings after consultation with the Director of Personnel Services. Although each Sister still receives her assignment in August each year at the Ceremony of Apostolic Missioning, there is usually no surprise in the envelope, rather the card contains a confirmation of her

---

6. S. Amata Fabbro, Oral History, 2010. Marywood Archives.
7. S. Aquinas Weber at the Sixteenth General Chapter, June 15, 1972, Opening Address, Marywood Archives, Drawer 01641.

assignment and an affirmation from the Prioress in these words: "Go forth in confidence, for God will give you the gift of preaching. You will lack for nothing."

Another practice that changed in the new realm of collegiality and subsidiarity was the scheduling of daily meals, prayers, and recreation. Where once the schedule for each day, known as the *horarium* in convent parlance, was determined by the Prioress and sent out to all the Sisters, now the Sisters at each convent would determine their own schedule of prayer, meals, and recreation. This was determined at a house meeting and written in a contract known as a Community Living Agreement. Periodic house meetings throughout the year were set to review the contract and to discuss current issues around living in community.

In the Annals written in the early days of this new way of living together, the Sister Annalist noted:

> We voted on a collegial type of government for the year and then set up our horary (daily schedule).... Coordinators were elected for Liturgy, Bursar (treasurer), Contact Person, Car maintenance and Guests. It was also decided that we would have monthly house meetings chaired by a volunteer and a monthly celebration of birthdays and feast days prepared by another volunteer. Our work on the living agreement was based on last year's contract.[8]

Unaccustomed to candor, with little experience in actually facilitating a meeting of this type, the house meetings were a mixed success. For some the house meeting was an opportunity to grow as a group of mature women supportive of each other; for others it was a perfunctory meeting to fulfill the requirement; for still others it was an opportunity to air grievances of one kind or another.

A former Prioress describes the attitudes well:

> I think that in those years we were questioning the hierarchical structure that we had of a Superior and Sisters.... We recognized that Dominican spirituality is supposed to be in a circle. We each take our turns being elected to lead the circle. But then when the time is up, we go back into the circle

---

8. Annals of St. Alfred's Convent, Taylor, Michigan, 1973-1974, Marywood Archives.

Life in Common

and other people lead and so on. So that spilled over into how our convents were operated. For some of those years, we didn't use the word "Superior." We used "Coordinator," or whatever, for the one who would guide the house. Nobody was supposed to have more authority than anybody else. That was a growing movement, and they were tough times, tough times for Sisters, tough times for Leadership, during those years. But we grew through it and matured with it, in my opinion.[9]

"They were tough times, tough times for Sisters, tough times for Leadership." Sister Marjorie Vangsness

These were tough times indeed, and not just at the level of the relationships within a convent. Parish-owned parochial schools, a major source of employment for many Sisters, were closing their doors as the hoped-for financial boon by way of Proposal C failed to gain voter approval.[10] Eventually, parishes renovated the buildings that had been convents for use as parish centers and offices for catechetical services and adult education initiatives. Catholic families were leaving the city parishes for life in the suburbs. The people moving into the cities were neither Catholic nor in a position to pay tuition for their children's education, which was free in the public schools.

Sisters searched for work and housing — often this meant that Sisters would need to live singly or with one or two others. So it was that Sisters found themselves living with members of other congregations or living singly in an apartment in order to be in ministry.

The 1984 Chapter affirmed the position that "our source of bonding as a community is found in the sharing of common goals in our lives and ministries rather than the formulation of congregational com-

Sr. Agnes Thiel, leader and advocate for senior citizens

---

9. S. Marjorie Vangsness, Oral History, Marywood Archives, p. 13, April 9, 2008.

10. A poignant finality to anticipated financial aid was found in the annals of Immaculate Heart of Mary Convent, in Grand Rapids, Michigan, November, 1970: "In spite of months of prayer and hard work, Proposal C was passed prohibiting aid to private schools." Marywood Archives.

mitments to specific institutions or places."[11] Ministries diversified; justice and peace issues emerged as the new focus, as did an emphasis on enablement of laity, team ministry, and collaboration.

Area Structure

Srs. Ann Thielen (left) and Thaddeus Kowalinski engage in intense discussion.

With the new model of collegiality at the local level, a structure was needed to enable communications between Sisters working on the missions and the Congregational Leadership who were operating out of the Motherhouse (central headquarters) in Grand Rapids. In 1980, the Committee on Governance recommended the establishment of Areas, each with its own duly elected Coordinator, as a vehicle for greater participation and improved communication. The Chapter of 1984 approved this new structure and Areas continue to function as of this writing (2014). The purposes of the Area are threefold. First, the structure is meant to encourage unity and love among the Sisters; second, the Area is designed to promote the life of study; third, the Area is to facilitate participation in the governance of the Congregation and, for a time, it was the means for electing members to the General Chapters.

Area meetings, held at least two and usually three times each year, further the sense of unity and friendship especially in smaller and geographically distant groups. In this manner, the Area structure has fostered unity and love among the members as the Sisters come to know each other better through these gatherings.

During the Area meetings, the members discuss a topic chosen by the group and/or engage in the study of a topic that pertains to an upcoming decision, such as regarding a corporate stance.[12] In some cases, the Prioress and Council provide materials for study, while in other cases, the members decide what they specifically wish to explore. Either way, the Dominican emphasis on study continues to be a part of every Area meeting. As members

---

11. Chapter Briefs, 1984, Marywood Archives.
12. A corporate stance is an official position taken on an issue of importance and approved by a two-thirds majority of Sisters.

deepen their ability to listen and share ideas, the time-honored Dominican value of *disputatio*[13] is honed and members grow in appreciation for others, even those with whom they may not agree.

Through the elected (or occasionally appointed) Area Coordinators, two-way communication is established between members of each Area and the Prioress and Council. The Area Coordinators serve in the capacity of advisors to the Prioress and her Council as well as providing support for members of her Area in matters relating to the mission and ministry of the Congregation. When Area Coordinators and Leadership Team meet several times each year, matters of governance are discussed, advice is sought, Area meetings are planned, and best practices are shared.

In actuality, the functioning of the Areas varies with the Area itself, which may

The first Area Coordinators: (front row, left to right) Srs. Patrice Konwinski, Margaret Hillary, Mary Navarre, Stephanie Heitz, and facilitator Sr. Catherine Harmer, MMS, PhD; (middle row, left to right) Srs. Joan Thomas, Lisa Marie Lazio, Teresa Houlihan, Theresa Bray, and Orlanda Leyba; (back row, left to right) Srs. Margaret Thomas, Carmelita Murphy, Mary Ellen Novakoski, and Jean Reimer

have as many as fifty or as few as ten members. Area groups may be located close to the Motherhouse or hundreds of miles away. Recent advances in technology facilitating remote communication may change the structure of

---

13. *Disputatio* is an ancient Dominican practice of listening to an argument with a charitable stance and an "ear" to what may be true in a position contrary to one's own. Far from mere polite agreement, the debaters pursue a deep understanding of each other's position, make distinctions where needed, and maintain a goal of seeking truth with mutual respect and greater understanding rather than animosity.

some Areas in the near future, but the purposes of the Areas are essential to the living of the common life.

The General Assembly

In addition to the creation of Areas, another recommendation of the Committee on Governance was the idea of a General Assembly, the first of which was held in 1986. Scheduled to meet between General Chapters, the General Assembly was to "to be a source of unity, love and strength. . . . It is a forum for sharing, discussing, exploring and celebrating the life of the members."[14] For the first General Assembly, each Area played a significant role in planning, suggesting themes, creating Area banners, engaging in common study, and executing specific events. Part working conference, part "family" reunion, the first General Assembly resulted in a resounding affirmation of the willingness of the Sisters to be together and to work together. The title given to the Assembly, *Dominican Women: Embracing Today, Creating Tomorrow*, rang true to the experience. In the Annual Report, the long-term effects of the first General Assembly were articulated:

> Of even greater significance was the outcome of the working sessions in which so much was accomplished: the life and mission of the Congregation was renewed; substantive material from which to prepare directional statements for Chapter was provided. This data could shape our congregation's agenda for the next six years and it is this particular feature of the Assembly that is the basis for the theme: *Forging a Vision*. Of particular importance is that each of the Assembly's reporting groups noted peace and justice to be firmly fixed at the heart of Congregational life. This clearly manifests that deliberate efforts have been and are being made to strengthen and deepen a common understanding: for us as Dominicans, justice is the other face of truth.[15]

"For us as Dominicans, justice is the other face of truth."
1998 Annual Report

Following this inaugural event, the second General Assembly in 1992 identified Direction Statements and corresponding strategies for the Con-

---

14. *Constitution & Statutes*, #66, p. 38.
15. Annual Report, February 1988, Marywood Archives.

gregation. The first three Direction Statements called the Sisters to foster a contemplative stance that all Earth is sacred and interconnected; to stand in solidarity with people who are materially poor; and to commit themselves to be open to encountering the Holy in themselves, each other, and people of all cultures and lifestyles. Each of these commitments was followed with specific strategies for implementing them, and they have informed Sisters' decisions about ministry since the day the statements were promulgated.

Two additional Direction Statements were added in 1994 in which the Sisters committed themselves to stand with other women who suffer from oppression, poverty, and violence, and to act as advocates for children in local, national, and international communities. Together these Direction Statements have continued to unite the Sisters in their efforts on behalf of justice. In the Chapter newsletter at the close of the meetings, Sister Lenora Carmody reported: "We left Chapter with a deeper awareness of the openness to the Spirit and the collaboration with others that will be needed if we are to live out the commitments we had made or reaffirmed."[16]

Gathering Days

Each August all members of the Congregation gather at Marywood to celebrate the feast day of the founder, St. Dominic de Guzman, and to join the Jubilarians who are honored with a festive Eucharistic celebration and a

Gathering around the Peace Pole in front of Marywood

dinner prepared for them and their family and friends. It is a joyous occasion and an important means of fostering love and unity among the Sisters. Most importantly, this large gathering, like a family reunion, is an opportunity to bond together as Sisters and friends finding strength in a common faith and

---

16. S. Lenora Carmody, OP, Secretary for the General Chapter, General Chapter Briefs, July 5, 1994, Marywood Archives.

unity as a community serving the people of God with the resolve that comes from a life holding so much in common.

It was during the Gathering Days in August 1990 that the Sisters participated in a ceremony in which each member of the Congregation received her copy of the new *Constitution and Statutes*. The document received approbation from the Vatican office, Congregation for Institutes of Consecrated Life and Societies of Apostolic Life, on May 31, 1990, the Feast of Our Lady of the Sacred Heart, the Patroness of the Congregation. Nearly twenty years in the writing, the document provides the most fundamental basis for the Sisters' lives together. It articulates the identity of the Sisters as Dominican Women Religious and delineates the charisms and structures by which the Sisters live and minister. Thus was brought to completion the work begun over twenty years before at the direction of Vatican Council II.

Many ways and places to pray together

Committees, Task Forces, and Commissions

"It is only through sharing our views, our perceptions, our insights that we can arrive at a more complete reality of truth."
Sister Aquinas Weber

In the 1969 Chapter of Affairs (as opposed to a Chapter of Election, this Chapter focused on the particular business of the Congregation) Sister Aquinas Weber opened the meeting with these words:

Real communication requires of us: freedom, humility, and acceptance of the fact that the view which we share is limited, is incomplete. No one, be he bishop, priest, layman, Religious — sees reality as it is. It is only through sharing our views, our perceptions, our insights that we can arrive at a more complete reality of truth.[17]

Sharing views, perceptions, and insights meant then, as it does now, that people need to meet with each other over extended periods of time. Without anyone realizing it, the age of meetings, of newsprint and markers, of focus groups, of booked evenings and weekends, of crowded calendars had begun. Committee work, task forces, and commissions enabled all Sisters to participate in visioning the future together. It was a new kind of discipline to prepare for, attend, and contribute to meetings. Someone had to call and facilitate the meeting; someone had to take notes, type them up, and distribute them. However arduous the tasks of endless meetings, it was the primary method Sisters had and have to determine their future according to their insights and dreams. The Vatican Council II's principles of subsidiarity and collegiality demanded, and the "coming of age" supported, the trend that Sisters make the decisions that affect their lives, and that they do it in consultation with one another while honoring the tradition and authority of the Church in which they serve.

Sisters meet to discuss the future.

The decree *Dignitatis Humanae* from Vatican Council II, with its insistence on human freedom from coercion, was not lost on the Sisters. Early during the 1969 Chapter of Affairs, one of the Sisters, a gifted teacher, carefully laid out for the delegates the principles of human dignity and freedom. Reflecting on that day, she recalled:

Central to that position[18] was the role of the dignity and worth of every human being with particular emphasis on freedom and the ability to choose;

---

17. *Religious Life: Lived Reality*, p. ii.
18. "That position" refers to the structures, policies, and practices formulated in *Religious Life: Lived Reality* in response to the renewal called for by Vatican Council II.

that one would choose a vowed life, one would choose service, one would choose common living. Because freedom was such a central concept, we had a formal presentation on the concept of freedom from a philosophic perspective, which I was very honored to present. Freedom wasn't, "Do your own thing" or "Choose what you want." The presentation dealt with what freedom truly entailed to make a fully developed human person.[19]

The balancing of freedom and personal responsibility was on everyone's mind and heart. Mistakes would surely be made, but trust and goodness were at the heart of the matter. And the Sisters embraced the challenges before them with energy and enthusiasm.

In her opening remarks during the Nineteenth General Chapter, 1982, Sister Teresa Houlihan said: "A preferred future is our option and opportunity."[20] To this end, all Sisters were invited to participate according to their tastes and abilities in a primary group, a task force, a board, a committee, a commission, or any other structure that would include them in decision making. This was no time for passivity. All Sisters were to become involved in the formation of their preferred future. In this way, the Sisters responded fully to the call of the document *Perfectae Caritatis* to return to the charism of their founder, study the Scriptures, and read the signs of the times in which they lived.

More meetings to discern God's call (left to right): Srs. Lisa Marie Lazio, Joellen Barkwell, Evelyn Schoenborn, Joan Thomas, and Catherine Anderson

"A preferred future is our option and opportunity."
Sister Teresa Houlihan

---

19. S. Teresa Houlihan, Oral History, 2009, Marywood Archives.
20. General Chapter, 1982, June 12, Minutes of Session I, Archives 4.2 II Govt. A.

Newsletters — a Structure to Promote Unity

The newsletter *Rapport,* a vehicle for expressing opinions and clarifying thinking on matters relating to the renewal of Religious Life, supplanted circular letters from the Mother General which had been a regular feature in the life of the Congregation for decades. *Rapport* morphed into a more professional-looking magazine known as *Tessera* which included articles by both Sisters and laity. That in turn evolved into yet another means of communication among the Sisters — *News and Notes* and a separate publication known as *Dominican Futures* which focused on the development of benefactors. Finally, in the spring of 2010 the current magazine known as *Mission and Ministry* was inaugurated. It combines reflective pieces, news on ministry, and articles on topics relevant to development efforts. The use of technology, especially e-mail, has increased the frequency and ease of communication as well as reduced costs of postage and printing.

Concluding Observations

A shift is clearly evident in the structures supporting common life that evolved with the renewal of Religious Life following Vatican Council II. The locus of authority, while still officially vested in the Prioress and her Council, now is seen to also exist in the members themselves. Consultation with membership has become more and more an expected and regular practice of governance and responsibility of life lived in common. Whatever can be handled at the local level needs to be resolved there. Wherever one Dominican Sister resides, all reside. Each Sister has rights and responsibilities to share in the governance of the Congregation at the local, regional, and Congregational levels. Today Sisters continue in the fundamental values of shared common life in new ways, with new structures to accommodate the needs of this day for the times in which we live.

Living and Loving Day by Day

"This is how all will know that you are my disciples, if you have love for one another."

JOHN 13:35[1]

COMMUNITY LIVING IS an apostolic call embedded in the Constitution of the Congregation.

> Each of us is called to acclaim the gifts, acknowledge the needs and nurture the growth of one another. We strive to be patient with one another, to forgive one another and to seek forgiveness, to give generously and to receive gratefully.[2]

These beautiful words express the sincere desire of members of the Congregation to live together in peace and harmony. The reality of doing so is a life-long journey.

In this section on community living, the actuality of living community life in the twenty-first century is briefly compared with the customs of fifty years ago. Just how the transition occurred is treated in the bulk of the chapter. Through study, discussion, and experimentation, a new way of living

---

1. *New American Bible* in the edition, *Anselm Academic Study Bible*.
2. *Constitution & Statutes*, #22, p. 7.

community as active apostolic Women Religious in mutual and interdependent relationships is now the norm for the Sisters, and it does not look like the former way at all.

One Roof or Many Roofs

About one-half of the two hundred plus members live on the Marywood Campus either at the Motherhouse or Aquinata Hall, the newly renovated building for assisted living. The few Sisters needing skilled medical care reside at the Marywood Health Center. Meals, housekeeping, and maintenance are provided for everyone on the Marywood Campus. The reality for these Sisters is that of a large institution, although small "neighborhoods" are formed within each of the larger houses to facilitate a more homey atmosphere and supportive living groups. There are also several apartments in the Marywood building where a few Sisters live either singly or with one, two, or three others. These Sisters may prepare their own meals or join the main house depending on their wishes or needs.

Srs. Roberta Hefferan (left) and Janet Brown making music

Of the members of the Congregation not living on the Marywood Campus, some live in houses with three or more. Currently, about twenty-five Sisters live in one of four residences that house groups of three to five members. Other Sisters live singly or with one other due to the needs of their ministry or for personal reasons.

Living under the same roof, sharing life with other Sisters in close proximity, was the norm for most Women Religious fifty years ago and for many centuries before that. In those years, the schedule of each day allowed about one hour of verbal communication, and no doubt, this restriction on verbal interaction had the potential to reduce overt tension and possible conflicts. An appointed Superior was responsible for resolving any nascent disputes and keeping order. The ordinary horarium or hourly schedule for the day began with a bell calling the Sisters to rise, wash, and dress in order to be in chapel by 5:30 a.m. for group meditation, morning prayers, and Mass. Breakfast followed in silence except for the voice of the appointed lector who read from an approved spiritual book during the meal; then each Sister began her assignment for working throughout the day. The noon meal was in silence, although an assigned lector read an excerpt from a spiritual book for the Sisters' edification. This was followed by the afternoon work detail, usually teaching, nursing, or housework.

Between the ending of the work day and the supper hour, there was time for the recitation of the rosary, Vespers (evening prayer), a quiet walk outside, preparation for the work of the next day, or spiritual reading. Then supper, again in silence, except for the lector who read from another spiritual book, followed by one hour of "recreation," which was the time when talking as well as sewing, and playing cards in the company of the Superior and the other Sisters was the custom. This was followed by Compline, the night prayer.

Cooking, grocery shopping, and laundry were the responsibilities of the Sister/Housekeeper if one was available. In later years, these tasks were often hired out to a lay woman in the parish. Light housekeeping duties such as vacuuming and dusting were assigned to the Sisters to be done once each week on Friday afternoon, after the close of the school day. Financial matters were handled by the appointed "bursar" under the Superior's supervision. Yard work and maintenance were the responsibility of the maintenance men of the parish or school. This regimented schedule, with oversight by the Superior, left little time or opportunity for disunity, conflict, or jealousy. The majority of an individual's hours were spent either in a ministry or in a reflective mode of interiority. It was a traditional schedule and lifestyle followed by monastic or cloistered nuns for centuries and still maintained by a few Congregations to this day. Many women lived their entire adult lives in this manner and were happy and fulfilled in it. Many others were ready for a change.

For about eighty percent of the Congregations of Women Religious in the United States this monastic worldview and uniformity did not withstand the changes that came about as the result of both the *aggiornamento* (updating) of Vatican Council II, as well as the Sisters' own desires and readiness to change their lifestyles to better fit with the demands of new ministries and contemporary life.

As the Sisters responded to the call of *Perfectae Caritatis* to return to the sources of their founder and the Gospel, and to read the signs of the times, the variety of ministries expanded, daily schedule and living configurations changed, and life, as the Sisters had known it, was never the same. Few Sisters could fit their new jobs into the school day schedule that had been the norm for years. New ministries in areas such as religious education, parish administration, social work, and advocacy required work in evenings, weekends, and through the summer months. The monastic schedule of the previous centuries was no longer feasible. The *diaspora* of Sisters living far and wide had begun.

The demands of the times called for the skills of mature and interdependent relationships.

The principles of subsidiarity and collegiality, two new concepts promoted by Vatican Council II, were greatly needed as Sisters negotiated their work and life together in new ways, adapting, experimenting with decision making at the local level and collaborating with each other on an equal footing rather than subjecting all decisions to the Superior of the convent. In brief, the demands of the time called for the skills of mature and interdependent relationships.

All of this was much easier talked about than accomplished for several reasons. Among the difficulties were the dispositions of individuals developed in their own family of origin, and the fear of change itself. There was

Music to play as well as to pray (left to right): Srs. Joan Williams, Dolorita Martinez, and Therese Rodríguez

also the difficulty that many Sisters had little experience in direct communication or conflict resolution either from their homes or their earlier years in the convent. Then, too, there were no current models to look toward as examples of adults in active apostolic ministry living interdependently in this "new world" of the late twentieth century. For many Sisters, their family of origin, as faith-filled and loving as it may have been, did not provide the modeling or skills for this new way of being together.

Even if every young woman who entered had come from a perfectly functioning home and was mature, balanced, and healthy — the changes would have been difficult. But of course, such was not, nor ever could be, the case. Sisters come from diverse families with all of the strengths, flaws, and foibles therein.

Among the Sisters in the Grand Rapids Dominican Congregation, a few come from either extreme poverty or modest affluence; most Sisters are from middle income, working class families. They hail from small towns or rural families in Michigan or New Mexico, with a few from other states. Entering at a young age from homes where parents were the ultimate arbiters of disputes to a Congregation where a Superior was responsible for harmony in the house left the individual Sister with little practice in the skills of conflict resolution, open communication, or relationship building.

For example, one Sister recalls being silently aggravated by the extreme frugality of a classmate who saved every inch of thread, scraped every molecule of peanut butter from the jar, and never wasted a drop of water. Only when family stories were shared years later did the annoyed Sister come to understand the anxiety that can accompany true deprivation. The frugal Sister's large family lived in a dirt floor house and ate mostly potatoes supplemented by what her father could kill in the woods or find dead on the road on the way home from foraging.[3] The aggrieved Sister, on the other hand, had never known any food source except the local grocery store. With little opportunity to listen to each other's stories, frustration could set in, passive-aggressive behaviors were not uncommon, and misunderstandings could and did happen.

Sociologists estimate that many young women and men entering religious life in the boom years of the 1950s came from seriously dysfunctional

---

3. Recalled in a private conversation wherein the speaker wishes to remain anonymous.

families[4] where large numbers of children of first- and second-generation immigrants had an all too brief childhood. Young girls were often expected to take on the responsibilities of child care, field work, cooking, and cleaning. The prolonged childhood and adolescence of contemporary society was unknown. The families of many who entered in the 1940s and 1950s had experienced both the Great Depression and World War II.

While it is a reasonable assumption that those who entered and persevered in Religious Life responded to an authentic call, it is also reasonable to recognize that human motivation is seldom singular or simple, whether it is to enter Religious Life or to choose a spouse. The young woman entering Religious Life in her late teens/early twenties might also subconsciously be motivated by a need to feel safe or to avoid marriage and parenthood without the stigma of spinsterhood. In some instances, a desire for higher education or to please a parent was part of the motivation for a decision to enter Religious Life. Some Sisters reflect on their yearning to wear the beautiful habit as the first allurement to Religious Life. They looked up to the women who were their teachers and wanted to look like them and be like them. Still others were drawn to the notion of a higher calling than that offered by the married or single state of life according to the teachings in the Church prior to Vatican Council II.

The reasons for entering are seldom the reasons for remaining, however, and the changes that came with the response to Vatican Council II soon dismantled Religious Life as a place to delay maturation, personal responsibility, or adult relationships. Only the single-minded desire to be a seeker of God's will for her could and would sustain the individual in her vocation during these turbulent years.

Reflecting on the great exodus from the Congregation that happened during her tenure as Prioress (1966-1972), Sister Aquinas Weber recalled:

> Some of them left, I think, who came during the time when the rush to religious communities was on [in the 1940s and 1950s]. For some [Religious Life] was a safe haven, and once we loosened, they no longer felt comfortable in that milieu, and so it would be better for them to go back home and start

Only the single-minded desire to be a seeker of God's will for her could and would sustain the individual in her vocation during these turbulent years.

---

4. Reference by Marilyn Wussler, SSND, M.S., in "Don't is a Four Letter Word," *Human Development* 10, no. 1 (Spring 1989), p. 19.

life in a new way for them. And we did not try to hold them. We encouraged them [to leave] if they didn't feel they belonged there.[5]

An issue of conflict more intense than any other was that of clothing. Strongly symbolic and highly visible, the habit or dress of the Sisters had varied little over the centuries. Although the head dress (veil) was modified to improve peripheral vision after a fatal car crash (1955) in which the older style veil was implicated in the accident, the habit remained essentially unchanged from medieval times. The second session of the fifteenth Chapter of the Congregation took up the controversial issue in June of 1967. A committee studied the matter of the Dominican habit. They considered the need for change, the expense involved, the influence on external witness, the experience of other communities, the reaction of the laity, and the continuity of the Dominican tradition. Sister Aquinas's letter of June 8, 1967, on this subject set a tone for tolerance, although a nuance of exasperation can be detected in her choice of words in the second paragraph:

> Some are eager for experimentation and wish to see it carried on extensively this summer. At the opposite position are those who do not wish to change anything about our habit or veil, and who want an end to any experimentation whatsoever. Somewhere between these two groups are the Sisters who want some modification of the habit or veil or both. It is obviously unthinkable that all three groups will be completely satisfied, regardless of what we do or don't do about experimenting.
>
> First, Sisters, let us get this clothing business in perspective. It is not, nor can ever be, the most important area of renewal and adaptation. In fact, it has no real meaning in terms of renewal, which is interior and spiritual. Secondly, those who are strongly opposed to any change in clothing have indicated anxiety lest they be forced to change against their will. To repeat: any and all experiments are just that — try-outs. No one will be able to force change on anyone else in this matter. This kind of decision — to change our attire — can only be done as it was the last time — by community vote.

> "Sisters, let us get this clothing business in perspective. It is not, nor can ever be, the most important area of renewal and adaptation."
> Sister Aquinas Weber

---

5. Gary Eberle, *Going Where We Are Needed* (Grand Rapids: Aquinas College, 2013), p. 31.

Even if change is made, why shouldn't those preferring the old form be free to retain it if they wish?[6]

In response to this letter, some Sisters did begin to experiment. The annals from the Immaculate Heart of Mary Convent in Grand Rapids report a nonchalant attitude toward the experimenters:

With the arrival of Mother's letter, three of our Sisters thought they would launch out into new wardrobes. Sister Margaret William and Sister John Mary hope to look "new" from head to foot by the end of the summer. Sister Stanice is trying a new veil.[7]

Clothing, since it was an outwardly visible sign, was given a long period of experimentation. There were set guidelines for requesting habit modifications and secular clothing and for reporting on all experiences, so that a final decision would be based on solid experiential foundations. All such changes emphasized personal responsibility, consideration of others, dialogue, and greater understanding among Sisters.

Seamstresses within and outside the convent assisted in the external transformations. There was a great deal to learn as Sisters struggled with minor and major changes in clothing. One Sister recalls an embarrassing moment on that learning curve.

How I changed from the habit to blue suit was.... It [the modified habit white dress] was made out of our old habit material. When I first wore it the tenth graders saw my briefs... through the thin, worn habit material.... In the afternoon I came back with a blue suit on. That was the last day of my wearing the white.[8]

Today, Sisters wear secular clothing, modified habits, or full habits without comment or pressure to do differently. As Sister Aquinas promised in

---

6. S. Aquinas Weber, letter to the Sisters, June 8, 1967, Circular Letters, July 1966–June 1968, Marywood Archives.

7. Immaculate Heart of Mary Convent Annals from 1966-67, Marywood Archives.

8. S. Elaine LaBell, OP, Oral History, June 28, 2008, Marywood Archives, Transcripts 2008-529-2011.018, p. 28.

her letter of June 8, 1967, no one was forced to change against her will. The *Constitution and Statutes* of the Congregation state the right of a Sister to wear the Dominican habit or not:

> We reflect our religious commitment by our appreciation of simplicity within a context of beauty, by our dress and demeanor. As a witness to poverty and as a sign of consecration for mission the Sisters wear either the Dominican habit or simple, appropriate attire for our lives as Grand Rapids Dominican Sisters.[9]

Wearing or not wearing the habit was not the only controversial change. Another revolutionary idea was that of living in a house without an appointed Superior. How could a Sister live a vow of obedience if there was no one to obey every day? One of the first forays into this new kind of living occurred with a group of five Sisters requesting to experiment with intentional community living in a non-convent setting. In 1968, five Sisters[10] from the Grand Rapids area who lived in four different convents wrote a letter to the Prioress and Council asking for permission to engage in an experiment in community living which would be marked by the innovative concept of complete collegiality in governance. This meant there would be no appointed or elected Superior. In other words, as the Sisters themselves stated, "We wish to try collegiality on a basis of equal-status . . . since we think this may assure an even greater sharing of needs and decisions, a greater awareness of others, and an increasing sense of responsibility and giving."[11]

In their letter of May 3, 1968, they wrote: "We are by intent, a compatible group, varying in temperament and ideas, but deeply united in goals, ideals, united in our concept of dedicated religious living."[12] Their time spent reading, praying, and discussing the essence of community life led to their eagerness to try an intentional community. They would strive to be open in communication, accepting of each person, willing to share their faith journey, personal life, and apostolic commitments which would vary in that

> **They would strive to be open in communication, accepting of each person, willing to share their faith journey, personal life, and apostolic commitments.**

---

9. *Constitution & Statutes*, #12, p. 27.
10. The original five were: Sisters Patricia Milan, Jacqueline Bennett, Killian Bowler, Helen Bueche, and Jacqueline Hudson.
11. S. Patricia Milan letter on behalf of the group, Marywood Archives.
12. Letter to the Leadership Team, May 3, 1968, Marywood Archives.

they would not be in daily ministry with the Sisters they lived with, as had been the custom in the past. Their vision was to be active and hospitable Christian witnesses in a racially integrated neighborhood and local parish. They would, by word and example, foster mutual respect and understanding among themselves and their neighbors. They desired to be a part of the neighborhood and parish — in their own words, a place where "people feel more at home rather than in awe."[13] These pioneer women faithfully filled out community questionnaires, gave rationales for their quest, researched rental properties and leases, projected the financial needs, and supplemented their ministry income with the salary of one Sister working in the public school system. The first "non-convent" was a rented five-bedroom house in a middle-income neighborhood in the southeast quadrant of Grand Rapids about one and one-half miles from Marywood.

Although the individual members of the house changed over the fourteen years of its existence, the aims and purposes of the community remained the same. They had their share of adventures with landlord stories, break-ins, and summer jobs as babysitters, tutors, and piano tuners. Their schedule included morning and evening prayer, a monthly Mass at the house, as well as a weekly fast day that benefited the United Farm Workers. Through formal and informal communications with the Prioress and Council, reports at Chapters, and articles in the community newsletters, they spread the word about this new way of living life in common in an intentional community without an appointed Superior. Theirs was the first, but not the last, house where all

Sr. Jackie Hudson, peace advocate and piano tuner

13. Letter to the Leadership Team, May 3, 1968, Marywood Archives.

members shared the governance of the house and participated in the common ministry of presence and service in the neighborhood.

In time, the practice of an appointed Superior gave way to an elected House Coordinator. Collaboration among the Sisters in the house became the method for taking care of specific areas, e.g., communications, cars, personal needs, and finances. The responsibility for the welfare and congenial spirit of the house fell on each member of the household rather than on the appointed Superior.

The ease with which this transition in government occurred is quite remarkable, and the notice of it recorded in the annals of Saint Alfred Convent in Taylor is typical of the reports of other convents:

> On August twentieth, Sisters gathered together to set up a temporary government. [Tasks and names are then listed.] Several weeks later, the Sisters met to elect permanent Coordinators.[14]

With the changing times and economic conditions of the 1960s and 1970s, parish schools closed, Sisters' ministries became more diverse, Sisters assumed greater responsibility for their ministry, some Sisters opted out of classroom teaching, and consequently housing options outside the usual convent setting became the norm.

The Sisters continued to grapple with the meaning and ideal of Dominican common life, lived in community, yet not always in close physical proximity.

The Constitution states that

> Dominican common life is a call to apostolic community. It witnesses the Gospel mandate to "Love one another as I have loved you" (Jn. 13:34). It is a source of support and encouragement for our ministry of preaching and teaching. We come together to celebrate the word of God in prayerful praise; we partake of the strength of shared faith and charism; we contribute and share our talents, abilities and material goods for the sake of the mission.[15]

---

14. Annals from St. Alfred's Convent, Taylor, Michigan, 1969-70, Marywood Archives.
15. *Constitution & Statutes,* #20 and #21, p. 7.

Nevertheless, the question remained: Can this be realized if Sisters do not live together under one roof? Study of the meaning and means of common life continued with the work of a committee known as the Coordinating Committee on Common Life. In its recommendations to the General Chapter in 2000, this committee affirmed that common life lived together under one roof was the ideal in the Dominican tradition, even while recognizing that living singly is sometimes necessary. The committee offered two recommendations. The first was that Sisters wishing to live singly make a formal request invoking the principle of dispensation — a time-honored practice of the Dominican Order. Their second recommendation was that the Sisters living singly formally connect with an established house of Grand Rapids Dominicans for shared prayer, study, and socialization.

Although neither recommendation had much effect on daily life, the report recognized the fact that the Sisters' "deep affection and love . . . is evident whenever we come together in moments of great joy or suffering."[16]

The Sisters in their own lived reality concluded that while community life is the source of identity and shared charism, it requires neither uniformity nor proximity. Without negating the value and challenge of living and loving together under one roof, the Sisters themselves by word and deed proclaimed that the "joyful sisterhood based on the shared blessings of faith and the mutual enjoyment of the lives and gifts of the others"[17] was not dependent on common walls, but common hearts.

One Sister reflected on a discussion that helped her group see the distinctions that were emerging in the challenge of living community in a new way:

> I can still remember being at one of those study days and S. was in the group. We were talking about this. We started evolving into "community" and "common life." I can remember S. saying, "Oh that's it!" I thought, "S.'s got an insight here." She said, "Common life means holding all things in common, contributing to the good of the whole. But common life does not mean that we all have to get up at 5:00 in the morning and we all have to go to bed at 9:30 at night and we all have to be for prayers at this hour. Com-

While community life is the source of identity and shared charism, it requires neither uniformity nor proximity.

---

16. Recommendations to Chapter 2000 from Coordinating Committee on the Common Life, Archives, Box 33.1.
17. *Constitution & Statutes*, #24, p. 7.

mon life means something deeper than the horary (the daily schedule). It's holding things in common (the stipend coming in to the community)." That whole sense began to evolve. I can still remember being in that group when suddenly it came to her. Then she explained it to the rest of us and that made so much sense of what we were grappling with.[18]

Over the ensuing years, more and more Sisters, by necessity or choice, live singly in apartments or with one other Sister. They continue to find ways of bonding with each other through visiting, celebrations, use of technology, regional meetings, General Assemblies, Chapters, and committee work. It is not uncommon for Sisters living singly or with one other to make connections with other small groups for prayer, socializing, and study on a regular basis.

Asked about the changes in living together over the years, one senior Sister reflected:

> I think that we see the other Sister in our Community more as a person, a person with dignity, a person capable of making her own decisions, respecting where they are in their ministry and their prayer life. I think we have come a long way.... I think there is more of an ability to confront each other. Before, you held it all in (with all the silence). Now I think we see each other as human. The good Sister isn't the one who kept perfect silence, or the Sister who always did the right thing.[19]

Another Sister reflected on the opportunity to experience friendship both within and outside the community as a result of the changes following Vatican Council II. Previously, fear of same sex attractions led to rules that prohibited the development of a "particular" friendship (code word for an exclusive relationship appropriate to marriage) even among members of the same community, let alone with individuals outside the community. When asked about the differences between the two eras in Religious Life, she recalled:

18. S. Margaret Hillary, Oral History, September 8, 2009, Marywood Archives, Transcripts 2008.589-2011.018, Folder 2009.06.03, p. 35.
19. S. Amata Fabbro, Oral History, July 1, 2010; July 20, 2010; and July 22, 2010. Marywood Archives, p. 80.

Well, we can have friends. You can be my particular friend. I used to think, "What kind of friend do you have if it's not a particular friend?" I have strong friendships with people, with our Sisters and others. I have a lot of friends out there. I love them dearly and they love me back.[20]

It takes a while to learn the skills of direct adult communication and mutuality. In her book on the subject of Community Living in Religious Life, Sister Barbara Fiand suggests practical ways to honor that long and difficult process:

(Left to right) Srs. Teresa Gallmeier, Alice Wittenbach, and Nancy Malburg share an interesting point.

> We may discover that though we can share our perspectives, we cannot necessarily live together indiscriminately any more, for our needs will reveal themselves as widely divergent and may need to be addressed in different settings. Intentional communities will have to be considered seriously, and some of us may need to live alone at least for some time.[21]

The high value for devoting time, energy, and resources in nurturing relationships and quality of life was recognized, in the Direction Statements of the General Assembly of 1992, and expanded two years later in 1994.

We commit ourselves to be open to encountering the Holy in ourselves, in each other, and in people of all cultures and lifestyles.

---

20. S. Bernice Garcia, Oral History, July 23, 2010; August 19-20 & 30, 2010, Marywood Archives, Transcripts 2008.589-2011.018, Folder 2010.0363, p. 79.

21. S. Barbara Fiand, SNDdeN, *Where Two or Three Are Gathered: Community Life for the Contemporary Religious* (New York: Crossroad, 1992), p. 53.

Recognizing the need for help in "encountering the Holy," faced with the reality of Sisters who were lonely and lost in the transition, becoming cognizant of the long-term effects of trauma and loss, the Prioress and Council (1994) determined to do something more specific to help our own Sisters suffering from emotional distress.

The S.I.S.T.E.R. program begun under the administration of Sister Barbara Hansen offered peer support to Sisters suffering from the stress of changing life situations by reason of ministry, health, or unresolved familial issues. The acronym S.I.S.T.E.R. stands for Spiritual Intercession Specialist Teams for the Enhancement of Human Resources. Sisters Barbara Hansen, Prioress, and Ann Walters, Councilor for Life Development, along with a consultant/psychotherapist, designed the program to train Sister listeners in the skills of non-judgmental empathic listening. In teams of three, these Sisters offered to serve those in need through weekly hour-long listening sessions. The goal was a more integrated and happier life for the Sister being served. An additional benefit was that Sisters on the team became skilled in empathic listening and much more tolerant of and loving with each other. The teams of three Sister listeners were supervised by the psychotherapist or a social worker. This supervision was critical in order to keep the Sister listeners from becoming either problem solvers or judgmental of the Sister being served. Supervision also helped the Sister listeners keep their own personal issues separate from the Sister being served by the team.

About eighty Sisters were trained in empathic listening, although only a small number actually became team members. This training in itself had a ripple effect in the Congregation. Sisters were able to listen to each other and be present in a positive way that tended to diminish gossip, judgment, and negativity. Although the program only lasted about six years, the effect has been longstanding with greater compassion and acceptance of each Sister for the other and a more integrated way of recognizing and living through painful life issues and transitions.

The transformation from the traditional, more interior way of living monastic life under one roof buffered by silence and the oversight of a Superior to that of apostolic women living an interdependent life, growing in relational mutuality, under many roofs did not happen instantly. It happened over years and through much conversation, trial, error, and questions. There were no models for this new way of being together in community. As Barbara Fiand remarked in her book on community living:

> The art of interdependent relating . . . is "virgin territory" on the map of human development, and though good intentions always help, the day-to-day working out of it is a painful business.[22]

There are many ways of living Community Life: alone, with one other, in a small group or a large institution. Whatever the path, the way is always with deep connections; love and care for one another whether or not it is lived in the same house. While living Community Life is an essential part of Religious Life, it has come to mean mutuality of care in a life-long commitment rather than physically living in the same space. Where once silence, rules, and a high degree of conformity was the mode for living Community Life, today that is no longer the case.

Today, Apostolic Religious Life in America is clearly for women who have navigated the trials of childhood dependency and the adolescent turbulence of fierce independence and are now capable of the give and take of adults living and dying in interdependence and mutuality. Whether the Sisters live in a large house of fifty or a small group of four or singly in an apartment or house; whether they dress in a full or modified habit or contemporary clothing, real community is found in the relationships they have with one other and the Congregation as a whole. Each Sister chooses in her daily life to be a part of that "joyful sisterhood," whether living singly, with one other, or with many others.

---

22. Barbara Fiand, *Living the Vision: Religious Vows in an Age of Change* (New York: Crossroad, 1990), p. 91.

Concentric Circles

Enlarge the space for your tent,
spread out your tent cloths unsparingly;
lengthen your ropes and make firm your pegs.
ISAIAH 54:2

IF VATICAN COUNCIL II opened the window to freshen the stuffy air of entrenched practices, the Dominican Sisters in Grand Rapids metaphorically opened their doors, windows, and hearts to include more and more groups of individuals, some vowed, others not, into their Motherhouse, chapel, and circle of friends and acquaintances. The reunion of former members and the development of the Associate Life phenomenon are two examples explored in this chapter. In addition, the Sisters joined groups with whom they shared roots in the Dominican tradition. Both the documents of the Council and the culture of the time supported this widening of the tent stakes.

The documents of Vatican Council II issued the invitation:

> Independent institutes and monasteries should, when opportune and the Holy See permits, form federations if they can be considered as belonging to the same religious family. Others who have practically identical constitutions and rules and a common spirit should unite, particularly when they have too few members. Finally, those who share the same or a very similar active apostolate should become associated, one to the other.[1]

---

1. *Perfectae Caritatis*, #22.

Concentric Circles

Not only the documents and spirit of Vatican Council II, but also the signs of the times and the spirit of the generation spoke to the rightness of this expansion and the dismantling of the "us and them" mentality. For example, the thinking of the Jesuit priest Pierre Teilhard de Chardin, philosopher, paleontologist, and geologist, had begun to mitigate the Augustinian notion of original sin and to challenge the dualism of the Graeco-Roman tradition that asserted matter was corrupt and spirit alone was holy. Pierre Teilhard de Chardin, on the other hand, proclaimed with conviction that by reason of creation and still more by the fact of incarnation, everything on earth is holy.[2] His writings, once condemned by the Church, and then affirmed by later pontiffs, began to change attitudes about Earth and human relationships to it. No longer a "vale of tears," Earth became again the garden of God to be cared for and enjoyed by humans.

> **By reason of creation and still more by fact of incarnation, everything on earth is holy.**

Also seeping into the peripheral consciousness of the culture was the re-emerging notion of the connectedness of all creation. In his first letter to the Corinthians, St. Paul had recognized this phenomenon in his reference to the Body of Christ as composed of many parts, but one Body. Now in contemporary times, the idea of the relationship among parts and wholes was affirmed in the sociological and scientific realms, especially in quantum physics. Cletus Wessels, OP, describes the impact of this understanding on relationships and systems, e.g., marriage, religious congregations, and the Church itself.[3] Wessels explains that the theory states that while there are many wholes which are also parts, each of these wholes/parts, when combined, transcends to a deeper, greater entity. Without getting caught up in the terminology of quantum physics, one can readily see that isolation or separation from human relationships as a form of holiness is challenged by this thinking. Both/and replaces either/or, as described by Sarah A. Conn, clinical psychologist and lecturer at the Harvard Medical School:

> The sense of the uniqueness of the individual that has emerged over the past few centuries is not to be thrown away. It is to be taken with us as we awaken

---

2. Pierre Teilhard de Chardin, *Divine Milieu* (New York: Harper and Row, 1960), p. 66. "... by virtue of the Creation and, still more, of the Incarnation, nothing here below is profane for those who know how to see."

3. Cletus Wessels, OP, *The Holy Web: Church and the Universe Story* (Maryknoll, NY: Orbis Books, 2000), pp. 55-67.

to our place in the whole. The individual self is . . . simultaneously both a whole, with special qualities and experiences that need to be honored, and a part of a larger whole, whether it be a family, a community, a bioregion, or the living planetary ecosystem. There is a danger in overemphasizing any one of these qualities. If we develop rigid boundaries around the self-as-whole, then we separate ourselves from the world and are unavailable to the nourishment essential to aliveness and growth; the capacity for mutuality and engagement is diminished. If, on the other hand, we develop diffuse boundaries and experience only the self-as-part, then we can be swept away by the larger whole, losing the ability to give feedback to the system from our unique perspective. The capacity for mutuality and engagement is again diminished.[4]

This rather lengthy introduction to the chapter on concentric circles gives us a glimpse of the theological, ecclesial, and scientific thinking that has emerged since the close of Vatican Council II. As the Church herself is ever ancient, ever new — so is the understanding of God's mystery. In her book *The Emergent Christ,* Ilia Delio, OSF, merges the new science with the ancient mystery of God's plan for all being:

> Jesus' dynamic process of whole-making was not imposed but was offered in response to needs based on relationships of mutuality, dialogue and openness. Jesus sought to create whole where there were divisions — whole people, whole communities, wholesome living — for the glory of God.[5]

Prior to 1966, Sisters generally limited their friendships to those within their Congregations, and on a daily basis, with members of their immediate local community. The phrase "fraternizing with the laity" was used to reprimand a Sister who was thought to be flaunting this expectation and conversing too frequently with those outside the Congregation. More often than not, it was the Major Superior and her Council who negotiated with church organizations and the laity to carry on the business of the ministry. Vatican Council II issued an invitation to broaden the base. All

---

4. Sarah A. Conn, in Theodore Roszak et al., eds., *Ecopsychology: Restoring the Earth and Healing the Mind* (Sierra Club Books, 1995), p. 164.
5. Ilia Delio, OSF, *The Emergent Christ* (Maryknoll, NY: Orbis Books, 2011), p. 65.

were invited to join together in order to build the Kingdom of God here on earth.

In two instances, non-vowed persons were invited to form a closer union with the Sisters, and in several other cases, the Sisters formed alliances and closer connections with Dominicans outside their immediate Congregational circle.

Former Members

Before Vatican Council II, members who left the Congregation were seldom heard from again. Their disappearance was often a source of grief and pain for those who remained with the felt loss of a friend, a Sister, a "comrade in prayer"; those who left felt the same loss from the other side; and in some cases bitterness was a part of the grieving process. For one former member, that realization came sixteen years after her departure. She wrote after the first reunion of former members:

> I realize now, after sixteen years, that my grieving the loss of Community was not fully [mine] alone, because you as Community had to grieve the loss of me. In all my years away, caught up in my own pain, I never considered myself a loss to you. But now I know there existed two sides to our parting.[6]

> **"But now I know there existed two sides to our parting."**
> Elaine M. Newton

The reunion of former members occurred as the result of the entering class of 1959 who, upon reaching its twentieth anniversary of admission into the Congregation, decided to change the situation that had caused such unresolved pain among members and former members. Sisters Marguerite Cool, Regina Mary Goeldel, and Susanne Tracy formed a planning committee. They sent out invitations far and wide and on Saturday, September 8th, 1979, twenty-nine Sisters and former classmates gathered at Marywood. It was a joyous reunion.

Amidst hugs and "How are you's?" the years of separation melted. Among the comments were, "I never thought I would ever step foot in Marywood again but here we are!" Conversations covered the way-back-when stories

---

6. Elaine M. Newton (Sister Rose Karl 1964-1972) Marywood Archives, Folder AR 33.1.

to updated tales on current life events in 1979. Thank you notes flowed in following this first-of-its-kind opportunity. The Class of 1959 continued the tradition with a thirtieth year gathering in 1989 and a fortieth in 1999.

Inspired by this successful experience, the General Chapter in 1980 approved and enacted the following:

> Proposal: That we establish a program for continuing associations with former members of our Congregation who wish to maintain ties with us. The program would be coordinated by a Sister reporting to the Director of Religious Development. It would include invitations to former members to pray for and with us, to receive occasional communications from us, to correspond and to come [back to Marywood] for days of recollection.
>
> Rationale: Our love for those who have shared our lives should continue to be expressed in tangible ways. Some former Sisters already desire to maintain ties with us. Others might be desirous if we took the initiative. This program could lead to reconciliation with some who may have negative feelings toward the Congregation. Both we and the former Sisters would benefit spiritually.
>
> Implementation: A Sister would be appointed to begin a program of corresponding with former members and working out ways in which they could associate with us. Sisters already corresponding or associating with former members could inform her and possibly offer suggestions.[7]

Sister Jean Milhaupt (Maris Stella) accepted the responsibility for initiating the program. Sisters Jude Bloch, Madelyn Hronek (Marie George), and Mary Ann Otway (Gregory Ann) volunteered to assist. Former members Carol Hale, Karen Kania, Charlene McNerney, Kathleen Sullivan, and Carolyn Ehr gladly consented to form a working committee.

This undertaking launched regional gatherings throughout Michigan in Grand Rapids, Saginaw, and Traverse City as well as Albuquerque, New Mexico where Sister Bernice Garcia reported:

---

7. Chapter Proposals submitted to the June session of the 1980 Chapter, Marywood Archives, AR 4.2.

And sharing it was! Throughout the day you could hear: "and how/where is Sister ———. These are my children. . . . I want you to meet my husband. . . . Sister is now in New Mexico and her name is . . ." A delightful time was had by all. It was moved that this type of gathering become a yearly celebration. It was unanimously accepted by all those present.[8]

Former member Janet Johnson Welsh (left) enjoys meeting her old friends, Srs. Diane Dehn and Janet Brown.

In 1981, a Directory of Former Members was compiled. Several years later through the dedication of former members, Laura Loehnis (Marie Frances) and Margaret Kaiser (Francis Bernadine) plus the word processing services of Sandra Walraven, a booklet was published entitled, *Whatever Happened to . . . ?* It was well received as it opened the possibility for former members to re-establish ties with Sisters and other former members.

Former members Ruth Beckman Grinstead and Sally Schad Gelderloos remember by-gone days with Sr. Lorraine Rajewski.

8. Marywood Archives, Box 33.1. Government Committees/Remembering Committee [Former Members].

At one reunion held at Marywood, Prioress Sister Teresa Houlihan led a heartfelt prayer for reconciliation. Asking forgiveness, seeking reconciliation, the prayer names the pain and claims the power of healing. It bears repeating in full here:

> As a Community, we come this day to ask forgiveness for any of the misunderstandings, for any pain and hurt that may have been experienced or inflicted while you were a member of the Community.
>
> We ask Jesus to enter into those areas of pain and hurt, those areas where you were misunderstood, and in His love to minister to you now as you needed to be ministered to then. For there is no time or distance with the Lord, but all is present to Him in the Eternal Now, and we ask that in His great love for you, and for all those who are not able to be here, to touch and heal over those wounds, those scars, so that from this day forth you will be set free and not have to carry the burden of them anymore. As we extend and receive this mutual forgiveness and acceptance, we pray all in the healing power of Jesus' Name. Amen.[9]

"From this day forth you will be set free and not have to carry the burden of those wounds anymore."
Sister Teresa Houlihan

Sr. Mary Pat Beatty and former member Eileen Moss

One significant follow-up of the committee was to provide a periodic newsletter that was entitled *Remembering, Reaching, Responding*. It became a gold mine for sharing, providing a venue for notes/letters, giving information about lectures and programs during the summer, giving notification of deaths, and offering other topics of interest.

April 22-24, 1988, marked a retreat for former members entitled "Women

---

9. Marywood Archives, Box 33.1.

Searching and Thirsting." At the close, a former member, Judi Neiman (Thomas Francis), had this to share on her evaluation:

> What dimensions of the weekend were most significant for you? That I accepted the grace and courage to come back and face that formation in my life I loved the most but yet feared the most because of the pain. Leaving was similar to a divorce or death and I never had the chance to close that door and say good-bye. Yet in my spiritual journey since, I discovered you never separate yourself from your pain. They have been transformed into a new ministry. Most significant was the non-judgmental and accepting attitude of the Sisters, the environmental changes and greeting old classmates and friends.[10]

Former members and Sisters: (front row, left to right) Helen Gancarz, Sr. Carmelita Switzer, Mary Anne Micka, and Alice Falkowski; (back row, left to right) Sr. Anne Monica Shalda, Sr. Ann Terrence Wieber, Millie Hathaway, and Ruth Beckman Grinstead

Another attendee stated:

> When I walked up the front steps of Marywood Friday night, I was filled with fear and apprehension. What would it be like recalling the happiest and most bitter moments of my life? My fears were allayed when I was warmly greeted by Sisters much younger than I. . . . I was home![11]

In responding to suggestions for future gatherings, another former member, Judy Karafa Spencer, wrote:

> It's exciting to think we could do this again. It means that this isn't just a

---

10. Marywood Archives, Box 33.1.
11. Marywood Archives, Box 33.1.

one-time welcome and then forget. Even if we didn't have another weekend like this, the fact that you are willing to consider it means a great deal to me. Acceptance! That's the key word for me this weekend. We are okay — even though we left the order. Thanks.[12]

By 1994 the committee reflected, reviewed, and realized that most of the goals and directions set by the 1980 Chapter had been met. The multiple opportunities for reunion and reconciliation had benefitted many former and current members alike.

In light of this assessment, the committee recommended that the Remembering Committee continue with a primary focus on communication. They made it known that all former members would continue to be a special part of the Grand Rapids Dominican family. The welcome mat would always be out and the committee members pledged to remain willing to assist in any way that would enhance ongoing spiritual development.

The reunion in 2010 on October 9th saw sixty-three former members gather with current members to celebrate a life once shared. As one former member wrote in her thank you note: "It is one thing to have a 'reunion' — but it is quite an accomplishment to experience community and being part of the family. You were able to achieve that!"[13]

Currently, some former members have become Dominican Associates, while many others stay in contact through frequent communication via e-mail.

Dominican Associate Life

Although there had been Dominican Laity (Third Order) affiliation with provinces of Dominican men, the phenomenon of association directly with the spiritual legacy of women's Congregations was a new movement sweeping the country. And so it was that the next concentric circle was waiting in the wings. After such a positive experience in renewed relationships with former members, the possibility of openness to others who desired a closer

---

12. Evaluation of "Women Searching and Thirsting Retreat," April 22-24, 1988, Archives.
13. Marywood Archives, Box 33.1

affiliation was appealing. Some lay women and men felt such an affinity for the spirituality of the Dominican Sisters, they desired a closer, more formal union than presently existed.

In March of 1984, Sister Wanda Ezop, Linda Housewert, and Madeleine Kane (two longtime friends of the Grand Rapids Dominicans) began meeting to discuss the possibility of designing a plan through which the Sisters and lay persons might associate more formally. Unfortunately Sister Wanda was diagnosed with terminal cancer about the same time, which put these plans on hold.[14]

The cause was re-ignited by the Chapter of 1988 and the inaugural meeting of the Co-Membership Committee on July 21, 1989.[15] Sister Diane Zerfas was the new formation director for the Congregation at this time. Reflecting back on this new moment, she said:

> When the Co-Membership Committee was convened I joined because I didn't want whatever this might become to be a part of my job description — not the highest of motives but a valid one. How God laughs at us! Not only was this a dynamic group of people but it became obvious very quickly that they were *already* Dominicans in spirit and action. As Mary Vaccaro and I wrote the first documents for the Associate Program, we realized that we were not "making people Dominican." We were discovering that they already were Dominican. Their love of study, commitment to prayer, love of the community and experience of ministry enhanced the charisms of the Congregation and were mutually supportive for Sisters and Associates. My strongest memory of that first year was the affirmation that the Congregation felt in hearing the Associates' stories of our influence in their lives and of the joyful response to our gentle invitation to Dominican Life for lay women and men, friends of God.[16]

"We were discovering that the Associates were *already* Dominicans in spirit and action."
Sister Diane Zerfas

The committee struggled to find a suitable name for the initiative. They wanted to name the group in a way that would effectively show the mutual

---

14. S. Wanda Ezop died June 1986 from cancer.
15. The following members were present at that first meeting: Sisters Laurena Alflen, Deborah (Teresa) Gallmeier, Mary Lucille Janowiak, Carmelita Murphy, Joan Thomas, and Diane Zerfas. Lay women who attended were Madeleine Kane, Val Keller, and Ann Webb.
16. Marywood Archives, AR 28.2 Dominican Associates 1992.

relationship and contributions of both Sisters and Associates and not designate it as just another program. In time they came to a consensus that *Dominican Associate Life* was the best way to identify this way of being part of the Dominican Family.

It took three years of prayer, dialogue, and much rewriting before the Co-Membership Committee was ready to present the working paper to the Prioress and Council. Approval came on July 16, 1991. The next step was the implementation process that included structures, timelines, and consultations with vowed members every step of the way.

During February 1992 members of the committee made presentations at the regional Area Meetings — allowing plenty of time for questions and discussions. Through this collaborative procedure which respected the thoughts and feelings of all members regarding the new enterprise, the concept of Dominican Associate Life was accepted. The first commitment ceremony for Dominican Associates took place during the General Assembly in the summer of 1992. Because of major renovations taking place on the Marywood grounds, the ceremony occurred at Aquinas College on July 29, 1992.[17] Three of the first Dominican Associates share their vivid memories of those early days of searching and hoping and wondering and waiting. Charmaine Kulczyk recalls her journey:

> We moved to Grand Rapids in January of 1971 from Gary, Indiana. Sister Rose Callahan drafted me to work with her in the ministry of religious education for developmentally challenged children and adults.... This work brought me into frequent contact with other Sisters and in the 1980s I began to inquire if there was an Associate Program available. I felt a fit, a homecoming of sorts whenever I was involved in anything Dominican. I met Sister Diane Zerfas in the fall of 1990 as we collaborated on a Diocesan Adult Education series. I was invited to several prayer/brainstorming/discernment gatherings.... We grew in community and the Commitment Ceremony of July 29, 1992, was a welcome into the Dominican Family that remains one of the most significant experiences of my life.... Dominican Days bless us in

---

17. The first twelve to make their commitment were: Marguerite Erlandson, Fran Georgeff, Edward Heille, Madeleine Kane, Valerie Keller, Cassandra Kroondyk, Charmaine Kulczyk, Dorothy Ledrick, Cynthia Trenshaw, Alison Heins, Father Phil Shangraw, and Mary Vaccaro.

Concentric Circles

ways too numerous to count. . . . Being Dominican is being fully alive. Being Dominican is my journey home.[18]

"Being Dominican is my journey home." Associate Charmaine Kulczyk

Mary Vaccaro remembers:

I began my association with the Grand Rapids Dominican Sisters in 1967 when I entered Sister Adrienne's Montessori Kindergarten class at Marywood. Since then I have known Dominican Sisters as teachers, classmates, co-workers, co-prayers, mentors and friends. They have been for me role models of what women can do and be, and of what non-ordained ministers can do and be. They are women who study, pray, teach, serve, preach and lead. Most of all they are models of women who are free — even and perhaps most especially when they are in prison. . . .[19] It has been lovely to dance with you these past twenty-five years. . . . I look forward to continuing the dance.[20]

"The Dominican Sisters have been for me role models of what women can do and be." Associate Mary Vaccaro

Finally, Cynthia Trenshaw recalls:

Dominican Associates (left to right) Carole Nugent, Cynthia Trenshaw, and Fran Georgeff meet during August Dominican Days Gathering.

In the late eighties I was one of five or six Grand Rapids women who began gathering in our homes to satisfy our yearning to be together in silence and in prayer. Several of us attended Mass at Dominican Chapel, and sometimes we registered for workshops offered at Marywood. Each time I showed up, I was amazed and humbled by how many Sisters I so admired welcomed me and remembered my name. I felt as if I belonged there. Some of the other women in my circle felt the same. And so we asked if there

---

18. Marywood Archives, Box 28.2.
19. Referring to the witness value of Sisters who serve prison time for civil resistance against nuclear weapons.
20. Marywood Archives, Box 28.2.

might be a way that we could officially be attached to, or even become a part of the Grand Rapids Dominicans.

As I recall, it took much persuasion and many, many months — during which we learned how frustratingly wonderful the process called "discernment" could be — before we and a few other like-minded folks were finally invited to make our first tentative commitments as Dominican Associates. God's delightful joke was that neither we nor the Congregation knew what that really meant! But there we were, in 1992, twelve newly-minted Associates, both women and men, both Catholic and non-Catholic, with our enthusiastic love for our adopted community received in equal measures of joy and perplexity! May we Associates always be carriers of God's humor and of divine paradox for our beloved Grand Rapids Dominicans.[21]

> "We learned how frustratingly wonderful the process called 'discernment' could be." Associate Cynthia Trenshaw

Initially, some Sisters resisted the development of the Associate Life program. They feared that the Associates would "take over" or that the Associates wanted the benefits without the responsibilities of Religious Life. The witness of the Associates themselves, their generosity in service, their enthusiasm for prayer and study, their patient endurance during times of turmoil eventually persuaded the critics that there was nothing to fear, and much to gain by embracing this newest circle and including them into the joyful sisterhood and brotherhood of the Dominican Family.

> There was nothing to fear and much to gain by embracing this newest circle of the Dominican Family.

By the year 2000, the Dominican Associates numbered thirty-nine committed women and men, and by the year 2012 more than one hundred members claimed Dominican Associate Life as their own. The energy and blessings already felt by the turn of the century enhanced the conviction that this special way of being Dominican had lasting value for Sisters and Associates alike.

The Parable Conference

In pondering the potential of a collaborative venture with fellow Dominicans, Sister Ann Willits, member of the Sinsinawa Dominicans, said simply, "We can do so much more together than we can apart." The birth of Parable began with a conversation in 1975. The Sinsinawa General Council and some

---

21. Marywood Archives, Box 28.2.

members of the Dominican men's St. Albert the Great Central Province sat down and talked about collaboration, its meaning and purpose.

The summer of 1976 saw over seventy Dominican women and men gather for a conference on Dominican Life and Mission. The Word in Scripture was celebrated, preached, studied, prayed, and lived. Papers were given, ideas were exchanged, and friendships were formed. A permanent national Conference of Dominican Life and Mission was birthed. The name *Parable* emerged as a fitting title for the conference whose purpose was to promote the preaching of the Word of God as Jesus had in his lifetime — often using parables to make his point. Sister Diane Kennedy from the Sinsinawa Congregation was the first director.

In 1979 Sister Carmelita Murphy joined the Parable team and served in a leadership capacity until she was elected to the Council of the Grand Rapids Congregation in 1984. In time the two initiating groups expanded to include twenty-six Congregations of vowed Sisters, the four provinces of men, ten monasteries of nuns, and eight groups of laity. During 1985, over three thousand persons participated in Parable events and projects. The 1986 calendar of events included thirty-one retreats and conferences which were staffed by over one hundred Dominican women and men.

One form of retreat was entitled "Encounter with the Word." These retreats were staffed by four to six Dominican preachers (women and men) and a liturgist; countless numbers of Grand Rapids Dominicans participated in these around the country. A few Grand Rapids Dominicans were members of the teams. Among them was Sister Mary Ann Barrett, who recalled:

> I found every Parable retreat to be an experience of wonder and mystery. The gathering of Sisters and Brothers from different congregations offered a unique encounter with the Word of God in each. The insights, the prayerful exchange of life experiences, the shared commitment to prayer and study broadened my appreciation of our family. The feminine and masculine voices of preachers gave a fullness to the daily readings. I always came away with renewed vigor to live the Word more faithfully. The quiet sitting with the Word together, in the same sacred space, joined in Spirit often brought me to tears of thanksgiving for the calling to Dominican life and ministry.[22]

> **"The feminine and masculine voices of preachers gave a fullness to the daily readings."**
> Sister Mary Ann Barrett

22. S. Mary Ann Barrett in e-mail December 28, 2011, to S. Susanne Tracy.

Another meaningful and well-attended Parable-sponsored program was the *Lands of Dominic* pilgrimage. From the inaugural 1984 trip with Sister Carmelita Murphy on staff and two Grand Rapids Dominicans as participants to the final 2008 journey with ten Grand Rapids Dominicans on board, a total of seventy-six Grand Rapids Dominican Sisters were enriched by this experience. The brochure announcing the pilgrimage states:

> We invite you to study, pray and celebrate the vocation and charism of our founder, friend and brother, Dominic de Guzman. As his followers we shall travel in the spirit of mendicant simplicity. Many of the towns to which he was called and sent will be our stopping places in Spain (Caleruega and Osma), France (Toulouse, Carcassone, Prouille and Fanjeaux) and Italy (Bologna, Siena, Florence and Rome).[23]

In the anticipated excitement about such a pilgrimage, participants were cautioned, "But, this type of travel is demanding of physical and psychic energy because of the long days, rough walking, carrying suitcases and sharing rooms with a bathroom down the hall."[24] Such warnings were received with a grain-of-salt as most Sisters assumed they would manage — and for the most part they did.

When asked what remains meaningful in recalling the 1994 pilgrimage, Sister Kateri Schrems pondered:

> The three week immersion in Dominican people and places offered indelible experiences. Highlights from Spain include sitting atop the [hill] Pena Jorge overlooking Caleruega, peering into the bodega [cave on a hillside where wine is stored] of Jane of Aza [the mother of St. Dominic], using and being blessed by water from the same stream that refreshed and served the Guzman family in the late 1100s.
>
> In southern France the Sisters/Associates on the Pilgrimage sang the *Tantum Ergo* and *O Sacrum Convivium* at the tomb of Thomas Aquinas in the Toulouse Church of the Jacobins and chanted Evening Prayer within the cloister at Prouilhe, walked from Prouille to Fanjeaux (seeing along the way a

---

23. Marywood Archives, Box 7.2, Folder on Parable.
24. Marywood Archives, Box 7.2.

statue of Dominic covered with bees) and explored the Castle of Carcassonne while hearing about the thirteenth century presence of the group known as the Cathars, the very group Dominic sought to convert away from heresy.

Then Italy! City after city and church upon church — San Remo and the Pisa bridge, Bologna's tomb of Dominic with the angels of Michelangelo on both sides of the altar. Siena with side trips to Florence and Orvieto. Finally Rome where Catherine came alive on the steps of Santa Maria Sopra Minerva and pieces of the history of the Order, Church and civilization spun into threads for life's tapestry![25]

Fran Georgeff's memories bubble with enthusiasm:

A view in St. Catherine of Siena's hometown in Italy

> It was 1998 and having been an Associate for six years, I was about to embark on a Dominican trip of a lifetime. Expecting to have other Grand Rapids Dominican Sisters along to share the experience, I found myself the lone representative of the community. I knew the history for as anyone who has gone on the trip knows, a member of each Congregation is to give a brief history of their part of the Dominican family tree.
>
> What a thrill to visit and walk the path that Dominic would travel daily from Fanjeaux to Prouille and immerse oneself in the struggles, exhilaration and growth of the Order. For me the most emotional, prayerful and life giving experience took place in Siena. "Overwhelming" hardly touches the surface of what transpired the day I spent with Catherine of Siena.
>
> Early in the morning after breakfast . . . , I took the short walk to the Church of St. Dominic. Mass was the first piece of the puzzle, then a visit to

---

25. S. Kateri Schrems in an e-mail to S. Sue Tracy January/February 2011.

every nook and cranny of the church of which the bookstore and the altar of Catherine with its relics were a part.

The niche where Catherine spent much of her time became my place of prayer, meditation and journal writing for the next seven hours. Emotionally, I was spent with tears falling at various times. She had entered my soul and spirit. The joy was to be a part of me forever. Even as I write this down I can visualize the place on the right side of the church, the worn pew and the pillar she would lean against. The entire trip gave my Dominican spirit a boost to last the ages but the experience with Catherine was a priceless gift.[26]

> "The joy was to be a part of me forever."
> Fran Georgeff

Other offerings of Parable included study tours to Central America. Many years included a trip to Guatemala and either El Salvador or Nicaragua. Sister Honora Werner, a Caldwell Dominican, who was a primary organizer of these immersion experiences, had this to say:

We would spend about a week in each place. We arranged in advance through the Friars and Sisters missioned there to meet key people to learn the history, the resources, the challenges, and their view of the present reality. We prayed daily on the road, in the retreat centers/convents where we stayed, and with the people.

The years we visited these countries were times of violence, fear and extraordinary courage. The witness of people who had been killed, injured, and/or detained and those who grieved for them touched us deeply. We think our presence offered the Friars, Sisters and their people a sense of our trying to be in solidarity with them.

At one point we were in San Salvador when the U.S. invaded Iraq the first time. The people were horrified and at first did not want to speak with us. However, as they thought about it, they thought that we would not be the type of people to support such aggression and violence against those with whom we disagree. What a witness they were for us![27]

Among the Congregation's participants was Sister Mary Brigid Clingman, who shared the richness of this opportunity January 7-21, 1991, in El

---

26. Fran Georgeff, Associate, in an e-mail to S. Sue Tracy January/February 2011.
27. S. Honora Werner in an e-mail to S. Sue Tracy January 20, 2012.

Salvador and Guatemala. After numerous riveting encounters, she summed up the Guatemala week in this way:

> In bidding us farewell, Vitalino (the director of a medical clinic in Guatemala City who planned the week for the group) reminded us to know what we have seen with our own eyes. He reminded us of his exile in the United States and the great fear we have of communism. He does not understand that fear. The people of Guatemala do not understand the words "communism" or "capitalism." They do, however, understand the words "hunger" and "misery."
>
> Vitalino challenged us to return to our country to speak the truth as we have seen it, as we have learned; to work for the Kingdom promised by Jesus for justice and peace. But that we need to build the reign of God in our own country. U.S.A. is not heaven. It has money and is overdeveloped and it can look on the Guatemalans with eyes of pity and sadness. He said, "Struggle — do not sit with your arms crossed! Hope because thousands of Guatemalans have died but we are not sitting with our arms crossed. We are in the struggle. The seeds of the martyrs are planted in the problems of misery and poverty. Therefore we have hope. What is the hope of the people of the United States?"[28]

A collaborative project among the Provinces of St. Albert the Great (Central) and St. Martin de Porres (Southern) and two Congregations of Dominican women grew from the seeds of this Parable-sponsored study tour. In January 1992, an informal conversation between Sister Carmelita Murphy and Dominican Friar Father Jim Barnett stirred interest in forming a collaborative venture for ministry in Central America. Subsequently Sister Joan Williams was asked to discern the possibility of being a part of this venture. The site was Honduras, a country with the dubious distinction of having the highest rate of intentional homicide in the world.[29] Sister Joan began her ministry in San Pedro Sula, Honduras, on May 27, 1998, and was joined by Sister Doris Regan, a Dominican Sister of Columbus, Ohio (now Dominican Sister of Peace), on September 9, 1998. Together the two Sisters serve the poor through education,

> "The seeds of the martyrs are planted in the problems of misery and poverty."
> Sister Mary Brigid Clingman

---

28. Clingman, notes from her trip, confirmed in e-mail October 15, 2013.
29. United Nations Office on Drugs and Crime.

pastoral care, and visiting of the sick and imprisoned. Sister Joan keeps the Congregation updated on life as it has evolved, including occasional hurricanes and governmental unrest. The presence of the two Sisters widened yet another circle of Dominican life. In a real sense, a part of each Sister went with Sister Joan as it does when any Sister is called to a new land and ministry.

Thus, without exaggeration, Parable's offerings of retreats and study tours resulted in an immense and intense expansion of awareness and involvement for Dominican life in Michigan. There was no going back. Destiny was moving the Congregation towards stronger bonds with the larger Dominican Family in the United States, Europe, Central and South America.

It wasn't just the invitation of Vatican Council II for individual Congregations to associate with those who have a common spirit and similar ministries; it was a deep desire to recognize that Dominican Sisters held a great deal in common with one another. This recognition was fueled by the experience of sharing histories through storytelling on the bus trips through Europe as part of the *Lands of Dominic* Pilgrimage sponsored by Parable. All who made the trip remarked on the amazing similarity in founding stories as their Congregations were formed to serve the immigrant Church in America in the nineteenth century.

Dominican Alliance

Under the umbrella of concentric circles, just such an association came about as a result of conversations among Dominican Congregations in the midsection of the country. The history of the Dominican Alliance was synthesized by Sister Joan Scanlon, a Dominican Sister of St. Catherine, Kentucky.[30]

> Initial conversations about a "closer union" among Dominican Women's Congregations began in the nineties. In 1996 at the Dominican Leadership Conference meeting in Sinsinawa, four Congregations (Akron, St. Mary New

---

30. St. Catherine, Kentucky, was one of seven Congregations of Dominican Women Religious that reconfigured into one Congregation known as Dominican Sisters of Peace in 2009.

Orleans, Kenosha and Springfield) began talking about an alliance of Congregations that would collaborate for the sake of the mission.[31]

This phrase, collaboration *for the sake of the mission,* had been and continues to be the *raison d'etre* of all efforts toward mutual growth and collaboration. It is spelled out more fully in the mission statement of the Dominican Alliance, which guides collaborative efforts and is stated here:

Itinerant Dominican women,
committed to collaboration,
link their energy, resources and
personnel to preach the Gospel.

The Dominican Alliance remains a non-canonical organization, enabling members to collaborate on issues of common interest around ministry. Basic Congregational identities remain intact, even while members forge working relationships to foster ministries and/or collaboration in a given area of interest. These interests usually result in long-standing committees: African Connection, Dominican Associates, Communications, Corporate Responsibility Investment, Eco-Justice, Kaleidoscope (for newer members of Dominican Congregations), Justice, Peace and Care of Creation, Promoters of Preaching, Vocation/Formation. These focus areas allow a cross-fertilization of ideas from Sisters eager to pool their dreams into realities on behalf of justice. The committees link members with similar interests through special projects, study, and retreats.

In spite of the valuable benefits that the Dominican Alliance offered, the Grand Rapids Dominicans did not immediately participate. Through many Area meetings the Sisters grappled with the pros and cons of joining. Interest in the Dominican Alliance peaked and waned. Caution, without outright dissent, brought the topic to the table with regularity. Despite acknowledging its worthwhile intent, the Congregation was not ready to join the Alliance until the year 2005 under the leadership of the then Prioress, Sister Maribeth Holst.

By 2012, the composition of the Dominican Alliance had changed sub-

---

31. S. Joan Scanlon, OP, www.oppeace.org/dominican-alliance.

stantially with the union of seven Congregations into the newly founded Congregation named Dominican Sisters of Peace in 2009. The Grand Rapids Dominicans, along with Dominican Sisters of Sinsinawa, Racine, Houston, and Kenosha/Taos, did not join the reconfiguration, but remain active participants in the Dominican Alliance. More recently the Dominican Sisters of Adrian have joined the Alliance.

The Dominican Leadership Conference

The Dominican Leadership Conference was founded in 1935 to be the networking organization for elected leaders of Dominican Congregations and Provinces in the United States. The Dominican Sisters ~ Grand Rapids joined this conference from its earliest days and collaborated in the mission of the group, which was to unite and support the Dominican leaders of Congregations of both women and men. In 2010, after seventy-five years as a leadership conference, the group reorganized to allow space for the creation of a new organization: the Dominican Sisters Conference. The new design will provide the apostolic Sisters an organization that serves both the leaders and members of Dominican Congregations. Over time this new configuration will make it possible to create closer bonds among the other branches of the Dominican Family such as the Friars, Nuns, Laity, and Associates.[32]

Federation of Dominican Sisters U.S.A.

In an effort to involve more Sisters and Associates in matters relevant to Dominican life, and to build relationships among the members, the notion of a national federation of Dominican Sisters and Associates emerged. Chapters of the Federation were based on geographical location. Both Sisters and Associates were encouraged to join.

The founding date was May 15, 1999, when leaders and members of twenty-three Congregations committed themselves to gather on a national

---

32. Anne Lythgoe, OP, http://www.domlife.org/2010Stories/dlc_meeting_maryknoll.htm.

level and form a "new dance" for U.S. Dominicans. The Federation of Dominican Sisters U.S.A. was born.

As with the Dominican Alliance begun three years earlier, this group was a non-canonical union wherein each Congregation kept its own identity and autonomy. Federation chapters met in regions and all regions gathered once every three years for a national convocation.

From its inception the intent of the founding members was that the structure of the new Federation would be simple, allowing it to unfold at a natural pace in an organic manner. Its purpose began and continued as a national dynamic union to support the preaching mission of the Order.

When Sister Barbara Hansen was asked about her participation in the early development of the Federation, she commented:

> There had been an interest and movement among many U.S. Dominican congregations for getting closer. During my years in leadership this was the work of the Closer Union Committee within the Dominican Leadership Conference structure.... Seeking union has taken many shapes: the gathering of Dominican Sisters International in 1995 and 1998, the Alliance, and the Dominican Sisters Federation USA formed in May 1999. Will we become Dominican Sisters USA? Dominican Sisters International? To use Mother Eveline's metaphor, we know not on what shore the ripples will land. But we Dominican women will continue to make ripples![33]

Occasionally individuals were confused about the differences between the Federation and the Alliance. The Federation was a national organization with members in all fifty states, while the Alliance is regional, originally comprising Communities in the mid-section of the country along with two Congregations in the southwest. The Federation linked members through regional chapters and formed a common voice for participating U.S. Dominican Women and Associates. It was led by an equal representation of leaders and members and began with a desire to network all Dominican Women and Associates in the country. The original idea for the Federation was that it would be a networking vehicle for Dominican Sisters and Associates in the U.S.

> "We know not on what shore the ripples will land, but we Dominican women will continue to make ripples!"
> Sister Barbara Hansen

---

33. S. Barbara Hansen, in an e-mail dated February 26, 2012, to S. Susanne Tracy.

As of this writing, both the Dominican Leadership Conference and the Federation of Dominican Sisters U.S.A. have been incorporated into a new entity known as the Dominican Sisters Conference. But that is a story for another time in the great unfolding, and enfolding of the Dominican Family and its mission to praise, to bless, and to preach the Good News of Jesus Christ.

Collaborative Dominican Novitiate

When the word *novitiate* is spoken, the majority of the Sisters quickly and easily recall an enclosed, i.e., cloistered, experience on the Motherhouse grounds. The novitiate year provided an in-depth year of immersion in the customs, history, and daily life of what it meant to be a Dominican Sister of Grand Rapids with its particular history and unique spirit.

By the mid-1980s, a new view of this formative base was widened as connections with other Dominicans were blooming. Sister Teresa Houlihan, Prioress at that time, and the formation director, Sister Carmelita Switzer, were present at the foundation of the risky initiative of bringing Dominican novices of several Congregations together under one roof. The initiative appeared risky because it had not been done before, but it appeared to offer a potential way to stretch new members into an experience of the larger Dominican Family to which all belonged.

When asked to share her place in this promising venture, Sister Carmelita responded:

> At the first one [meeting] we considered the possibility of a Common Novitiate. At the second meeting we made a decision and a commitment to participate. At that point an Advisory Board was formed and took over the planning. . . .
>
> The spirit of both meetings I attended was intense and exciting. For a number of years novice directors from across the country had brought our novices to Sinsinawa (Wisconsin) for a three week Dominican Formation Conference each May. We worked together planning those programs and brought in Dominicans from across the country to present different topics related to Dominican history, spirituality and mission. Those weeks gave

novices a chance to grow in an experience of Dominican Family with shared common life, prayer and study. That experience gave great hope for the value of a Dominican Novitiate. We saw potential for novices developing a deep sense of Dominican Family. We knew that together we could offer a much more integrated experience than any one of us could do alone.

At the same time there were points of tension as each local Congregation realized it would be letting go of cherished traditions. As we shared, it became clear that the Novices would change through the experience of a common novitiate. I suspect some wondered how a Novice would bond with the local Congregation after the exciting experience of the larger Dominican Family. Many wondered what would be given up or lost. The decision was not an easy one. At times the anxiety in the room was palpable. However, after *much* discussion, prayer, and reflection the decision was made to move ahead. Each Congregation was asked to choose whether they would join. The group who were there jokingly called themselves the "Founding Mothers" maybe to lighten the spirit. Grand Rapids chose to join.[34]

The purpose for the Collaborative Dominican Novitiate (CDN) is stated in its handbook:

Sr. Maureen Geary, prioress and preacher

> Dominican women will collaborate on a common canonical year for novices in order to: 1) provide a richer program; 2) encourage a supportive peer group; 3) share the giftedness and resources of the Congregations involved; 4) promote the Charism of the Order; 5) help shape the future of the Dominican family. The program is to comply with the canonical requirements for year-long novitiates.

Sister Maureen Geary, among the first to participate in the Collaborative Dominican Novitiate, recalls her experience. Her reflection bears reproducing here, for it captures the experience of others who have enjoyed the experience of the CDN since that day.

---

34. S. Carmelita Switzer, OP, in response to an e-mail sent to her by S. Sue Tracy in November 2011.

When I entered the Congregation in August 1987, I had no idea that winds of change were blowing.... During my first months I learned about Dominican history, including "other" Dominicans.... Our Candidacy program (at that time we were called Associates) included conferences at Weber Center, which was run by the Adrian Dominicans. *But I had entered the* Grand Rapids *Dominican Congregation.*

By late winter of 1988, we learned that it was likely that a Common Dominican Novitiate (it was originally called "common" and later changed to "collaborative") would be opening in August in St. Louis and that our canonical novitiate year would be spent there.

I think my first reaction was puzzlement: we had a very good thing going here in Grand Rapids, so why would I need to go to St. Louis to be with other Dominicans? My skepticism and even resistance carried through all the way to our arrival in St. Louis. But almost immediately upon entering the CDN . . . I knew this was very right and I embraced the opportunity. In that inaugural year we had two novice directors (one from Amityville and one from Sinsinawa) and there were ten novices. . . . We bonded well as a "novitiate class" even as we had our struggles. . . . We each took one class per semester at Aquinas Institute (or St. Louis University) and spent one day a week in a ministry — mine was visiting the residents of the Little Sisters of the Poor Home, which I loved.

Once a week we attended an intercommunity novitiate program that included women and men from various congregations. We had class at the CDN on the vows and the Rule of St. Augustine. We studied the Constitution of each congregation — noting similarities and differences in spirit, ministerial focus and community living, etc. while following the thread of our common Dominican roots. We had presenters — often a Dominican woman and man — on social justice, prayer and other topics. We learned [to sing] the Salve and the O Lumen. We prayed morning and evening prayer together and celebrated Eucharist at the chapel of the high school where the CDN was originally located or in our own chapel. Sunday worship was at various churches — some novices were attracted to multi-cultural parishes, others to various neighborhood parishes. Yes — this was a real Novitiate; just one with expanded membership.

At our first prayer together we each contributed some rich soil from our home congregation. We mixed this good Earth and planted plants for our chapel — to be nurtured with our common history. During the course of the year the novice directors and prioresses of each Congregation visited at various times.

We heard through the grapevine that there was some concern that novices might be attracted to a different congregation and want to transfer! As we prayed, studied and talked together we often marveled that each of us seemed to be in just the place she belonged. The charism was *one* and yet had *many* flavors.

It was a blessing to experience the novitiate with a wider group with which to explore our call to religious life. We also spent two weeks with the men of the central province, learning more about Dominican history together. We celebrated major feasts and had meals with the student brothers and the community at Aquinas Institute. Many Dominican women lived in St. Louis and we had ample opportunity for interaction with them as well.

My experience of the CDN launched me into the large Dominican world. At the end of our year we took a road trip and visited about a dozen motherhouses, including the monastery in Guilford, Connecticut. I was able to walk the holy ground of vast numbers of Sisters, learn their roots and hear their stories as well as their dreams for the future. All of this led to my personal desire to make Parable retreats, attend Dominican gatherings/conferences of women and men from around the country, and later to interact through my work as Promoter for Justice and the Parable and DLC [Dominican Leadership Conference] Boards. The people who sustain me in this wonderful and challenging life come from our Grand Rapids Congregation and many other congregations and provinces.

I truly do not know any other way to *be* Dominican except this way that I was formed in the Dominican Family. The interaction in the CDN and since then affirms my call to Dominican life. I embrace my Grand Rapids Dominican roots and I affirm the nourishment I have received through my broad Dominican connections. It is a wonderful Family, and I am so grateful the Dominican Sisters of Grand Rapids have embraced their long, wide and deep Dominican heritage.[35]

While Sister Maureen was immersed in the canonical novitiate, Sister

---

35. S. Maureen Geary in e-mail November 11, 2013.

Mary Donnelly, who had entered the Congregation the year prior to Sister Maureen, was involved in a program at the House of Studies for Dominican women in St. Louis known as Siena House. This housing, a convent rented by the Sinsinawa Dominicans, was available for Sisters in their second year (non-canonical) novitiate wishing to study at Aquinas Institute. Sister Mary Donnelly reminisced about her time there:

> As I reflect on my experiences at Siena House, I now realize that this was my first real experience of Dominican Family. There were nine of us from eight different Dominican Congregations and I was amazed at how different we were in some ways, and how much alike we were in others. We shared the same Dominican charism, yet each en-fleshed it as a unique expression of the events and people who helped to shape our individual congregations.[36]

Through initiatives such as the Dominican Leadership Conference, Parable Conference, the Dominican Alliance, the Federation, and the Collaborative Dominican Novitiate, vowed Women Religious began to know and bond with one another in the extended Dominican Family. Two other groups came into the concentric circles of Dominican life — in this case involving both vowed and non-vowed women and men who, nonetheless, shared affinity with the spirit of Dominican life.

Dominican Institute for the Arts

Preaching can take many forms, words being but one. Dominicans often claim to "preach with their very lives." In 1997, Dominicans with a creative artistic bent came together and the Dominican Institute for the Arts, the DIA, was born. Writing in the St. Martin de Porres Southern Province newsletter about this event, Armando P. Ibáñez, OP, proclaimed yet another opportunity for Dominican women and men to bond with common focus — this time for those immersed in the world of art. One month later twenty-two Dominican artists and appreciators of arts met under the title of the *Gathering of Dominican Artists* in Mission San Jose, California. The Spirit was

---

36. S. Mary Donnelly in e-mail November 6, 2013.

palpably present and the artists testified to God's presence through their works of art and their lives. The Dominican Institute for the Arts was born.[37]

Sisters Francetta McCann, photographer, and Phyllis Mrozinski, sculptor, were part of the DIA from its initial meeting. Their responses sing out their enthusiasm at the prospect of creating a vehicle by which fellow Dominican artists could celebrate their artistic and God-given gifts.

Sister Phyllis recalled the first meeting, affirming what others experienced:

> The Holy Spirit was very present at that first meeting in Oakland [Mission San Jose]. It was Sister Dolorita, our Vicaress at the time, who strongly encouraged me to attend the meeting. I suggested that Sister Francetta also attend. It was a diverse group in attendance, male and female, lay associates and Religious. All were artists. Occupations varied. At the end of that gathering a Steering Committee of six was formed. I was one who was chosen. Each was given a task to work on for the next gathering.[38]

Sister Francetta McCann mused on her experience:

Sr. Phyllis Mrozinski, preaching through the art of sculpture

> While looking around the room at the Dominican Priory [Mission San Jose] in Oakland, California, I thought, I'm both privileged and honored to be a part of the first gathering of twenty Dominicans, including a few Associates, from various areas of the world such as England, France, California, Ohio and Michigan as a core member. It was a *glorious* time filled with prayer, song, and gratitude.[39]

Again a concentric circle widened for Dominican Family life and growth — this time for the artist preachers in the Order. Not always fully understood or appreciated in their individual Congregations, these gifted women and men found in the Dominican Institute of Arts a place where they could celebrate their diverse gifts and feel at home and supported.

---

37. Armando P. Ibáñez, OP, in *Preacher's Exchange*, vol. XI, no. 3 (Summer 1997); a publication of the Southern Dominican Province, Raleigh, North Carolina.
38. S. Phyllis Mrozinski in e-mail to S. Sue Tracy November 23, 2011.
39. S. Francetta McCann in e-mail to S. Sue Tracy.

The Mellow D's

Before the DIA came into existence, but of similar minds and hearts in artistry, a group of members and former members, came together in 1971. It was an inauspicious beginning — singing Christmas songs for a group of elderly Sisters. A relative of one of the Sisters heard them sing and asked if they could sing at her wedding. A guest at the wedding asked if they could sing at *her* wedding and on and on and on! And so it came to be. The Mellow D's (D for Dominicans) sang for over twenty years at church and civic organizations, ecumenical services, scriptural prayer events, retreats, parish events, funerals, memorial services, anniversaries, and public concerts.

Mostly singing at events in Grand Rapids, they also sang in Illinois and as far away as San Diego, California. They charged no set fee, but used free will offerings toward the expenses of transportation, instruments, tuning, repair, and the purchase of musical scores. And always, a portion was set aside to give to the disadvantaged, for as the title of their 1981 album stated: "You Are Special." They meant it! Everyone is special in God's loving eyes.

The Mellow D's, preaching through music: (back row, left to right) former member Ann Westerman and Srs. Marilyn Holmes, Joan Thomas, Jackie Hudson, Jackie Bennett, and Nancy Brousseau; (front row, left to right) Srs. Stephanie Heitz, Vera Ann Tilmann, and Mary Ann Ferguson

Through their song, vibrant voices, and infectious joy these women preached the Gospel message of God's bountiful love for each person.

In the summer of 1991 the Mellow D's received commendation from the Grand Rapids Diocesan Office for Worship, in a letter dated August 2, 1991:

The ministry of the Mellow D's deserves special commendation during this, their twentieth anniversary year. Whether within the Congregation, or Diocese, or in the presence of civic groups their music has led others in praise and thanksgiving; they have ministered comfort and hope; and they have offered both an invitation and challenge to live the Gospel. We all must call to mind that when they minister within the liturgical assembly, they significantly contribute to the re-shaping of our image of God and promote the transformation of the human person through the particular content and style of their music.[40]

40. Marywood Archives AR 25 top.

Dominican Volunteers USA

As early as the 1970s there were programs sponsored by various congregations of Dominican women for volunteer ministry geared toward young women and men who were recent college graduates. Sister Kathi Sleziak recalls the early days of the program in the 1990s when she worked in collaboration with other Dominican Sister Congregations to consolidate the individual programs into one national organization to serve the Dominican family.

The proposal for a national program received enthusiastic support from the Dominican Leadership Conference (DLC), and in 2001 the Dominican Volunteers USA was organized. Since then the program has grown in numbers and diversity of ministry. Volunteers live in intentional intergenerational communities of Dominican women or men whenever possible throughout the United States. They serve those in particular need in areas of teaching, administration, social services, public policy advocacy, immigrant rights, nursing, and organic farming. Alumni of the program invariably describe the experience as life changing — their faith is strengthened and the values of the Dominican Family for prayer, study, community, and service permeate their choices forever after.

Closing Thoughts

In this chapter some of the major movements of collaboration since Vatican Council II have been highlighted. These examples are far from the total picture of efforts to cooperate with one another in the Dominican mission to Praise, Bless, and Preach. Other groups such as Dominican Sisters International, Dominican Leadership Conference, the Colloquium of Dominican Colleges and Universities, and the McGreal Center for Dominican Historical Studies (an organization that promotes the research and writing of the history of the Order of Preachers in the United States) have each yielded rich and deep connections among members of the larger international community of Dominicans.

Dominican Sisters and Dominican Volunteers USA: (back row, left to right) Sr. Ann Walters, Fr. Ron Kreul, OP, Sr. Kathi Sleziak; (front row, left to right) Srs. Jean Reimer and Jessica McKenzie, Bill Taft, and Sr. Mary Ann Barrett

Nearly fifty years have transpired since the closing of Vatican Council II. The stakes of the tent have been set out wide to embrace all who acknowledge a kindred spirit with Dominican life. A new century has begun, with no way of knowing what other circles will be opened, what possibilities will find fulfillment in this Dominican way of life that has endured for over 800 years.

PART IV

Ministry: Essential to Dominican Life

I N THIS SECTION on ministry, the stories of three long-standing ministries are told. Each situated in a distinctive geographical region, the three places have engaged the Sisters and the people there in relationships that have had profound and enduring effects on both. The Sisters will agree that the Congregation would not be the same without these three places so dear to their hearts: Aquinas College, New Mexico, and Chimbote, Peru.

The first essay relates the remarkable story of the growth and change at Aquinas College in Grand Rapids, Michigan — still flourishing, still offering a premier liberal arts education. Reinventing itself in the face of tremendous challenges in the early 1960s, the College developed creative programs for the traditional college-aged undergraduate, mature adults, and senior citizens. High school and elementary school students benefited from special programs designed for them during the summer and from a reading clinic during the school year. Graduate students profited from carefully crafted programs, and the neighborhood around the College itself was revitalized. Grounded in the four Dominican essentials of prayer, study, community, and service, and committed to preparing all — the young and not so young — through the exhilaration of lifelong learning, Aquinas College is truly a "jewel" in the minds and hearts of the Dominican Sisters ~ Grand Rapids.

The second story is about the beloved Land of Enchantment known as New Mexico, so far from Grand Rapids, Michigan, yet so dear to the hearts of all through the gift of the enchanted land, the generous and joyous people, and particularly through the women who entered the Congregation from

New Mexico and are a blessing to the Congregation to this day. The Sisters' work in schools, hospitals, parishes, and social work is noteworthy, but pales in comparison to the beauty and depth of the cultural exchange between two peoples — one close to the Rio Grande in the Southwest, the other near the "Grande Rio" — the Grand River in western Michigan.

The third place of import for the Sisters of Grand Rapids is also the furthest from home. Here is a story of horrifying events, unremitting hope, new births, floods, famine, earthquakes, and terrorists. It is a compelling narrative that speaks to perseverance, courage, and deep faith on the part of the Sister missionaries and the Peruvian people alike. And it is an ongoing love affair of two peoples in two lands who have come to know and care for one another.

The next part of this section on ministry relates the broadening horizons and flourishing ministries of the Sisters from the late 1960s forward. This story describes the breathtaking diversity among the new ministries embraced during these years. For those who ask, "Where have all the Sisters gone?" this chapter answers the question, "They are everywhere."

The remarkable story of the rise of social consciousness among the Sisters in the 1960s and the decades that followed is the subject of this part. Far from the enclosed protection of a semi-cloistered life, Sisters took to the streets, the neighborhoods, the slums, and the barrios. Wherever injustice was flagrant, Sisters were found with their sisters and brothers protesting for better living conditions and human rights.

The transition of the west wing of Marywood from an academy for girls to a center for spirituality and conferences along with the expansion of the prayer community to include the Sunday Assembly in the worship space of the Campus is relayed. Here is an ongoing saga of adaptation to meet the needs of the people for the times in which we live.

Sisters adapted to the changing times in the Church and culture, not unlike their founder St. Dominic, who did precisely this in his own time. Lastly, the expansion of ministries is delineated as the Sisters answered the call to minister in new places and ways. While the terminology changed, the underlying mission to preach the Gospel in both word and work remained the same.

Aquinas College in Changing Times

"Do you understand what you are reading?"
He replied, "How can I, unless someone instruct me?"
ACTS 8:30-31

Introduction

The 1960s and 1970s marked a period of profound change in virtually every institution and every aspect of life in the United States. It was a time of social and sexual revolution, of political unrest, the Vietnam War, and Vatican Council II. Aquinas College, a small Catholic liberal arts college sponsored by the Grand Rapids Dominican Sisters, sailed into the headwinds of this turbulence teetering on the edge of serious financial difficulties.

The college was unquestionably Catholic. Its curriculum required eighteen credit hours of Theology and nine credit hours of Philosophy. A large group of dynamic Dominican Sisters were members of virtually every department — faculty, staff, and administration. Dominican priests were part of the faculty and built strong bonds with students. Catholic lay faculty joined the Dominicans in the creation of a traditional Catholic culture manifesting itself not only in prayer and liturgy, but in May crowning processions, retreats, rosaries, and many signs of traditional Catholic practices. The essentials of Dominican life, i.e., prayer, study, community, and service, saturated every aspect of college life, including curriculum, extracurricular activities, and the very ethos of the institution.

It was the hearts' desire of the Sisters to establish a four-year, coeducational Catholic liberal arts college, as a natural capstone to an extensive system of schools staffed by the Sisters. They endowed the college both physically and fiscally. The Marywood Archives document financial transactions of loans and the transfer of monies from operating funds. Letters from Mothers General reported achievements and developments at the college with pride. At the same time these missives often regulated frugality throughout the Congregation as each Sister in the Congregation made sacrifices to keep Aquinas College going.

A Time of Change or Demise

In the midst of these turbulent years of the 1960s and with the college in uncertain times financially, Monsignor Bukowski, the diocesan priest appointed president of the college by Bishop Joseph Pinten in 1937, retired after thirty-eight years of service. In 1969, in what appeared to be a dramatic change, the first lay president of Aquinas College, Dr. Norbert Hruby, took office. Formerly the vice president of Chicago's Mundelein College, he was chosen by the Aquinas Board of Trustees, which had been expanded to include business men in addition to the Sister officers of the Congregation. Some members questioned the competency of the Sister Trustees if they had to involve lay persons in the hiring process for the highest officer of the College. Yet, this was a natural outcome of how the early leaders of both the Congregation and the college had been developing a leadership style. Following a national pattern, Sisters in administrative positions had been quietly consulting trusted lay men and women as they made decisions guiding the growth of their insti-

Sisters who had served or were serving at Aquinas College in 1984

tutions and Congregations. So while it appeared to some that naming a lay man as president was a radical departure from the norm, it was simply recognizing the depth and breadth of resources already being used by wise Congregational leaders.

A Different Kind of Campus Revolution

Dr. Hruby agreed to take the position on the condition that he would immediately mandate a college-wide Self-Study to assess its ability to survive and meet the challenges of the future. Small liberal arts colleges were becoming anachronistic in the turbulence of the late 1960s. Aquinas College would not be exempt from that threat. Indeed, urban unrest erupting in riots, anti-war protests, and student rebellions ending in the deaths of four students at Kent State occurred just days before the end of the Aquinas College Self-Study. These deaths along with the assassinations of three national leaders, including the president of the United States, marked the end of a sense of innocence of the mid-century. The era of quiet, liberal arts colleges where young adults extended their adolescence through the protected environment of *in locus parentis* was over.

The college-wide effort of the Self-Study involved every member of the Aquinas community. Together they faced broad questions such as whether the college deserved to survive and what difference an Aquinas education made. They also asked very specific questions about everything from curriculum requirements to living arrangements on campus. All this radically changed and invigorated the curriculum, revised the governance structure, and reshaped the entire institutional culture.

Dr. Norbert Hruby, President of Aquinas College, and Sr. Jean Milhaupt in procession at a graduation ceremony

Led by Dr. Lee Jacokes, professor of psychology, five study groups were formed: Governance; Faculty Rights and Responsibilities; Student Rights and Responsibilities; Teaching Resources and Theory; and Learning Resources and Theory. Every full-time faculty member was on a committee. Students were also full participants in committee work. From February 26, 1969, to March 16, 1970, the college worked through three phases: gathering and asking questions, answering questions, and finally making decisions, culminating in a plenary session for the entire college community.

A grant from the Grand Rapids Foundation permitted committee members to travel to twenty-nine colleges, observing the best practices in the areas they studied and then reporting on what they had learned. A board of several nationally known scholars visited the college during this period to help committee members think through questions, ponder solutions, and propose a path to the future.[1]

A radical revision in curriculum allowed more student choices and individualizing of programs. It marked waves of many more curricular revisions to come before the turn of the century, which involved humanities programs, science initiatives, the Baldwin Observatory and its curricular influences, and a developing business program. In every instance, the core values of the "Sisters'" college, i.e., the Dominican essentials of prayer, study, community, and service, remained at the core of the changes in the curricular and cultural life of the college community.

Among these changes were the development of study abroad opportunities such as the Ireland Overseas program and English as a Second Language program. The confluence of the ideas for a methods course in teaching English as a Second Language, the skills of Sister Thomasine Bugala in teaching languages, and the work of Father Graham McDonnell created opportunities for students to teach English in Japan over the years.[2]

There were far fewer required courses in the revised curriculum emerg-

---

1. Interview with Dr. Lee Jacokes, September 2011.
2. Fr. Graham McDonnell, a former Maryknoll missionary, now Japanese diocesan priest, contacted S. Anne Keating, Academic Dean, in 1971 to inquire about the possibility of Aquinas students spending a year in Japan teaching English as a Second Language. With the cooperation of several departments at the college, S. Thomasine found herself in Japan in 1972. Sr. Thomasine spent 23 summers teaching English to the Japanese people; she taught in the Maryknoll Program, revised and wrote textbooks, and made tapes for teaching English.

ing from the Self-Study. New scheduling was adopted and opportunities for life-experience credit were allowed. A bicameral governance structure was voted into place, with the faculty voting to step away from the power they had once exercised. They would now share power with administration and students in the structure known as the Academic Assembly. Rules for student life were changed. The more public displays of Catholic culture such as May crowning of the Blessed Virgin Mary and religious processions diminished, but not the spirit and faith of Catholicism. Overt signs and practices lessened, but living, breathing examples of how exemplary Catholics live and how they preach the Gospel with their lives remained a strong reality.³ Dominican influence was maintained as the foundation and bulwark of the institution. Sisters were a strong presence at committee meetings discussing the nature of the Catholic college and the goals and objectives of the institution.

Sr. Thomasine Bugala teaching English during summers in Japan

In the midst of student rebellions across the country, Aquinas College held its own brand of "revolution" — quiet, inclusive, and effective. The Self Study of 1969-1970 was a great watershed in the life of the institution. This review of the college's life and culture not only answered the question of whether Aquinas deserved to exist with a definitive Yes! But it also redefined what a Catholic liberal arts education could be. This endeavor enabled Aquinas to change to meet the needs of the students for the times in which they lived. The Self-Study and its aftermath opened the way for a period in which innovation and fresh, new programs set Aquinas apart for its creativity and invitation to students of all ages.

Aquinas College held its own brand of "revolution" — quiet, inclusive, and effective.

---

3. Interview with Lee Jacokes, September 2011.

MINISTRY

Continuing Education

The college began to turn its energies to increasing its student population by serving potential students who had not had the opportunity for a college degree. The Career Action Program was one of the first Aquinas programs to invite adults to complete their college degree in Business Administration and enhance their careers. With an innovative format of courses scheduled once a week on Saturdays plus evenings for twelve weeks, it was an opportunity accepted by nearly 500 students by the second year of its implementation.

A companion program soon followed. Encore targeted women who had left college for work or for raising a family. Now in their mid-thirties or early forties, with children in school, they had an interest in pursuing or completing their degrees. College staff were especially sensitive to scheduling these students in classes that would be convenient for their responsibilities at home, and they were directed to coursework with faculty who understood their hesitancy to be in classes with traditional age students. Even though this program enhanced enrollment, it also marked an example of Aquinas's awareness of the concerns and needs of women. As both programs flourished, a new area of Continuing Education emerged with other initiatives such as IDEA, Individually Designed Education for Adults. Developing from the 1971 Aquinas Summer School without Walls, these initiatives enabled more of the adult population, even those returning from the armed forces, to complete their degrees.[4] Here was another step toward Aquinas's Directed Studies Program, combining independent study with on-campus class meetings.

Men return to complete their degrees in the Career Action Program at Aquinas College.

4. Patricia Kozal, *A Brief History of Continuing Education at Aquinas College, 1989*: An In-House Report summarizing the Activities of the First 20 Years of Aquinas' Degree Completion Programs designed specifically for Adults, paper presented at the college's celebration of National Continuing Education Week, March 12-18, 1989. Marywood Archives.

These new initiatives in Continuing Education for adults found their full complement in the Emeritus Program. In 1971, the White House Conference on Aging emphasized life-long learning as a right for persons of all ages. With this as its foundation, Mr. R. Paul Nelson, Director of Continuing Education, commissioned a market study of the senior population in this area. A consultant, Dr. Carl Pettersch, dean of Graduate Studies at the University of Western Connecticut, conducted the study and determined an educational program for seniors could be an initiative Aquinas might undertake as a genuine service to the senior population. Under the leadership of Sister Agnes Thiel, OP, Emeritus College developed as a non-degree program for those fifty-five and older, tapping into a senior population possessing a range of interests and habits of life-long learning. Emeritus has been heralded as one of the first programs for seniors in the country. In 2008, the college received a grant from the Osher Foundation and Emeritus was transformed into the Osher Lifelong Learning Institute at Aquinas College (OLLI).

Women like this student return to complete their degrees in the Encore program at Aquinas College.

Besides serving a traditional age population, mature adults, and seniors, Aquinas also targeted young people and developed another visible commitment to life-long learning. In 1969-1970, the college focused attention on supplementing the education of disadvantaged youth. The positive effect of the Upward Bound program rippled throughout the high school student population in the Grand Rapids Public School system. Academic service to young people continues in the Aquinas Reading Clinic for kindergarten through fourth grade students; science camps for grades four through six, and jazz camp for those in the eighth grade through college, to name a few opportunities. The Dominican legacy of study and life-long learning shone through the multiple opportunities at Aquinas for all age groups and interests, including the graduate level.

Continuing education for all at Aquinas College.

MINISTRY

AIRS — Aquinas Institute for Religious Studies

In a collaborative venture between Aquinas College and the Grand Rapids Dominicans a program for Sisters was transformed into a program of academic service to the Grand Rapids Diocese. It began in 1952, when the first Theological Institute sponsored by the Congregation was begun at Aquinas College and housed at Catholic Central on Sheldon Street in Grand Rapids. The purpose was to "better qualify the Sisters as Catholic educators and expand their vision of religious life."[5] This program, originally named Institute for the Spiritual Formation of Sisters, was initially meant only for the Grand Rapids Dominican Sisters, and was taught only by Dominican priests. Through the joint auspices of the Dominican Sisters and the Dominican priests at Aquinas College, the program evolved into the Aquinas Institute for Religious Studies or AIRS. Students took courses in dogmatic and moral theology, Sacred Scripture, and canon law. This four-summer course sequence, successfully completed, merited a Certificate in Theology. In 1964, two additional summers of study in religious education were added to the curriculum, giving an opportunity to complete a Master's in Religious Education.

Senior citizens continue their education at Aquinas College in the Emeritus Program.

Growth in student numbers in the program caused its location to change several times until it nestled itself in the beauty of the Aquinas campus in 1969. Courses were offered in a new program of five summers, and expanded in 1971 to include laity with the recognition of their needs in preparing to minister in the Church. Within a short time, courses were scheduled

Young students get a summer boost toward a college education in the Upward Bound program at Aquinas College.

5. *Aquinas Magazine,* Spring 1983.

during the academic year as well as during the summer. In addition to areas of concentration in religious education, Scripture, and theology, an opportunity for concentration in pastoral ministry was added. The program was renamed Aquinas Institute of Religious Studies (AIRS).

AIRS became diverse in student population as well as instructors. Students came from all over the United States and faculty came from Ireland, Germany, Italy, and China. Close bonds of community were formed among students and faculty. In the thirty years of its flourishing, 315 Grand Rapids Dominican Sisters, 165 Women Religious from other congregations, 138 priests, Brothers and lay men and women were educated in this great learning community for work in Catholic parishes and schools.[6]

Sister Joan Thomas, long-time administrative assistant for the program and then director, shares this insight: "AIRS existed at a time when programs like this were few in number. Our faculty stretched the minds of all as we pursued truth together. The essentials of study, community, prayer, and service were mightily impacted!"[7]

Although AIRS officially ended in 1983, Aquinas College continues to work with the Diocese of Grand Rapids to provide classes which apply toward Youth Ministry certification, Director of Religious Education (DRE) training, and diaconate preparation. It now offers a certificate program in ministry in addition to a Catholic Studies minor.

Welcome to the Neighborhood

While the college offered courses for the academic and professional formation of Sisters and lay ministers in the Church, the Dominican penchant for service was also exercised in the relationship of Aquinas to its neighbors. The once peaceful and prosperous neighborhood around Aquinas College, known as Eastown, went through a major change. Crime was on the rise; more and more single-family homes had become rental properties owned by slum landlords. Wilcox Park, a green space adjacent to the campus, was

---

6. *Aquinas Magazine*, Spring 1983.
7. Joan Thomas, O.P., interview, April 24, 2012.

becoming a dangerous place. Empty storefronts pocked the business district and people were afraid to be out in Eastown at night.

The Aquinas community was threatened by these changes, and Dr. Hruby knew that the future of the college would be at risk if nothing was done. At his initiative, faculty and staff of the college became involved in reversing these changes. Among them were an anthropologist, Linda Easley; urban geographer, Thomas Edison; and community organizer, Michael Williams. They undertook a study of the neighborhood together with Aquinas students, Grand Rapids urban planners, the Grand Rapids Board of Education, and the Grand Rapids Housing Commission, concluding that without the involvement of the college in the neighborhood, there would be little hope for change and revitalization.

Sisters Aquinas Weber, member of the Eastown Board, and Jean Paul Tilmann, of the Geography Department, played a significant role. Sister Aquinas recalls visiting every merchant to discuss the situation that had led a once-thriving area to become marred by boarded-up buildings with poor lighting at night, making it a seedbed for crime. A local merchant, Mr. Jim Geib of Hammer and Cortenhof Hardware, joined her and Sister Jean Paul in talking to then Mayor Lyman Parks and the Grand Rapids City Commission about the situation, pointing out that some of those boarded-up and empty buildings belonged to the city itself. The group, including the Sisters, took them on a bus tour of the area, showing them the problems firsthand and pointing out a lack of police presence which exacerbated the difficulties.[8]

The neighborhood is revived through the Eastown program: (seated, left to right) Linda Easley, Thomas Edison, and Michael Williams; (standing, left to right): Dr. Norbert Hruby and Sr. James Rau.

8. S. Aquinas Weber, Oral History, May 14, 2012, Marywood Archives.

Police patrols increased; the Sisters joined in organizing the first Eastown Street Fair; a food co-op was established, and local leaders emerged to begin the first neighborhood association in Grand Rapids.

In light of this, merchants and members of the neighborhood joined leaders of the college community in 1973 to develop the Eastown Neighborhood Association. A year later the W. K. Kellogg Foundation provided a grant of $129,836 over a three-year period to support three goals: College-Community Liaison; Community Development through Organization; and Institutional Development at Aquinas.[9] Sister Aquinas Weber was named administrator of the grant. Urban Studies became part of the Aquinas curriculum and faculty worked with association members to revitalize the neighborhood. With Sister James Rau as editor, Linda Easley, Thomas Edison, and Michael Williams wrote the book *Eastown! A Report on How Aquinas College Helped Its Local Community Reverse Neighborhood Transition and Deterioration*. With the expiration of the grant period, the college moved back from its leadership role and the merchants continued their joint work in the neighborhood association. Today, the area is thriving with new businesses and a robust urban life. The process and the neighborhood association became a model for others in the city and beyond.

Srs. Jean Paul Tilmann and Aquinas Weber meet the merchants in Eastown.

---

9. Linda Easley, Thomas Edison, Michael Williams, *Eastown! A Report on How Aquinas College Helped Its Local Community Reverse Neighborhood Transition and Deterioration* (1978), p. 3.

MINISTRY

The Neighborhood Beyond

The Dominican service ethic permeated student life. Hundreds of students participate in Campus Ministry service-learning opportunities in Haiti, Peru, Dominican Republic, Honduras, and the Pine Ridge Indian Reservation in South Dakota, to name a few. Three annual events — *Project Unite* within Freshman Orientation; *Into the Streets,* a week of volunteering; and *Heartside Pride Cleansweep* — mark significant opportunities for students to widen their horizons and open their hearts in service. Service Houses were also organized to support small student groups focusing on a common project for the academic year.

With the presidency of Mr. R. Paul Nelson, Dominican essential values were highlighted as hallmarks distinguishing Aquinas College from other institutions. They were explained in the President's talks to donors and to potential students. Despite the decreasing numbers of Dominican Sisters on campus, there is a continuing embrace of the essentials of Dominican life by the college community.

As the numbers of Dominican Sisters in full-time ministry at Aquinas

Sr. Aquinas Weber and Mr. Jim Geib, a local business owner in Eastown, confer on actions to make the neighborhood safer and more prosperous.

College decrease, the importance of faculty and staff imbued with the Dominican spirit has increased. To that end the Sisters offer an annual subsidy to support a member of the Aquinas faculty or staff to attend the Summer Study Program in Fanjeaux, France, where Saint Dominic lived and worked. Here they study with faculty, administrators, students, and staff from Dominican colleges across the United States, and return with deeper understanding of the Dominican story and a greater motivation to nourish the tradition of the Order at Aquinas College.

Conclusion

Reflecting back over the decades of the existence of Aquinas College, we have harvested lessons from the strength of those four essentials and from a deep understanding of how they have guided the institution through waves of change. Over the years, Aquinas College has been transformed. The Sisters' dream for a Catholic and Dominican liberal arts college has been realized far beyond their expectations. That dream has reinvented itself with the changing times, always anchored in the Dominican essentials of prayer, study, service, and community as guiding principles. Ingrained in the very fabric of the college's culture, they move Aquinas into its future.

Sr. Diane Dehn advising a student at Aquinas College

New Mexico — Dominicans in the Land of Enchantment

"Your people will be my people...."
RUTH 1:16

Introduction

In 1925, with an adventurous spirit and trust in God, the Congregation sent four Sisters to New Mexico at the invitation of Father Peter Kuppers, a priest working in New Mexico.[1] Many more Sisters were to follow. By the 1960s the Sisters had lived and ministered in New Mexico stretching from Socorro in the south to Ranchos de Taos in the northern region and Bloomfield in the northwest corner. From the beginning to the present day, schools, parishes, and hospitals have been staffed and enriched by the presence, dedication, faith, and gifts of these Sisters from New Mexico and Michigan. Well over four hundred Sisters have served in New Mexico from the beginning to the present day. Since the middle of the 1960s their ministry and presence has reached beyond Catholic institutions to public schools and other agencies.

This is "a story within a story," a story of faith and challenge, of adventure

---

1. Mona Schwind, *Period Pieces,* p. 115. Mention is also made of a tradition among the Sisters that in the 1920s a mission to China was contemplated, but was deferred with the invitation to New Mexico.

and surprises, of giving and receiving that continues to generate life in New Mexico and in this Congregation. In this telling, the reader will observe the unfolding of ministry in New Mexico from the mid-1960s, and in this historical view, gain new perspectives and understanding — a possibility so aptly articulated by author Eudora Welty: "The events in our lives happen in a sequence in time, but in their significance to ourselves they find their own order: the continuous thread of revelation."[2]

The Spanish philosopher José Ortega y Gasset once said, "Tell me the landscape in which you live and I'll tell you who you are."[3] The landscape of New Mexico, nicknamed the Land of Enchantment because of its beautiful scenery and rich history, has shaped and formed, in one way or another, the native New Mexicans who followed a call and joined the Dominican Sisters of Grand Rapids, Michigan. Likewise this land influenced and changed the Sisters who served in and came to love this enchanted land and its people.

The mountains with their strength and constancy give a sense of God's presence in all of life. The expansiveness of the sky and the land, as far as the eye can see until the Earth and sky meet, leaves one with wonder and awe at the majesty of all creation and the unfathomable goodness of the Creator. The demands and challenges of the desert and the surprising abundance of

The mountains with their strength and constancy give a sense of God's presence in all of life.

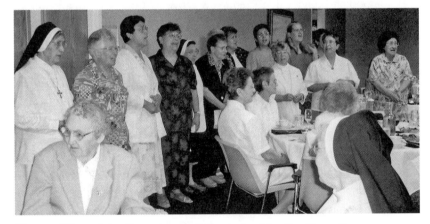

Sisters of Hispanic heritage share their joy and celebrate with music.

2. http://www.successories.com/iquote/author/3551/eudora-welty-quotes/2.

3. http://www.gbod.org/site/apps/nlnet/content2.aspx?c=nhLRJ2PMKsG&b=5900487&ct=2932733.

life and color in spring fuel the heart and soul through the challenges of life with a deep trust in God's providence and hope that out of suffering, some good can come. A saying testifies to this common wisdom of the folks: *No hay mal que por bien no venga.* (There is nothing bad from which good cannot come.)

Vocations from the Land of Enchantment

From the land and its people, twenty-seven young women entered the Congregation. Fortified with deep faith, a strong sense of family, a love of creation and life, young women from New Mexico responded to the call to "Come and See" — a common mantra for congregational vocation directors. Come and see if this life is a good fit for you. Their travel to Michigan was not without fear. They left the familiar and went into unknown territory. Sisters recall their early experiences in Michigan. "I missed the sky and mountains. It never seemed to stop raining. It felt like the sun would never appear again." "I had to get used to eating things I had never heard of, like sauerkraut and Brussels sprouts. The first time sauerkraut was served I refused, saying it was no good and obviously rotten. Now I love it." One Sister in an attempt to make up for the loss of red and green chili used an abundance of pepper on her food. An elder Sister told her that she should not consume so much pepper because it was bad for her passions! "I said that I had been eating hot red and green peppers all my life and there was nothing wrong with my passions." Laughingly she adds, "I didn't know what my passions were, but I wasn't having any trouble." Eventually hot chili sauce took its place next to the salt and pepper on the dining room tables at Marywood.

Eventually hot chili sauce took its place next to the salt and pepper on the dining room tables at Marywood.

Sisters from New Mexico brought with them a heritage of *fiestas: las mañanitas* (morning songs), *las posadas* (celebration nine days before Christmas), *las piñatas,* and *las luminarias* (candles in bags that line the walkways during Christmas). A variety of foods found favor in Michigan: *sopaipillas* (a light pastry), *pozole* (a kind of soup), *enchiladas, frijoles* (beans), *chili verde o rojo* (green or red chili), *tortillas de harina o de maíz* (wheat or corn flatbread). But it wasn't just that tasty, new foods found their way into the life of Grand Rapids Dominicans; a special southwestern brand of hospitality also wended its way into the very fabric of the Congregation. The Sisters from

New Mexico

New Mexico came from families where hospitality was a way of life. *Mi casa es su casa* was not just a nice saying. The door was always open . . . be they friend or neighbor or stranger. All who came were welcome at the table. And that is still true today, for the Sisters are renowned for their warm hospitality.

In addition to deep family ties and hospitality, a sense of *milagros* or miracles was and is a story line in the families of New Mexico. Exclamations such as *Bendito Sea Dios, Jesus, Maria y Jose* (Blessed be God, Jesus, Mary, and Joseph) as well as expressions such as *Santa Maria Purisima* (Holy and Pure Virgin Mary) undergird the faith that was passed on from generation to generation. References to God were personal and intimate, e.g., *Tatito Dios* (Daddy God).

Michigan sights were astonishing to the New Mexican arrivals. Lush, abundant flowering bushes, deep green carpets of grass, frequent rain, trees of every kind, ponds, rivers, and lakes were things to write home about. The dramatic change of each season was an experience of beauty. Falling in love changes you and you become a new person. The vocation to Religious Life, the beauty of Michigan, and the unfolding love of God enhanced and enlarged the heart of faith and the desire to minister to God's people, despite the challenges. And the challenges were many. Several Sisters agree that it was only grace that kept them in this strange place.

Falling in love changes you and you become a new person.

Sister Dolorita Martinez, who arrived from Truchas, New Mexico in 1955, recalls the challenge of languages. "Spanish was my first language in prayer. It was difficult to go from Spanish to Latin and then English. And for a long time we didn't know what language Father Charles Wilson was using when he led us in praying the rosary." (On this point, the native English speakers had a similar experience. Father Wilson, Dominican priest and Marywood chaplain, from Boston, Massachusetts, had an accent that was equally mystifying to Midwesterners and New Mexicans alike.)

Sister Orlanda Leyba came to Grand Rapids from Peñasco in 1962. She shared her memories in these words: "What I found most challenging was leaving my family and friends. What got me through those early years was that my whole life was programmed from morning till night and I liked that! I also loved the times of silence: meals, night, and silent retreat. Little by little the Holy Spirit gently led me to accept this strange house as my home and these women as my sisters, and my life has ever been so incredibly blessed!"[4]

4. S. Orlanda Leyba in an e-mail to S. Eva Silva in 2012.

MINISTRY

Ministry in the Land of Enchantment
(Could I Walk Back to Michigan?)

There was a parallel experience for the Sisters sent to New Mexico from Michigan. Some of them too experienced homesickness and felt challenged by dust storms, food, language, and, in some cases, the deep poverty around them.

Sister Peter Mary Korson, who came to love her time in New Mexico, describes her initial experience in Ranchos de Taos this way:

> My arrival at my new mission, located high in the mountains in Northern New Mexico, filled me with misgivings. In fact my heart sank. The remoteness, terrain, different landscape, strange buildings and poverty were such a contrast to what I had ever experienced. Needless to say, in a short time I not only became very lonesome but full blown homesick. It affected my sleep, my eating, my entire physical well-being, my prayer life and my sociability. I often thought of walking back to Michigan.[5]

> **"I often thought of walking back to Michigan."**
> Sister Peter Mary Korson

Sisters echo over and over again that once they overcame their homesickness, they fell in love with New Mexico and the people. Sister Helen Bueche writes:

> I missed the beautiful waters of Michigan's Great Lakes that had been so much a part of my life. However, this was replaced by the experience of the beauty and wonder of this Land of Enchantment. One of my greatest joys and inspirations was to watch the Sandia Mountains[6] take on many moods and personalities in a day. I watched in awe as the full moon rose over the Sandias and the setting sun illuminated the mountain from bright yellow to its illustrious watermelon color.[7]

Her poem captures a moment in her experience.

---

5. S. Peter Mary Korson, in an e-mail to S. Eva Silva 2012.
6. *Sandia* is the Spanish word for watermelon.
7. S. Helen Bueche in an e-mail to S. Eva Silva.

New Mexico

Watermelon Rock,
Tempting onlookers to taste
Your mouth watering beauty,
Served on an infinite blue platter.

Raising Awareness

Sisters from New Mexico came mostly from rural or small towns, not unlike the majority of Sisters who entered from Michigan, Canada, Ireland, Germany, and other places. Although quite distinct, there was a natural weaving and connection of this common background. Still, there were some tensions between the cultures, some unspoken assumptions that hinted at a separation, even of class distinction, between those whose home language was Spanish and those who spoke English in their homes. Also there was some tension between those from New Mexico who claimed Spanish ancestry and those who claimed Mexican ancestry.[8] And then there were Sisters from the east side of the state of Michigan who were the children of Mexican-American citizens who had settled in the Saginaw Valley having found employment in factories and farms there.

Fiesta at Marywood with Rafelita Silva, Sr. Bernice Garcia, Sr. Charlotte Mondragon, Sr. Eva Silva, Eduardo Silva, and Sr. Eileen Jaramillo

---

8. The question of racial identity is complex and sometimes an area of conflict between those who claim Spanish ancestry and those who claim Mexican ancestry. Spanish descendants of the conquistadores settled in New Mexico before the American colonies were established. When Mexico ceded territory to the US, it included vast sections of the southwest, including New Mexico. Sister Eva Silva notes: "We are Latinas, Hispanas, Mejicanas, Espanolas, Nueva Mejicanas. The story of migration and immigration gives evidence that we are enriched with the blood of the moro, visigodo, judio, gypsy, azteca, indio americano, and africano. Racially, we New Mexicans carry a mixed blood and proud histories."

Spanish was their mother tongue, but the Saginaw Valley, not New Mexico, was their motherland.

One day an awareness of the beauty of differences in the midst of shared celebration occurred. It began to melt some of the tensions and unite the Sisters from all places regardless of ancestry. It was music that made it happen. Music was and is an essential element of New Mexican life and Hispanic ancestry. Music was also important in the Grand Rapids Motherhouse, but it was more likely to be Gregorian chant or classical music. Although a few Sisters were known to enjoy dancing the polka to an accordion, such celebrations were much more the exception than the norm. Not so for the families of Hispanic heritage where a sacred hymn could segue into a secular ballad on a moment's notice.

It happened one day when Mr. Eduardo Silva and his wife Rafaelita joined their daughter, Sister Eva Silva, along with Sisters Bernice Garcia, Eileen Jaramillo, and Charlotte Mondragon, in a serenade of Spanish music during the Dominican Gathering Days in Grand Rapids. It was a real *fiesta* with music and dancing and food, fabulous food from New Mexican/Latina recipes with an abundance of rice and beans, chicken and tortillas. Something palpable happened that day; two language groups became acutely aware of the gift of the other. Nuevo Mejico met in the land of the Great Lakes and it was joy, esteem, appreciation all around. It was a new moment in the Congregation for all of the Sisters. The notion of family grew and together the Sisters could say: "¡Vive la fiesta!"

Standing (left to right): Sr. Orlanda Leyba, celebrating her Jubilee with family and friends, Srs. Emilia Atencio, and Therese Rodriquez; sitting (left to right): Srs. Thomas Estelle Bryan, Angelina Gonzales, Ann Perpetua Romero, Consuelo Chavez, Lorraine Rajewski; back to camera (left to right): Srs. Lucille Leannah, Ada Domínguez, and John Therese Kusba.

New Mexico

Mission & Ministries: Possibilities, Promises, and Vatican Council II

It has been nearly ninety years since the first Sisters were sent to New Mexico. Much has changed in the wake of Vatican Council II. Previously, ministry was primarily in schools and hospitals; now it expanded to other venues. Seismic cultural shifts changed everything in the decade known as the sixties. Responding to the Decree of the Vatican Council, *Perfectae Caritatis,* Sisters began to probe the depths of both Scripture and the early spirit of their founder, St. Dominic. They listened to the "signs of the times" and looked toward ministries that answered the cry of the poor and that matched their own skills and gifts. The Sisters began to ponder more deeply the meaning of Dominican life. With the Vatican Council II principles of subsidiarity and collegiality, unquestioning compliance flew out the window that was opened by that Council. Discernment, conversation, and discussion came in the door. Obedience, still highly valued, took on its root meaning of deep listening. Technically, a major superior could order a Sister to comply with an assignment, but the cultural milieu of the time did not support such action, and no elected superior was eager to act in such a heavy-handed way. The changes were felt in Michigan and New Mexico alike.

> **The Sisters began to ponder more deeply the meaning of Dominican life.**

Schools to Religious Education; Hospitals to Pastoral Care and Counseling

In July of 1966, there were nine parish elementary schools staffed by Grand Rapids Dominicans in the Archdiocese of Santa Fe. Ten years later, there were four such schools. The story of the merger there between Holy Cross Junior High and the McCurdy Methodist Mission School is of particular interest for the human drama and the opening of hearts to something new. This would not have been possible without the papal encyclical *Pacem et Terris*[9] and the cultural shifts in society. It was a revolutionary moment when Pope John XXIII said, "Finally, may Christ inflame the desires of all men [sic] to

---

9. *Pacem in Terris.* Encyclical of Pope John XXIII on Establishing Universal Peace in Truth, Justice, Charity, and Liberty. April 11, 1963.

break through the barriers which divide them, to strengthen the bonds of mutual love, to learn to understand one another and to pardon those who have done them wrong."[10] This shift to a more inclusive notion of church made the next part of the story achievable.

In northern New Mexico, the merger between the Methodist Mission School and Holy Cross Catholic School made heretofore unheard of collaboration possible. Sister Bernice Garcia, one of the teachers, wrote:

> I use a beautiful Lutheran text on Old Testament history. The life of Christ is taught to the boys by Mr. Pringle, Mission School Elementary school principal. We teach an ecumenical religion, with no doctrine as such, two days a week. On the third day we hold ecumenical services. Last week . . . several boys and girls led prayers and one boy even played a trumpet solo. It has been just beautiful. . . . I don't believe either of the schools can exist alone. We've found we have much in common.[11]

Sister Norena Downes made the observation: "We now realize what seems to be the crowning point of all our missionary endeavors. Thanks to Vatican Council II we have learned to understand and work with, not against, our Protestant brothers in Christ." Mr. Robinson, superintendent of the McCurdy Methodist School, expressed the following: "This merger is said to be the only one of its kind in these United States. May we ask your prayers for its continued blessing and success, and in the spirit of renewal let us pray that all peoples may be one — one fold and one Shepherd."[12]

> "Let us pray that all peoples may be one — one fold and one Shepherd."
> McCurdy Methodist School Superintendent Robinson

More recently, Protestants and Catholics came together to celebrate a formal reconciliation between them. In 1947, a Protestant group had sued the New Mexico State Board of Education for violating the separation of church and state because Sisters were teaching in the public schools. Priests and nuns had been teaching in New Mexican schools since the days before New Mexico was a state. The courts ruled in favor of the Protestants — a wrenching loss to the Catholics of the region. All lingering ill will was put

---

10. Pope John XXIII, *Pacem in Terris*.
11. Sister Bernice Garcia, OP, "Unity in Diversity in the Southwest: 1925-1971," Marywood Archives.
12. Garcia, "Unity in Diversity."

aside in a reconciling reunion between the two groups in Dixon, New Mexico, Sunday, May 23, 1999.[13]

In addition to ecumenical endeavors, necessity sparked yet another innovation; this one was specific to religious education. In 1968, the grade school was discontinued in the San Juan Pueblo and a Total Religious Education Center (TRE) was established. TRE, a national movement, invited the total community to be involved in its religious growth — children, youth, and adults. Religious education no longer ended with elementary school and sacramental preparation. Now it would extend to the years of high school and adulthood with programs such as Day with Christ, Christian Living Weekends, Bible Study, Charismatic Prayer, Cursillos, and Comunidades de Base or Base Communities.

Schools were not the only institutions slated for change. Sisters had once owned and staffed a tuberculosis hospital, Nazareth Sanatorium, in Albuquerque, New Mexico. The development of the antibiotic streptomycin in 1946 cured tuberculosis, a scourge that had plagued humankind since antiquity. The "San" changed to a psychiatric hospital the next year, 1947. In 1965 the number of Sisters serving as staff numbered twenty-six; just eleven years later, that number was two. The difficulty of administering a complex psychiatric institution was compounded by a governing board 1200 miles away. In addition, the deinstitutionalization of persons with mental illness became the standard of care after 1972 due to the advent of psychotropic medication and community mental health services. Consequently, Nazareth was sold and the Prior-

Nazareth Hospital in Albuquerque, New Mexico

---

13. *Albuquerque Journal*, May 24, 1999. For a nuanced treatment of this game-changing case see: Kathleen Holscher, *Religious Lessons: Catholic Sisters and the Captured Schools Crisis in New Mexico* (Oxford: Oxford University Press, 2012).

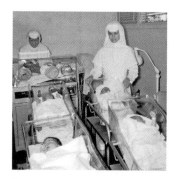

Sister-Nurses at Santa Rosa Hospital: Srs. Francis Borgia Goyette and Alphonsine (Elizabeth) Bishop

ess and Council in Grand Rapids determined that the monies from this land in New Mexico be used for ministry, especially in the service of those in New Mexico.

In addition to the "San," Sisters also staffed hospitals in New Mexico and for a few years in California. Sisters Ann Thielen and Elizabeth Bishop describe difficult and challenging schedules at Guadalupe Hospital in Santa Rosa, New Mexico, particularly on weekends when staff was minimal and the Sisters covered multiple shifts. The hospital was located on the Route 66 corridor and victims of tragic accidents were treated at the Guadalupe Hospital. Dominican Sisters staffed that hospital for about fifteen years. Recently a state-of-the-art facility was dedicated to replace the old Guadalupe Hospital. Sisters Angelina Gonzales, Ann Thielen, and Elizabeth Bishop attended the ceremony and Sister Elizabeth gave the invocation for the blessing of the new building.

Today, ministries continue in New Mexico through the work of the Sisters who live there and serve in hospice care, pastoral counseling, education, and therapeutic services.

The Gift That Keeps on Giving

The New Mexico land originally acquired through both the gift of a benefactor and purchase in 1927 was found to hold abundant minerals and water resources. Over the decades, what is fondly referred to in convent parlance as the *gravel pit* has "kept the wolves from our doors."

On July 28th, 1987, Dominican Land Company was established as a nonstock corporation to hold and administer property in New Mexico. Monies from land sold were designated for a special fund known as the Ministry Fund.[14] This fund was created and designated "to enable ministry to the poor, especially in areas where needs are not being met" and "to insure that our mission continues even as we age and our numbers diminish." The memo

---

14. Dominican Land Company; Statement of Cash Flows created November 7, 1994, Marywood Archives.

continues, "The primary purpose is to provide monetary assistance for vowed members of Sisters of the Order of St. Dominic Grand Rapids who are engaged in ministries which serve and empower the materially poor, promote systemic change to enhance the quality of life for the materially poor, or other ministries directed by the Sisters of the Order of St. Dominic, Grand Rapids and is not for the pecuniary profit of any member."[15]

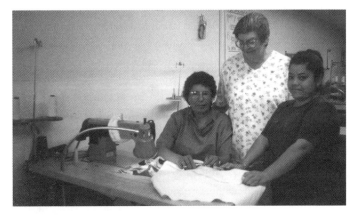

Sr. Bernice Garcia assists women at Southwest Creations Collaborative in Albuquerque, New Mexico.

The Ministry Fund continues giving to people in New Mexico as well as to others in need of assistance,[16] but there was one caveat regarding the use of land.

15. Dominican Land Company, Marywood Archives.
16. Some of the recipients of monies from the Ministry Fund are listed here:
   1. St. Pius X High School (Albuquerque) Tuition Assistance committee has given 97 Tuition Assistance Awards to students in the school.
   2. *Centro Mujeres De La Esperanza* was initiated in 1994 as a collaborative ministry project. It is located in El Paso, Texas. This three-pronged program assists women with HIV-AIDS, it helps women in need of practical information about economic issues, and it offers a life-planning program for women to clarify and set goals for their future health and happiness.
   3. The private practice of INNERWORK Psychotherapy and Counseling provides a reduced rate for clients according to need. Through this service to individuals and couples (offered in either Spanish or English), the therapist contributes to strengthening the fabric of families and communities, providing "a leaven in Church and society." The therapist also presents Sexual Abuse Prevention Workshops for the Archdiocese of Santa Fe, providing opportunities for healing the wounds of the institutional Church and of its members.
   4. The New Mexico Community Development Loan Fund is used exclusively to benefit low-income people in New Mexico. It helps those who might not otherwise have access to affordable credit. The Congregation collaborates with the New Mexico Council of Churches to fund such projects as the following:
      • Southwest Creations Collaboration. The SCC is a "vehicle to reach talented

Aware that land in New Mexico had been used for the detonation of the first atomic bomb, the Sisters were determined that land they had once owned not be put to such use. Therefore, they sold the land with a "string attached." The contract reads in part: "During the Period of Initial Use, neither the Owner of the Property nor any person occupying any portion of the Property shall use the Property for the research, development, production or deployment of weapons, weapons components or weapons systems."[17]

It is of great satisfaction that some of the land has been developed into what is known as the Balloon Fiesta Park with sports fields used year-round, a museum, and a field that is the site for the Annual International Balloon Fiesta. In 2011, well over 700,000 people attended the week-long events held in October. Each year hot air balloon pilots gather from around the world. As many as twenty countries have been represented. Hundreds of balloons soar each year; one year it was over 1,000. It is a joyful and family centered event.

Through the Ministry Fund, the people of New Mexico continue to benefit from the land once owned by the Dominican Sisters.

Closing Remarks

In their years of ministry in New Mexico the Sisters have made an incalculable contribution in schools, hospitals, parishes, and a number of public agencies and institutions, both in salaried positions and in numerous vol-

---

women who do not have the financial marketing or personal resources to start a business venture." SCC creates and sells Southwestern-inspired designs.
- "La Madrugada." A newsletter of the New Mexico Community Development Loan Fund reports in its fall issue of 1994 the story of how Max Turcios, an immigrant from El Salvador, was able to secure a loan through NMCDLF in order to buy a sander, a necessary tool for his Southwestern business. Before the loan he had no alternative but to rent a sander at a rate of a dollar per minute.
- The St. Elizabeth Shelter in Santa Fe. This program for homeless families was made possible in part by funding from the NMCDLF. "In 1992 the first loan was paid back and a second loan was applied for in order to buy an apartment complex for transitional housing for homeless."

17. Closing Memorandum of Dominican Land Company, May 18, 1998, Archives, Box 32.3.

New Mexico

unteer services. While the Sisters can name the places of ministry and the types of ministries they engaged in, they also recognize that they will never be able to measure the reciprocal life and love shared and engendered with the people of New Mexico. "Service," observes Rachel Naomi Remen, "has a life of its own . . . a single act of kindness may have a long trajectory and touch those we will never meet or see."[18]

It was a long way from Michigan to New Mexico, but now it is hardly any distance at all, for the land and people of New Mexico have stamped an indelible mark on the character of this Congregation. The mountain vistas of New Mexico and the vast lakes of Michigan have met and continue to mingle — two peoples, one God, one family, one Spirit. It is very good.

> "A single act of kindness may have a long trajectory and touch those we will never meet or see."
> Rachel Naomi Remen

Balloon Fiesta in Albuquerque, New Mexico

---

18. Rachel Naomi Remen, M.D., *My Grandfather's Blessings: Stories of Strength, Refuge, and Belonging,* New York: Riverhead Books, 2000.

Chimbote, Peru —
The Challenge of the Andes

*"Blessed are they who hunger and thirst for righteousness,
for they will be satisfied."*
MATTHEW 5:6

Through the last fifty years the people of Peru have experienced extreme floods, drought, deadly heat waves, earthquakes, terrorists, epidemics of diseases of horrific proportions, ongoing corruption, violence and death. What does it take to sustain hope in such circumstances?

The breathtaking story of fifty years of mission work in the city of Chimbote, Peru, a coastal town 250 miles north of Lima, is told in the pages that follow. The mission began with catechetical work. It soon expanded to include a maternity hospital with follow-up medical care, and a medical laboratory to serve the poorest residents of Chimbote. The operation also staffed a medical clinic and *Asilo* (home for the aged) on the grounds. Most recently, an orphanage has become a part of the mission. The entire compound is known as the *Centro de Obras Sociales* (Social Works Center) and through the years it has become, and remains, an oasis of hope for the people.

1960s "Sacrifice the Best . . ."

Even before the Second Vatican Council, the urgency for ministers in

Chimbote, Peru

Latin America was sounded by the hierarchy of the Catholic Church. Pope Pius XII created the pontifical Commission on Latin America in 1958, and that commission in turn implored the Major Superiors to send personnel and finances to serve the burgeoning population there. In a letter to the Sisters in 1961 Mother Victor described her experience of the appeal from her meeting at the National Congress of Religious held at Notre Dame the previous month. She wrote: "All [Vatican envoys involved in Latin American mission] exhorted us to give personnel — not merely what could be spared but to sacrifice the best . . . know the community will do its share . . . with this in mind I am asking for volunteers for this new mission work. . . ."[1]

The two volunteers chosen to begin were Sisters Marie Dominica Viesnoraitis and Herman Marie Maez. On October 29, 1962, they left for cultural and language training in Cuernavaca, Mexico. Chimbote, Peru, the site chosen, was one of the poorest cities in South America. Priests from the St. James Society were already working in Chimbote, and that connection was one reason Mother Victor chose the city.[2] Two other reasons were the extreme poverty of the people and the presence of Dominican priests in the area. The Sisters' work in Chimbote was to be catechetical, i.e., teaching the people about the faith of the Roman Catholic Church which was the official religion of the country. Few Peruvians had instruction in the faith, and fear of atheistic communism gripped both the country of the United States and the hierarchy of the Catholic Church in the 1960s.

Sister Herman Marie wrote of their 250-mile trip from Lima to Chimbote on March 12, 1963:

> We came to Chimbote by *colectiva,* which is a good name for this particular kind of transportation because the car goes right to its passengers' door to "collect" them. We had an excellent driver, thank God. The Andes are not baby mountains, you know! What a scenic drive! At times we're driving right along the Pacific and then away up in the clouds with the ocean hundreds of

> We were "exhorted to give personnel — not merely what could be spared but the best."
> Mother Victor

---

1. Letter of Mother Victor Flannery, September 11, 1961.
2. The Missionary Society of St. James the Apostle was founded by Richard Cardinal Cushing in 1958 as an international organization of diocesan missionary priests who volunteered to serve in Peru, Bolivia, and Ecuador.

MINISTRY

feet below. The mountains are unique. We are used to mountains with trees and other vegetation on them. Here they are bare and rugged, but colorful.³

One year after their arrival the Sisters attended The Second National Congress of Women Religious in Peru. Although over 700 Women Religious from all over the world were working in Peru, the poor were underserved. In her letter recalling this event Sister Herman Marie wrote:

Sr. Marie Dominica Viesnoraitis teaches school in Chimbote, Peru.

The meeting brought out the fact that hundreds of Sisters are here in Lima educating only eight per cent of all the children of Peru; that the Sisters must get out of their private schools and attend to the poor as well as to the rich; that more catechetical work must be done in the *barriadas* (slum neighborhoods); that the Sisters must be well educated before going into the field; that the habits (clothing) of the Sisters must be made practical in conformity with the Holy Father's request; that the Sisters must be more friendly with one another when they meet in the streets — that there must be more mingling among the various communities; that the Sisters must love the Church more than their own communities and customs. One could feel the workings of Ecumenical Council.⁴

Collaboration, renewal, the preferential option for the poor — this conference in a nutshell captured several of the principles of Vatican Council II.

Sr. Marie Dominica Viesnoraitis with children in Chimbote, Peru

The response of the Sisters all over the world was both ardent and swift. Although it may seem minor in the grand scheme of things, one of the immediate changes for the missionary Sisters was that of a habit that was more practical than the ankle-length white tunics that were the customary garb. A shortage of laundry facilities, coupled with long white habits and sandy, flea-ridden slums, necessitated the trial of a modified habit, shorter in length, belted at the waist, with a simple collar and simple sleeves with no flares. A sample was shared with Mother Victor

3. Collected papers of S. Margaret Mary Birchmeier, 2012, unpublished memoir.
4. Birchmeier.

for her approval when she arrived for a visit. The verdict was that it could be worn only in Chimbote and would need approval at the upcoming 1966 General Chapter. This opened the door for what was to come.

In 1963 Sisters Teresita Garcia and Georgiana Kowalski joined the first two missionaries to teach the teachers in the schools and eventually to operate a school for religious studies for teachers at the college level. They all lived in a convent built on land given to the San Martin parish where the church and rectory had already been constructed.

An *Asilo* (home for the aged) was on this same property; the condition of the "gift" was that the parish would take responsibility to care for the people in the *Asilo*. The priests soon saw a need for an outpatient clinic and this was established with the assistance of a nurse from the Peace Corps and a volunteer doctor. When the nurse's term was over in 1965, the priests approached Mother Victor for a replacement. Sister Veritas (Rosemary) Homrich was chosen to fill this position and arrived in Chimbote in June of that year (1965). As a registered nurse, she was assigned the task of taking care of both the *Asilo* and the outpatient clinic.

A home visit in Chimbote, Peru

Meanwhile, the priests, Father Jules Roos and Father Ray Moore, were also very concerned about the number of babies brought to them for Baptism who were already dead, and about the number of women who died in childbirth. Could they not do anything about the abysmal infant mortality rate and lack of maternal care? They could, they would, and they did. Letters flew home to Marywood in Grand Rapids, Michigan. Yes, they would not only spare Sisters to come as midwives, they would "sacrifice the best." Sisters Margaret Mary Birchmeier and Innocence Andres, certified in both nursing and midwifery, arrived in September 1965 to initiate a child and maternal care program. They found the Maternity Hospital unfinished — one wall and a concrete slab for a floor — and so they spent

The priests were concerned about the number of babies brought to them for Baptism who were already dead, and about the number of women who died in childbirth.

Sisters and children in Chimbote, Peru

Chimbote missionaries (left to right): Srs. Lillian Bockheim and Marie Dominica Viesnoraitis, Fr. Jules Roos, and Sr. Margaret Mary Birchmeier

the first year learning about the culture and customs as they knelt on dirt floors assisting women in rattan shacks giving birth in grim, unsanitary conditions.

The nurse-midwives needed a safe, sanitary, well-lit place to attend mothers during their deliveries. Prenatal care was also needed. The construction of the *Maternidad* (Maternity Hospital) was completed about ten months after their arrival and was a most welcome improvement. Even then, it was not an easy transition for the Sister-nurses.

One day Sister Margaret Mary recalls feeling particularly despondent: "I was feeling somewhat forlorn and was looking for someone with whom I could commiserate. While expressing my feelings to Father Jules Roos, I asked him how long he was scheduled to be in Chimbote. He responded, five years and I'm counting every day! I was overjoyed at finding someone who felt like I did." Sister Margaret Mary is still in Chimbote and only death could end Father Jules's days in his beloved Peru.[5]

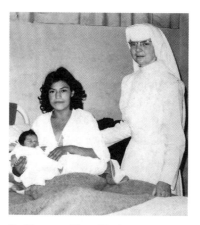

Sr. Margaret Mary Birchmeier caring for a malnourished infant

Sr. Margaret Mary Birchmeier with a mother and her newborn

---

5. Father Jules died February 16, 2013, at the age of 82 after nearly fifty years in Chimbote, Peru.

Chimbote, Peru

Sinking Roots

The seeds sown in the early 1960s were taking root. Prenatal care continued; home deliveries were replaced by safe, sanitary deliveries in the *Maternidad*. Although the home deliveries had been difficult and dangerous, the Sister midwives counted them a valuable experience in understanding the conditions and customs of the people so that they could serve them more effectively. One of the worrisome traditions was the family's disappointment at the birth of twins. The people believed that one of a pair of twins must die in order that the other would thrive. If they were of different sexes, the girl would be left to die; if the same sex, the smaller of the two would be neglected. Coaxing and providing formula did nothing to change this situation at first. Eventually, however, with better hope for a tomorrow, through education and long years of gentle care, the custom changed. Recently, the Sisters and people of the Social Works Center celebrated the weddings of triplets, two boys and a girl, who had been born prematurely in 1977 in the *Maternidad*. Years later, the "princess" of the trio and her two sisters-in-law all delivered healthy babies in the *Maternidad*. It was a joyful moment for the *Maternidad* community.[6]

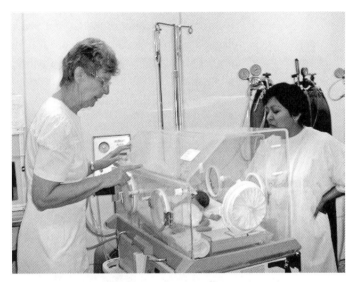

Sr. Margaret Mary Birchmeier and Betty Sandoval, certified midwife, watching over a premature baby in incubator

One of a pair of twins must die in order that the other would thrive.

The Sisters were working to the state of exhaustion, not only attending to the sick and pregnant mothers, but doing all the cleaning and laundry as well. Sister Innocence wrote in 1966:

6. Birchmeier.

Our *Posta Medica* (clinic) is open daily and the sick-poor come and go all day long. Hepatitis, typhoid fever, meningitis, skin infections, and all stages of involvement of tuberculosis, once so foreign, now take on the casualness of daily appearances along with bronco-pneumonia, coughs and colds, eye and ear infections. Our Peruvian doctor continues to come two afternoons a week for medical clinic.[7]

All but eradicated in the United States, tetanus, also known as lockjaw, plagued the people due to lack of sanitation. "Not a week passed without a mother showing up with a dead baby in her arms or one too sick to restore to health, most of them never celebrating their first birthday. . . . Saint Matthew's Gospel Chapter 25:35-40 no longer was just written words; hungry, thirsty, sick, homeless. They all had names and the Sisters lived and worked in the midst of them daily."[8]

Sr. Aurora Valerio with the Mothers' Sewing Club in Chimbote, Peru

With funds from the St. James Society of the Pittsburgh Diocese,[9] local women were employed as nurse aides and midwives. This freed up the Sisters to pursue prenatal classes and to begin a well-baby clinic for follow-up care.

In 1967 Sister Gerarda (Lillian) Bockheim, nurse, arrived to replace Sister Veritas (Rosemary) Homrich, who returned to the States;

Sr. Aurora Valerio with Peruvian women

7. Birchmeier.
8. Birchmeier.
9. The Diocese of Pittsburgh has been a major benefactor of the Chimbote mission from its inception in 1963.

and Sister Edemia (Aurora) Valerio joined the missionary band to assist with household tasks and to begin a sewing club. Out of this evolved a Mothers' Club with the intention of bringing women together to socialize, discuss common problems, and to improve their feeling of self-worth.[10]

When Sister Gerarda (Lillian) began her work in the *barrios,* she was determined to help the people realize the importance of hygiene as the first defense against parasites, tuberculosis, and other infections. She also treated many burn cases due to the flammability of the rattan shack housing and use of candles and kerosene lamps for lighting. Daily, Sister Gerarda visited a woman with third-degree burns on both legs and implored her to keep the area clean to avoid infection. One day she reacted with dismay when she saw two dirty boards holding down the sheet over the woman's legs. Why had they not heeded her admonition? she inquired. It seems the husband had placed the boards thus to keep the rats and mice from eating at the open sores while the woman slept. The conditions of the poor were unbelievably harsh. Yet, there was determination and hope for a better life.

Sr. Lillian Bockheim and Elizabeth Sanchez visit a family in their home in Chimbote, Peru.

While all this work was being done in health care, education in catechesis was also going on. The Sisters assigned to catechetical work had heavy schedules of classes teaching children, their parents, and the teachers themselves.

---

10. So effective was S. Aurora's Mothers' Club that the group raised money to initiate an on-site *cuna* (nursery) so that they could attend Sister's classes without the distraction of so many babies clamoring for their attention.

Sister Teresita Garcia and her colleagues, Sisters Marie Dominica Viesnoraitis and Jeannine Kalisz, began to implement a new catechetical program involving the parents of children preparing for the sacraments. This ambitious and innovative program trained "guide couples" and youth leaders in the catechetical work that had previously been left up to clergy, Religious, and catechists. This method was a great success and a fulfillment of the new age of the laity heralded by Vatican Council II.

In her letter to the Congregation describing her visit to Chimbote, Sister Norbert (Marjorie) Vangsness wrote:

> To my mind, the Chimbote group of Sisters is, up to now, our most striking example of a community of Sisters carrying on a variety of works ... each Sister, while excelling in her specialty, interests herself in everyone else's success as well as in that of all the religious in the city. Even the fact that we have no house in Lima helps, I think, to keep our Sisters in touch with American Sisters of other communities when they go to Lima.[11]

Sr. Maria Teresita Garcia teaches religion in Chimbote, Peru.

> "Each Sister, while excelling in her specialty, interests herself in everyone else's success as well as that of all the religious in the city."
> Sister Norbert (Marjorie) Vangsness

The admonition for mutuality and cooperation at the Second National Congress of Religious Women in Peru was being realized in Chimbote. On the civic national level, such collaboration was woefully absent as the military took over the government in Lima in the fall of 1968. Although relatively quiet, the coup resulted in restrictions, anxiety, and dangers, especially for foreigners. Curfews and a ban on assemblies of any kind were imposed. In case of medical emergencies, one was ordered to carry and display a white

11. Birchmeier.

flag. The Sisters needed to do this frequently as they attended patients in the *barrios*. Even then, they were frequently stopped and questioned. "The military ruled and they ruled with an iron hand."[12]

> "The military ruled and they ruled with an iron hand."
> Sister Margaret Mary Birchmeier

Work continued in the compound where the Sisters and their colleagues served the poor and the needy. A great boon to the enterprise was the contribution of an incubator from a group of women in the Catholic Diocese of Pittsburgh. It was a beautiful piece of equipment that would save the lives of many premature and sick newborns.

The need for a medical lab for the clinic and *Maternidad* became increasingly apparent. Sister John Cassian Logue, SSJ, a Sister of St. Joseph from Nazareth, Michigan, was looking for a place to use her skills as a laboratory technician. And so plans for the much-needed medical lab began to take shape. Before long the Sisters and staff of the Center greeted the arrival of Sister John Cassian, who arrived by ship in order to allow her to bring the supplies needed to set up her medical laboratory. She began immediately to prepare the building as well as to teach local women to assist as technicians for the long-awaited lab.

A Franciscan Sister from Pittsburgh, Sister Edith Mary Selik, OSF, a registered nurse, was also assigned by her community for a two-year stint at the *Posta Medica* in Chimbote. She was welcomed with open arms and described this way: "Her ready smile and her tremendous drive are a source of strength to us who are a bit numbed by the daily poverty and suffering about us which we have seen for so long." Sisters from three different Congregations — Dominican, Franciscan, and St. Joseph — were now living and working together on behalf of the poor

Medical laboratory in the compound in Chimbote, Peru

---

12. Birchmeier.

in Chimbote. Regrettably, Sister Edith Mary's stay, and indeed, her very life, would be cut short in the days to come, and Sister John Cassian would also suffer a setback in her goal to build and staff the laboratory.

The Earth Moved

The military coup developed into an oppressive dictatorship. The people had absolutely no say about their lives. Hardships piled up. Rice, potatoes, and kerosene — the basic necessities — became scarce. Curfews continued; monetary exchange and travel became more difficult and dangerous. Ironically, as the dictatorship closed its iron fist over the freedoms of the people, the Sisters at the Chimbote compound were implementing changes in the opposite direction in their community life. Heeding the Vatican Council II principles of collegiality and subsidiarity (all members have a share in the welfare of the whole community and a responsibility for it), the Sisters decided to share the responsibilities of the household — dividing the tasks of supporting community living, executing the responsibility of treasurer, and maintenance of the physical plant among them. They planned monthly meetings to resolve any difficulties. The goal was to foster a rich prayer life, common sharing, and a deep respect for individual ministries.

In spite of the restrictions of the military government, life in the compound was looking up — but nature had other plans. In January 1970, this desert area that knew little rainfall experienced tor-

The Ancash earthquake, also known as the Great Peruvian Earthquake, struck on Sunday May 31st in 1970 at 3:23 p.m. Along with the accompanying landslide, it was the worst catastrophic natural disaster ever recorded in Peruvian history.[1] This undersea earthquake twenty-two miles west of Chimbote registered 7.9/8.0 on the Richter scale. The trembling lasted about forty-five seconds, destroying more than seventy-five per cent of the city and causing 3,000 deaths in Chimbote alone; the landslide that followed from the mountain to the east caused an avalanche that roared down the mountain at speeds upwards of 150 miles per hour, burying two towns with all of their residents under tons of rock, ice, and snow. It is impossible to get completely accurate figures, but it is estimated that the death toll was more than 70,000 persons; property damage estimates are put at $530 million.[2]

1. http://earthquake.usgs.gov/earthquakes/world/events/1970_05_31.php
2. http://earthquake.usgs.gov/earthquakes/world/events/1970_05_31.php accessed November 18, 2012.

rential flooding. "Streets were flooded; slum areas swept away; roofs caved in; electric power cut; cars and buses immobilized. Damage ran into the millions of dollars."[13] But this was far from the worst of what the year 1970 had to offer. On a quiet Sunday afternoon, May 31st, there was a tremendously loud sound, and within seconds everything was moving, falling, and turning upside down. In less than a minute nearly everything was destroyed in the parish of San Martin and in the city of Chimbote.

It was a time of great sorrow. Two Sisters were crushed to death from the falling debris. They were Sister Gabriel Joseph Gussin, CSJ (Congregation of St. Joseph), who was teaching at the nearby Santa Rosa School, and Sister Edith Mary Selik, OSF, the Franciscan Sister from Pittsburgh who had joined the Dominicans at the Center. Sister John Cassian Logue was seriously injured. The Maternity Hospital, the *Asilo*, and several service buildings were completely destroyed.

Sr. Elizabeth Amman, visitor, and Sr. Lillian Bockheim visit the cemetery in Chimbote, Peru.

The outpatient clinic, Sisters' convent, and storage areas were severely damaged. Water and sewage lines were gone. Yet babies were on their way to be born, and although there was despair in the air, this was no time to depart. The lab was quickly converted into a maternity hospital. As soon as possible a temporary chipboard building was erected for providing a safe place for women to give birth. "Temporary" stretched into ten years before a new building could be erected. The luxury of grief and despair would need to be put on hold. Babies kept coming; the injured were in need of medical attention. One sad memory is that the old people had to be relocated to a

The luxury of grief and despair would need to be put on hold.

13. Birchmeier.

nursing home in Lima in order to make room for the injured in Chimbote. This effectively ended the presence of an *Asilo* in the compound.

The people were fearful that the Sisters would leave after the earthquake. "When are you leaving? Why stay? Everything is gone," one woman said. When Sister Teresita responded that they were not going, that Chimbote was their home too, the woman's eyes filled with tears. *"Su presencia nos da esperanza,"* she said. (Your presence is a sign of hope for us.)

> *"Su presencia nos da esperanza."* (Your presence is a sign of hope for us.)

Just fourteen months after the earthquake, the laboratory reopened under the able supervision of Sister John Cassian, who had recovered from her injuries in the earthquake; a new, albeit temporary, *Maternidad de Maria* (Maternity Hospital of Mary) was dedicated; the Well Baby Clinic for follow-up care was established; and the number of babies safely delivered since the opening in July 1966 was 3,100.

Natural catastrophe would not defeat the purpose and project of the Sisters. A political disaster, however, was looming in the wings. In 1975 the military dictatorship was passed onto another military man, General Francisco Morales Bermudez, who proved to be a more compassionate ruler. Although not yet a democracy, the new president promised free elections. He later opened the road to a return of democracy, and the people were more relaxed and hopeful after eight years of tension and restrictions. Unfortunately this was but the calm before another storm.

Sr. Maribeth Holst, Prioress at the time, visits clients at the clinic with Sr. Lillian Bockheim and Elizabeth Sanchez.

Chimbote, Peru

1980s Tilling the Soil

A tender story is told of an eight-year-old boy who appeared at the door of the *Maternidad*. He asked if they would take care of his sisters. Seeing no one with him, Sister Margaret Mary inquired where they were. He gestured toward his jacket. Sister opened the zipper of his jacket and found two little newborns wrapped in clean blankets. Each weighed about two pounds, but they were warm and their color, respiration, and heartbeats were favorable. The little boy had first taken them to the local hospital where he was told they had no service to help babies so small. A man at the hospital took the boy out to the street, found public transportation, and instructed the driver to leave the boy at the *Maternidad*. The babies were soon thriving under the skilled care of Sister Margaret Mary, and within a few weeks, little Sonia and Sofia were home with their mother and their brave big brother who had cared for them so tenderly.

> Sister opened the zipper of his jacket and found two little newborns wrapped in clean blankets.

The geo-political reality, however, was a sharp contrast to the nurturing of life that was and is the daily routine of the Social Works Center.

The new president was working hard to face the many economic and political problems inherited from the military regime, when climate change threw a "curve ball" into his plans. El Niño arrived with a vengeance. This phenomenon of warmer surface waters on the Pacific Ocean off the coast of Peru and Ecuador upsets the rich cool waters of the Humboldt current that is home to thousands of schools of fish, mainly the *anchoveta* upon which so much of the economy of Chimbote depended. This time El Niño arrived in December of 1982 and lasted over a year. It caused widespread flooding, heavy rains in some parts, and drought in other parts of the country. River valleys flooded, crops were destroyed, and the Pan

> El Niño arrived with a vengeance.

Sr. Lillian Bockheim visits people in the barrios (neighborhoods) in Chimbote, Peru.

American Highway, the only means of ground transportation into and out of Chimbote, became impassable with water and mud.

All of this brought greater desperation to an already impoverished people. Health-care problems escalated with skin diseases, typhoid, and dehydration. Babies and the elderly were especially susceptible to suffering and death. The fishing industry headed for bankruptcy; unemployment soared. All of these problems paved the way for a terrorist movement that had begun in the mountains and was now heading for the coastal areas. This terrifying movement based on the ideology of Marxist Communism was known as the *Sendero Luminoso* (Shining Path). Their leader, Abimael Guzmán, preferred the term *rebel*, but in truth he was a terrorist who was completely enamored of the Marxist philosophy of class struggle resolved in violent rebellion. A well-educated man and professor at the university, his methods included inciting youth from the working and poorest classes to engage in tactics of fear and terror in order to birth a classless utopian society. This included assassinating foreign missionaries and aid workers who, Guzmán declared, delayed the descent into chaos and isolation which was needed for the success of their revolution.

> **Guzmán preferred the term *rebel*, but in truth he was a terrorist.**

It was a terrifying time for the Sisters in Chimbote. One of them, Sister Lillian Bockheim,[14] recalls praying in their convent chapel during Holy Hour. She was nearly choked with fear when she and the others began to sing the hymn: "Be not afraid, I go before you always, come follow me and I will give you rest." It was a song that gave her courage to stand her ground and remain with the people in this unforgettable time of terror, led by a man who claimed that the way to the classless utopia of his dreams was a "river of blood." The people refer to his rebellion as the time of *chaqwa*, Quechuan for trauma and chaos.[15]

> **the time of *chaqwa*, Quechuan for trauma and chaos**

The acute needs of infants, young children, and others escalated during this decade. The numbers of infants and small children suffering from dehydration and malnutrition soared due to the consequences of widespread corruption and the ongoing terrorist activities of the Shining Path movement.

---

14. S. Lillian (formerly S. Gerarda), a registered nurse, arrived in Chimbote in 1967 and continues to serve in Peru as of this writing (2014).

15. Orin Starn, "Maoism in the Andes: The Communist Party of Peru-Shining Path and the Refusal of History," *Journal of Latin American Studies*, vol. 27, no. 2 (May 1995); accessed September 10, 2012, at http://www.latinamericanstudies.org/peru/shining-path.pdf.

Chimbote, Peru

With the election of President Alberto Fujimori in 1990 and the capture of the leader of the Shining Path, Abimael Guzmán, in September 1992, the people anticipated a restoration of peace and hope. But the days of terror and suppression of human rights were not over.

1990s Another Kind of Terror

During his first year as president, Fujimori implemented drastic measures referred to as "Fuji Shock." He met opposition to his measures by dissolving Congress and establishing what he termed an emergency government. This democratically elected president quickly became another dictator. The conditions degenerated for the people of the country. Migration of people looking for work, living in unsanitary conditions, scarcity of water, contamination of air and food, open sewers, extremely hot weather from El Niño — all were an open invitation for the next wave of suffering — cholera. Medical help and supplies arrived rather quickly. As a result, the death toll in Peru was estimated to be about 10,000, which was low relative to the estimate of cases — a little over one million. In Chimbote the number of cases in 1991 was 17,829 with nineteen recorded deaths.

Overpopulation is often cited as the cause of poverty and oppression. From 1996 to 2000, the Fujimori government oversaw a massive family planning campaign known as Voluntary Surgical Contraception. The United Nations and other international aid agencies supported this campaign. Nearly 200,000, mostly indigenous, mostly poor women were coercively sterilized during these years. A report from the British Broadcasting Corporation states: "most of the women interviewed said they were scared of talking because of threats made against anyone who spoke out."[16] Such was never the case at the *Maternidad,* where women were assured that no surgical sterilization would be done to them. Education and health care for women and men, not coercion and fear, are the best and most natural means of family planning in the experience of the Sisters and staff of the Center.

Trends over the past forty-five years have been recorded in birth ledgers

Nearly 200,000, mostly indigenous, mostly poor women were coercively sterilized.

---

16. Mass sterilization scandal shocks Peru, BBC News, July 2002, http://news.bbc.co.uk/2/hi/americas/2148793.stm. Retrieved September 10, 2012.

kept at the *Maternidad*. These statistics report that no longer are thirteen- and fourteen-year-olds giving birth; rather, now the mothers are in their twenties and thirties. Birth weights for the infants are higher and deaths of mother or newborns are rare. The overall health of both mothers and infants is greatly improved. Once the average family was about ten children. Today that number is more likely to be four or five. In over 90,000 births at the *Maternidad*, the mortality rate is lower than in many parts of the United States. All of these positive shifts are seen to be the result of many factors, not the least of which is education for women and men in the prenatal clinic, Lamaze classes, and the follow-up care offered through the Well Baby Clinic — a program that offers education, immunizations, and monitoring for the first year of a child's life.[17]

The 1990s brought another surprise to the Social Works Center; this one was and is a source of ongoing joy. Early one morning Sister Margaret Mary received a phone call from the judge in charge of the Orphans' Court. She was asked to receive an abandoned newborn until a permanent family could be found. Sister thought about the many consequences and tried to convince the judge that the Center was not equipped for this new challenge. The judge was not persuaded and reminded her of the fine reputation of the Center for the care of newborns. Thinking of the Congregation's early days of staffing Saint John's Home (an orphanage) in Grand Rapids, Sister Margaret Mary said: "Bring her out." So little

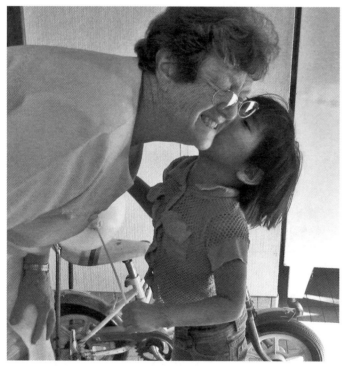

An orphaned child greets Sr. Lillian Bockheim with a kiss.

17. See chart of milestone births at the end of this chapter.

Carmen came — and then another and yet another until it became indisputable that yet one more ministry was begun. The personnel opened their arms and hearts to these little ones. A visitor, Father Gabriel Troy, wrote in his newsletter:

Sister Margaret Mary said: "Bring her out."

> She was approximately five months old when the Judge of the Orphans' court brought her to our hospital for shelter. She was filled with lice, scabies and parasites. She had rope marks around her little wrists and ankles from where she had been tied down on a garbage heap. We took her in. Since it was near the Feast of St. Michael we called her Micaela. She was weeks in treatment with us before she became a healthy little girl. Once she recovered from all her setbacks she gained weight quickly and became a thriving little girl. Micaela had big brown eyes and a winning smile and she won the hearts of all our workers. She was only with us three months when she was adopted by her new parents. Now a year and a half old, she occasionally visits us with her adoptive parents who are as thrilled with her now as the day they took her home with them.[18]

2000s Fifty Years and Holding

In his letter to the Bishop of Pittsburgh, the Bishop of Chimbote, Francisco Piorno, stated: ". . . the deep respect of the people of Chimbote for the *Maternidad* has been earned over time as a result of the quality of the services provided and the obvious and unlimited charity that for twenty-four hours of the day keeps the doors of the Social Works Center open."[19]

Meanwhile the work continues at the Center with Sisters Margaret Mary and Lillian and about 114 local lay persons serving in maternity, neonatal, orphan care, outpatient clinic, general medicine, and laboratory. Five days each week, two social workers comb the *barrios* doing home visits. Along the way they stop to visit those who ask for help for a relative or neighbor who is ill.

---

18. Birchmeier, "1990-2000 Blossoms Appear in the Midst of Terror," unpublished memoir.
19. "The Chimbote Foundation: A Bridge of Love and Hope," a brochure of the Catholic Diocese of Pittsburgh. Spring 2011.

Prenatal care continues with the education of mothers and fathers. Two days each week, midwives teach the parents to communicate with their unborn through songs and exercises. Lamaze training begins during the seventh month and involves both parents. Including the fathers has a positive effect on family unity, off-setting to some degree the "macho mentality" that can discourage fathers from involvement with their young children.

The orphans are cared for until suitable homes are found for them in Peru. High school students in a neighboring school run by Christian Brothers volunteer their time and attention with the orphans as part of their requirements for community service. This benefits both the orphans and the high school students who are learning to be attentive parents.

Conclusion

Those who have come to this city by the sea are changed. Some, like Sisters Margaret Mary and Lillian, have given their entire professional lives to this place of polluted air, scarce water, terror, poverty, and promise. Others come for a brief visit. In either case, one witnesses the hope for a better life shining in the eyes of the children and young people who have already seen too much sorrow. It is a life-changing experience.

Those who have never been to Chimbote in person, but who have had a part in this mission are also changed. It's hard to explain in words, but the deeds speak for themselves: a diocese like Pittsburgh that has its share of poverty and pollution generously shares its resources; a Congregation not known for missionary work has committed its best people.

One day Sister Kathi Sleziak, a Dominican Sister from Grand Rapids, was visiting the National Museum of the American Indian in Washington, D.C. Standing in line at the cafeteria, she began to chat with a woman next to her who spoke with an accent. As she often does in such situations, Kathi asked where she was from originally. When the woman answered Peru, Kathi exclaimed, "Oh, we have Sisters there in a Maternity Hospital in Chimbote, Peru." The woman responded in great surprise: "Why, that's where I was born!" The circle of life continues; we are one family.

Many improvements have been made at the Social Works Center, an oasis of hope, in the coastal city of Chimbote, Peru, in the past fifty years: a spacious outpatient clinic, state-of-the-art medical laboratory, a clean and bright maternity hospital, state-of-the-art equipment for prenatal, neonatal, and postpartum care; the Well Baby Clinic, physical therapy, Lamaze classes, expanded kitchen and laundry facilities, and most recently a new bright and cheerful place for the orphan children to be cared for with love and attention until permanent homes are found for them.

The old adage that it takes a village to raise a child takes on new meaning as the "village" in Chimbote includes the Pittsburgh diocese, the Dominican Sisters of Grand Rapids, and hundreds of local Peruvians who have come together believing that all life is sacred. Together they bring hope and health to the families of Chimbote, poor in life's basic necessities, yet rich in faith and courage and love.

Milestone Birth Records

Date	Number
October 17, 1984	20,000
February 1992	40,000
November 28, 1994	50,000
June 11, 1997	60,000
November 20, 2012	88,813
December 8, 2012	88,888
September 28, 2013	90,000

Baby boy named Emanuel was born at 12:45 p.m.

Dominican Center at Marywood

Remember not the events of the past,
the things of long ago consider not;
See, I am doing something new!
ISAIAH 43:18-19

JUNE 1989 FOUND the halls of Marywood Academy quiet. No uniformed children rushing to classes, no teachers' voices imparting wisdom, no interesting smells emanating from the science lab. As the chalk dust settled for the last time, alumnae and teachers gathered to celebrate the passing of an era. Laughter and tears flowed around the circle drive in front of Marywood with stories of rosary processions and Father Charles Wilson's East Coast–accented Hail Mary's, of Mrs. Schwartz's gym classes, of Sister Leonard's kindergarten, of piano lessons and concerts in Veritas Hall, of boarders and aspirants, popcorn balls, anise suckers, convent-made bread and cookies tasting of the wonderful Marywood kitchen. Old friends vowed to keep in touch.

When Marywood was built in 1922, the chapel held pride of place on the first floor with two large dining rooms below. Almost half of the building was designated for ministry — the education of young women. When the Marywood Academy High School closed in 1975, the Montessori School continued to flourish with a city-wide reputation for excellence and the grade school became coeducational. No longer could the students tease: Marywood Kin-

> **Old friends vowed to keep in touch.**

dergarten, "Where the boys are!"[1] Now what? How could the substantial buildings and beautiful grounds of Marywood be shared?

As often happens, the ending of one good thing became the beginning of another good enterprise. Three of the Congregation's Direction Statements captured the attention and hearts of the Sisters as they looked to the future uses of space on campus. In these three statements the Sisters committed themselves to advocate for children, to stand with women in their struggle for justice, and to be open to encountering the Holy in each other and people of all cultures and lifestyles. These were not *new* directions for the Sisters, for their work had always been about this — but these statements named an intentional commitment to seek ways to continue servicing the needs of women and children and of attending to the Holy in whatever ministry the Sisters might find themselves. The Marywood campus, and Dominican Center in particular, was to be a welcoming place for every woman, child, and man who walked through the doors.

As good Dominicans should, the Sisters commissioned a study. Sister JoAn Brown was asked to survey the needs of the Grand Rapids area. With her skills in administration and library research, and the help of Aquinas College professor Lee Jacokes, Sister JoAn surfaced three needs: a group home for men with mental illness, temporary housing for women and children in crisis, and a spirituality center. Since the Direction Statements called the Sisters to stand with women and children, it was appropriate to invite The Salvation Army to open the Family Lodge, formerly Aquin Hall, for women and their children seeking shelter from abusive situations. The Salvation Army noted that this was their first major collaboration with a Catholic entity and it was an overwhelming success.

The Direction Statement to tend the Holy in others moved the Sisters to consider what a spirituality center could look like on campus. Many suggestions were made. Members at Area meetings wrestled with the possibilities. The Leadership Team — Sisters Carmelita Murphy, Barbara Hansen, Jarrett DeWyse, and Margaret Schneider — worked with consultant Donna Fyffe to birth a spirituality center which would make Dominican spirituality available to a wider population.

The Sisters hope to deepen visitors' experiences of community, family life, and business relationships, and their sense of themselves as belonging to the family of God.

---

1. Previously, the school was entirely female except for the kindergarten, which accepted both girls and boys.

The essential elements of Dominican Life, namely, prayer, study, community, and ministry, are gifts to share. The Sisters wanted to share the prayer that permeates the campus, not just the chapels, but also the beauty of the gardens and grounds. Study, too, is a great love of Dominicans and so the Sisters explored ways to adapt this passion for study to the experience of adult learners and spiritual seekers. If people came to the campus, the Sisters hoped to deepen their experiences of community, family life, and business relationships, and their sense of themselves as belonging to the family of God. And where would these experiences take the guests? Back into society, spiritually strong, to make a difference in the world. So it was that a center for spirituality was a good fit with the values that Dominicans find essential.

Mark Clarke, of Dayton, Ohio, was hired in 1993 as the first director of Dominican Center at Marywood (DCM). He organized focus groups to connect with the larger Grand Rapids area and to surface hopes and possibilities for the Center. Renovations provided three conference spaces under the chapel in the main wing of Marywood, with two smaller spaces and a bookstore in the ground floor area. Three tracks were developed for Dominican Center: Leadership, Liturgy, and Bodyworks. A bookstore was also begun to support the programs. Mark Clarke organized business lunches called *Veritas* and facilitated strategic plans for area churches on the leadership track. Gregory Heille, OP, and musician Michelle Rego-Reatini, the chapel team, offered programs on prayer and the liturgical seasons for the prayer and ritual track. Sister Mary Jane Fedder was hired in 1995 to develop a bodywork track, providing therapeutic massage in a safe environment. This ministry also connected with Saint

Leadership Team 1988 (left to right): Srs. Jarrett DeWyse, Barbara Hansen, Margaret Schneider, and Prioress, Sr. Carmelita Murphy

Dominican Center/Marywood Team (left to right): Michelle Rego-Reatini, liturgist; Mark Clarke; Sr. Laurice DeRycke; and Fr. Joe Vest, chaplain

Dominic's tradition of prayer with the body. To support the program tracks, an endowment was started to subsidize income, and conferencing began to use the rooms more productively to cover the cost of space rental from the Congregation.

Mark Clarke met monthly with the Marywood House Sisters to share the progress in the Center. As one of the major "shareholders" in the project, the Sisters were very interested in making the Center a success and many of them volunteered to be hospitality ministers. Guests often commented on the hospitality and attributed it to the fact that the Sisters not only felt a deep sense of ownership for the building, but had loved, lived, and prayed in it for years.

Mark Clarke also met with the other departments on campus to work out balancing the needs of room setup and food service for guests with the needs of the Sisters who were already living on campus. With good will and hard work these issues were resolved and the Center provided a welcome to all visitors.

Mark Clarke and DCM's staff, with the guidance of the Congregation's Leadership Team, worked on developing a Mission Statement to guide the direction of the Center. Etched in the entrance to the ground floor and in the sensibilities of all who work here is the mission:

> We foster the growth and transformation of
> persons, communities and organizations
> through prayer, learning and collaboration
> in an inclusive, hospitable environment.

From these modest beginnings DCM continued to grow. In 1995 Father Paul Colloton, OP, and Sister Diane Zerfas became the Co-Directors of Pastoral Life for Dominican Chapel/Marywood and were shortly joined by musician Michelle Ogren. This team provided workshops and conferences for DCM on campus as well as throughout West Michigan in liturgy, prayer, RCIA (Rite of Christian Initiation of Adults), Vatican Council II theology, Liturgy of the Word for Children, and the preaching and preparing for the liturgical seasons. One highlight in 1998 was the collaboration with the Calvin Institute of Christian Worship, Aquinas College, Mary's Pence, and the Notre Dame Center for Pastoral Liturgy in celebrating the thirty-fifth anniversary of the liturgy document of Vatican Council II, *Sacrosanctum Concilium*. The memories of Sister Mary Luke Tobin, SL, one of only fifteen women auditors present at the Council, reminded everyone present of the excitement of those days and of the subsequent responsibility of the current day. The chapel was also filled on the day that Father Daniel Berrigan, SJ, shared his reflections on his book about the prophet Ezekiel with his own prophetic passion for peace and gentle humor. The peace and justice activists of the West Michigan area, old and young, concluded the event with the song "How Can I Keep from Singing?" — Fr. Berrigan's favorite hymn.

In 1997 Prioress Barbara Hansen invited Sister Nancy Brousseau to join the DCM staff. As Director of Spiritual Formation, Sister Nancy researched and developed year-long, multi-track programs advertised in three seasonal brochures: Summer, Fall, and Winter/Spring. The Spiritual Formation Program invited participants to explore their own spiritual lives with the assistance of the mystics and Christian spiritual giants. One strength of this program was having local experts in a given tradition share the insights of that tradition, e.g., a Benedictine shared Saints Benedict and Scholastica, a Franciscan spoke about Saints Francis and Clare, a Dominican taught about Meister Eckhart and Saint Catherine of Siena, a Calvinist told about John Calvin, a Methodist shared thoughts on John Wesley. Most of the participants had never read and prayed with these giants. The Beguines, women writers of the twelfth century, were particularly striking. The ecumenical mystic writers and participants made this program wonderfully rich and exciting for all. The underlying theme of this program was discernment. "How do I hear and respond to the Spirit in my life?" Noticing the Spirit's movements in the lives of others sensitizes the participants to the Holy Spirit's work in their own lives. This program was also offered for a few

Sr. Mary Luke Tobin, SL (third from left) meets with Srs. Lucille Leannah Diane Zerfas, Justyn Krieg, Marjorie Vangsness, and Helen Bolger.

"How do I hear and respond to the Spirit in my life?"

years in other locations such as Holland, Muskegon, Traverse City, Gaylord, Saginaw, and Toledo, Ohio.

Some participants felt a desire to continue their spiritual journeys in companioning and/or in the Spiritual Direction Practicum. Companioning is a two-year program that attunes the listening ear to friends, family, co-workers without becoming a problem solver. Using the prayer form *Lectio Divina*, each person responds by listening for the Word, given as gift by the Holy Spirit, in any situation: prayer, conversation, conflict, life. The first year focuses on personal transformation and the second year highlights social transformation.

Michigan and northern Ohio have been blessed with many spiritual directors formed in Dominican Center's Spiritual Direction Practicum. Rooted in *The Spiritual Exercises of Ignatius of Loyola* and *Lectio Divina*, developed by Sister Nancy, a practicum experience deepened the personal spiritual life and trained the director to listen deeply to someone seeking help on their spiritual journey. Most of the participants in this two-year program are convinced that this is the best experience in their spiritual lives. A discerning heart is always a blessing.

Dominican Center began offering other programs such as Group Spiritual Direction, Praying with the Mystics, Wednesday noon *Lectio Divina*, and Tuesday afternoon *Centering Prayer* with Contemplative Outreach of West Michigan. Silent directed retreats in Conway, Michigan, and Toledo, Ohio, made it possible for people to journey into silence and find God at their center. Individual directed and private retreats and days away were also made available using the overnight rooms at DCM. Pastors writing sermons, young mothers needing a break, sincere seekers discerning the next step in their lives have all made use of the quiet, prayerful setting which is Dominican Center.

All continue to be welcome at Dominican Center Marywood. As solid as the red brick building soaring over the trees, the offering of programs remains through recessions and financial challenges. Conference space has been one way, in addition to the endowment, to subsidize the spiritual development component at DCM. Of the Center, set back from the road, surrounded by old growth trees, some say, "The bricks are blessed by the prayers of the Sisters." Marywood continues to offer a time and space away from the hustle and bustle of the business world. It is a place to follow the

MINISTRY

example of Jesus who counsels his disciples in the midst of their ministry to "Come apart and rest awhile." Arbitration boards have found a peaceful ambience to offer a safe space for sensitive negotiations; business, medical, and educational organizations have found the hospitality to be conducive to in-service education. Retreatants have found the space and quiet to still their souls and enable them to deepen their relationship with God.

The Dominican Sisters of Grand Rapids rejoice in the good work of Dominican Center. As a corporate ministry of the Congregation, it is a living heritage of the Sisters on this site of both Academy and Motherhouse. From its inception it has welcomed all who wish to "tend the holy." The programs are rooted in the Dominican charisms of experiential prayer, shared study, and community building for the sake of making a difference in the world by witnessing the power of the Spirit through hospitality, gentle listening, and powerful speaking. In the words of a former Prioress, Sister Barbara Hansen, who was in office during the earliest years of the Center:

The Dominican Center has welcomed all who wish to "tend the holy."

> When I think of the [Dominican] Center, I think of its compassionate presence because society has a lot of harsh edges these days and there's something softening and welcoming about coming to Dominican Center and knowing

Ss. Diane Zerfas and Carmelita Switzer plan a program for the Dominican Center/ Marywood.

that whoever you are and whatever baggage you bring there and however broken you feel, that you will be welcomed there and that maybe while you're there someone or something . . . will help to heal a bit of the brokenness and you will feel then the compassion of Jesus Christ.[2]

The halls of Marywood are now filled with school teachers learning new methods, lawyers mediating between clients, spiritual directors walking with directees, program participants hoping to catch a glimpse of the Spirit in their own lives, participants in interfaith dialogue, yoga participants stretching for balance. The Marywood campus is alive with God at work, "tending the holy."

---

2. Sister Barbara Hansen in an interview July 10, 2003, unpublished.

Social Consciousness and Ministry

You have been told, mortal,
what is good,
and what the Lord requires of you:
only to do justice and to love goodness,
and to walk humbly with your God.

MICAH 6:8

THE OFFICIAL OPENING of the Second Vatican Council was October 11, 1962. By the time it closed four years later, the stained-glass windows of the Church were beginning to swing open, and a new era of "being church" emerged. On June 14, 1966, Sister Aquinas Weber was elected Prioress, the seventh in line from our foundress. The privilege and task of opening convent windows to the stirrings of the Holy Spirit being revealed in the documents of Vatican Council II fell to Sister Aquinas and her Council. Theirs would be the task of embracing the Dominican charism known as the *Holy Preaching*,[1] demanding intense work in the raising social consciousness and the Community response to it. Heretofore, the ministry of the Congregation had been primarily in education, with a few Sisters involved in nursing and social work. The logistics of the ministries and the personnel assignments had always been decided by the Prioress and her Council, who were elected

---

1. The *Holy Preaching* — this term first used by Saint Dominic in the 13th century to name the first community is the very reason for the foundation of the Dominican Order. Dominicans constantly preach the Gospel of Jesus by their lives through teaching, preaching, celebration of the arts, and service of whatever kind.

from the membership every four to six years. Now the vision of working for social change was to have a new direction with Sisters becoming more involved in decision making and forging into new ministries to effect systemic change. This was a new world for Women Religious in the 1960s. Social analysis applied to daily experience was a relatively novel concept, requiring rigorous discipline in study and honest self-evaluation. Dominicans, with a penchant for study and analysis, and a passion for the pursuit of truth, embraced the task with enthusiasm.

In the paragraphs that follow, the reader will encounter the ways in which the Congregation evolved from 1966. There was a gradual understanding and integration of the principles of Catholic social teaching into the fabric of the lives and ministry of all of the Sisters. Sisters began to recognize the broad spectrum of needs in the world, the possibilities for ministries, and the interconnection of one action with another, as well as the ultimate importance of every life in bringing about God's great desire for a just and peaceful world.

Prior to the 1960s, social and political issues were often considered concerns of the secular world. Sisters were not encouraged, expected, or in some cases, permitted to be involved in social and political issues. As a result of Vatican Council II, all of that changed. Now, "Sisters were asked to read about, think about and pray about public issues and relate them to Catholic social teaching. Intercessory prayers were not enough. Sisters were to respond to the needs of the world in concrete ways."[2] When Sisters read and thought about what they read, they found war, racism, and all kinds of injustice on their own doorsteps. They prayed, and they knew it was time to act. The call to action rang true in their own experience and in their emerging sense of themselves as members of the Church and the civic community. After the Sisters worked for many decades at the parish level or in Congregation-sponsored institutions, the benefits of collaboration became evident, increasingly necessary, and entirely welcomed.

Intercessory prayers were not enough. Sisters were to respond to the needs of the world in concrete ways.

---

2. Margaret Susan Thompson, Ph.D., "History of Women Religious in the United States," Audio CDs, Now You Know Media, 2009.

MINISTRY

1966-1972 Emerging Consciousness of Social Justice

Concurrent with Vatican Council II and the election of Sister Aquinas was the ongoing conflict in Vietnam. Sisters took to the streets to protest the escalation of this war, joining peace and justice organizations until the end of U.S. involvement in 1975. The civil rights movement was gaining momentum when Martin Luther King, Jr., became president of the newly established Southern Christian Leadership Conference in 1957. All of these events, the civil rights movement, the Vietnam War, and the teachings of Vatican Council II, significantly affected the emerging social consciousness of the Congregation as Sisters engaged in prayer, study, and public action on behalf of justice. The U.S. Bishops' documents gave energy and motivation to advance the cause of justice for all God's people. A compelling impetus for this came directly from the Holy See in Rome in 1971 when Pope Paul VI emphasized that the laity[3] have a primary call to create a more just world. The International Synod of Catholic Bishops issued a document that said, "Action on behalf of justice and participation in the transformation of the world appears to us as a constitutive dimension of the preaching of the Gospel."[4] *Preaching of the Gospel* — those words struck Dominicans in their deep hearts' core. Preaching the Gospel has been their foundational reason for existence since the thirteenth century. These words of the bishops further energized the Sisters in the direction of the *Holy Preaching* that shaped their communal vision for the future.

Preaching of the Gospel — those words struck Dominicans in their deep hearts' core.

1972-1980 Doing Justice

In 1972, Sister Norbert (Marjorie) Vangsness was elected Prioress. One of her first decisions had a major impact on the growing consciousness of justice issues. She became a member of the Social Justice Committee of the National Leadership Conference of Women Religious (LCWR). Through her participation in this committee, Congregational awareness of world and local injustices heightened. Many Sisters joined forces with Cesar Chavez

---

3. The laity consists of all members of the Church who are not ordained.
4. 1971 World Synod of Bishops, *Justice in the World*, #6.

and the United Farm Workers, supporting boycott efforts for labor reforms and union recognition.

A Sister who was missioned in Melvindale, Michigan, recalls that "upon one occasion I was arrested, finger printed and called before a Judge."[5] To see a Sister arrested was shocking, but this was only the beginning of the Sisters' willingness to pay the price for their commitment to justice. Another Sister recalls, "I can remember marching in protest and taking part in the grape boycott. We were downtown someplace and some man passed me. I didn't know exactly what he said, but it was that we were unpatriotic and he was very mad at us."[6] Sisters participated in sit-ins protesting local issues of racism in housing, another initiation into direct action. Still others attended the first NETWORK Workshop in Washington, DC. NETWORK is a social justice lobby founded in 1971 by forty-seven Catholic Sister Congregations in the United States. Today NETWORK continues its work as a powerful advocate on behalf of justice for men and women from every walk of life.[7]

NETWORK Lobby in 1984 (left to right): Srs. Susan Ridley, Marjorie Vangsness, Jeanne Marie Jones, and Jackie Hudson

The Sisters Respond to Papal and Episcopal Calls to Act Justly

The U.S. bishops launched an extensive two-year consultation process throughout the United States, involving thousands of Catholics and countless hours of conversations and deliberations. Sisters in their local dioceses participated in these hearings. This led to the Detroit Call to Action conference in 1976 with more than 100 bishops in attendance, along with 1340

---

5. Correspondence from S. Edith Marie Schnell, OP, 2011. This group included S. Edith Marie Schnell and S. Carol Gilbert as well as Cesar Chavez's daughter Sylvia and many others.
6. S. Marybride Ryan, Oral History, 2008, p. 16, Marywood Archives.
7. NETWORK's mission statement is "NETWORK — a Catholic leader in the global movement for justice and peace — educates, organizes and lobbies for economic and social transformation." See their website: http://www.NETWORKlobby.org/about-us (accessed November 9, 2012).

voting delegates and 1500 observers. The Sisters were there. A quote from the annals of Call to Action states:

> **"The Church must stand up to chronic racism, sexism, militarism and poverty in modern society."**
> Call to Action.

The assembly declared the Church must stand up to the chronic racism, sexism, militarism and poverty in modern society. And to do so in a credible way, the Church must reevaluate its positions on issues like celibacy for priests, the male-only clergy, homosexuality, birth control, and the involvement of every level of the church in important decisions.[8]

As the Congregation reflected on the works of justice, it became evident there was a wide spectrum of work involved in the establishment of a just society. Some members make prayer their primary contribution; others teach at various educational levels about justice issues; others hold positions in diocesan and peace and justice organizations; still others hold memberships in Pax Christi, Bread for the World, and NETWORK. Some Sisters work directly on parish committees; others choose to be actively engaged in programs addressing issues that touch them deeply; a few, working from an informed conscience, engage in civil resistance. Each member's work for justice is valued as a significant contribution to the understanding of the Christian message of justice and peace for all.

1980-1988 Peacemaking and Justice

In 1980 Sister Teresa Houlihan was elected Prioress and Sister Marjorie Vangsness joined the staff at NETWORK in Washington, DC. With the Congregational leadership of Sister Teresa and the social justice advocacy of Sister Marjorie, many more Sisters were lending their voices and actions to the cause of peacemaking and justice.

During the term of Sister Teresa, the Global Concerns Committee was given the task of raising the consciousness of the Congregation regarding peace and justice issues. To continue this work, the monthly newsletter *Op-*

---

8. Call to Action's mission statement states: "Call to Action educates, inspires and activates Catholics to act for justice and build inclusive communities through a lens of anti-racism and anti-oppression principles." Website address is http://cta-usa.org.

tion for Justice was published beginning in 1984. Its goal was "to establish a perspective on peace and justice which would encourage each member to address the issue with respect to her life and ministry."[9] On the twentieth anniversary of Dr. Martin Luther King, Jr.'s, "I Have a Dream" speech (1983), several Sisters joined 250,000 other peacemakers in celebrating the message and hope of peace at the Lincoln Memorial in Washington D.C.[10] The following year, Sister Susan Ridley began full-time ministry in peace and social justice in parishes and dioceses throughout Michigan.

In response to Catholics working with other peace groups on justice issues, a local Pax Christi chapter was begun in January 1983 by two Grand Rapids Dominican Sisters.[11] During its years of existence, Pax Christi members participated in nuclear weapons protests and supported and joined the Peace Ribbon Movement in Washington, DC. They also planned and conducted the January World Day of Peace prayer service at Dominican Chapel/Marywood for three consecutive years. In 1989 they helped plan a Faith and Resistance[12] retreat to prepare for acts of civil disobedience protesting the cruise missiles housed at two Air Force bases in Michigan.

During this decade, two historic documents, *The Challenge of Peace* (1983) and *Economic Justice for All* (1986), were published by the United States Conference of Catholic Bishops. Both were instrumental in encouraging participation in the national debate on justice issues. The American theologian Richard R. Gaillardetz summarizes the import of these two documents:

> The first document, the *Challenge of Peace* (1983), reflected on the particular ethical issues associated with modern warfare in a nuclear age. The second, *Economic Justice for All* (1986), brought to the foreground of public debate the ethical dimensions of modern economic policy. This willingness to engage contemporary American social, political and economic concerns sounded

---

9. S. Teresa Houlihan, Oral History, 2008-2009, p. 2, Marywood Archives.
10. The Srs. were Helen LaValley, Ardeth Platte, and Susan Ridley.
11. Srs. Mary Pat Beatty and Margaret Hillary, having been members of Pax Christi USA, started the Grand Rapids chapter.
12. Faith and Resistance retreats were developed to prepare people to examine their motives and to be fully aware of the potential consequences of engaging in acts of civil resistance. The process includes communal discernment so that participants were fully apprised of the possible outcome of their actions.

the final death knell for the insular, disengaged ghetto Catholicism of the pre-conciliar American church.[13]

Although most Sisters had been educated in Catholic parochial schools and in the kind of ecclesial atmosphere that Gaillardetz refers to as "ghetto Catholicism," the truth of the bishops' teaching rang true to their experience and they determined to preach the message. They taught and preached for peace and justice every chance they had — through teaching, presiding at prayer services, facilitating Bible study, marching in protest against racism, conversations with family and friends and with anyone who would engage with them. They also preached through the arts of music and visual depictions from designing greeting cards to paintings, sculptures, and liturgical dance.

Sr. Sue Tracy and others protest the Iraq War.

> They taught and preached for peace and justice every chance they had.

The refrain "preaching by our very lives" became a mantra of daily life.

Concurrently, Sisters were actively engaged in peaceful, nonviolent direct action. In 1983 a Grand Rapids Dominican Sister was featured in the Joplin, Missouri, newspaper when she, along with a local peace group, carried antinuclear weapons signs and handed out literature in front of the post office on tax day, emphasizing the amount of tax dollars being spent on the current military budget.[14]

In October of that same year (1983) Wurtsmith Air Force Base in Oscoda,

---

13. Richard Gaillardetz, Murray/Bacik lecture: "The State of the Church: 2011 Reflections on the State of American Catholicism Today." University of Toledo, Ohio. January 27, 2011.

14. S. Constance Fifelski, principal of McAuley School and St. Peter's Junior High in Joplin, Missouri.

Michigan, was the site of civil resistance by several Sisters.[15] Ironically, in one instance the Sisters were sentenced to jail on December 28, the Catholic Feast Day of the Holy Innocents. Such a happenstance no doubt added to the surprise of several guards who were former grade school students of the Sisters. At another time, Sisters were charged with trespassing while standing with members of the Shoshone Indian Nation in Nevada to protest their land being used for nuclear testing. All charges, however, were dropped at the request of the Shoshone Nation.[16]

Closer to home in Michigan, Sister Mary Brigid Clingman went to work for the Team for Justice, a program sponsored by the Archdiocese of Detroit. This work was dedicated to preserving the human rights of victims and offenders through advocacy within the criminal justice system in Wayne County. The Team for Justice and other justice organizations would eventually become the Detroit/Windsor Refugee Coalition with Sister Mary Brigid as the chairperson of the Board of Directors. Later changed to Freedom House (1994), this organization helped innumerable Central American refugees in their struggle to find asylum status in either the United States or Canada.

A rising consciousness of all corporate undertakings and ministries included assessing everything that the Sisters held in common. By 1983 a Philosophy of Investments Policy booklet with specific guidelines for investing was published. These guidelines included the following:

> The investment of community money may be an effective tool for supporting corporations and institutions fostering Christian values, but the preservation of principal and a reasonable profit will not be sacrificed for the sole reason of supporting a given institution because of the nature of its purpose. Conversely, money will not be invested in a high-return business for the sake of profit if the corporation is in violation of social justice practices. Should the community own equities and fixed income securities in such a corporation,

> **"Money will not be invested in high-return business for the sake of profit if the corporation is in violation of social justice practices."**
> A Philosophy of Investments Policy Booklet

---

15. Srs. Carol Gilbert, Ardeth Platte, and Edith Marie Schnell were forcefully removed from Wurtsmith Air Force Base in Oscoda, Michigan, for protesting and opposing weapons stockpiling. S. Maria Goretti Beckman was also arrested for trespassing at Wurtsmith as she also protested the arms buildup.

16. S. Maria Goretti Beckman, along with Srs. Helen LaValley and Jackie Hudson, was in this group of protestors.

the community will make efforts to correct the ills through means ranging from writing letters to the corporation to joining a coalition to bring about justice. Should these means fail, divestment of affected equities and fixed income securities takes place.[17]

The most current Statement of Policy and Investment Objectives is printed in Appendix 2 of this book.

In 1984 the first Dominican Conference on Justice was held in Caldwell, New Jersey. Two years later, the Justice Conference was hosted at Marywood in Grand Rapids. The Dominican Order's official Justice Promoter had been appointed to his role by the Master General (head of the international Dominican Order) in Rome.[18] In the *Option for Justice* September 1986 issue, the Prioress and Council stated that the two goals of this conference were:

(1) identify and pursue a Dominican response to peace and justice issues which is in keeping with our charism of prayer, study, ministry and common life, and

(2) provide a framework in which every member of the Congregation can see that her life and ministry do contribute to the work of justice.[19]

During the conference, the Sisters presented seminars enriching and expanding the keynote presentation by Brother Edward VanMerrienboer, OP.[20]

---

17. A Philosophy of Investments Policy Booklet: Guidelines for Investments. Summary of guidelines provided by S. Maureen Geary through e-mail in 2011.

18. Br. Edward Van Merrienboer, OP.

19. *Option for Justice,* no. 6, September 1986. Grand Rapids Dominicans in-house publication.

20. The presenters and topics were as follows:
U.S. Bishops' Pastoral Letter on the Economy by Marie Joseph Ryan, OP
Farmworker Movements by Lupe Silva, OP
Women and Peacemaking by Phyllis Ohren, OP
Hispanic Experience in the Church by Dolorita Martinez, OP
Justice on the Family Farm by Joyce Ann Hertzig, OP
Women in the U.S. Culture and Society by Marjorie Vangsness, OP
Central America by Jean Reimer, OP, and Carol Gilbert, OP
Teaching Justice and Peace in the Schools by Rose Karasti, OP.

Social Consciousness and Ministry

In 1984 as Sister Teresa Houlihan began her second term as Prioress, she also became a board member of Groundwork for a Just World, a social justice network founded by LCWR Region VII (Michigan and Indiana). Groundwork was charged with providing the organization's members with information and action ideas, mobilizing and networking opportunities, and workshops, presentations, and a newsletter.[21]

Groundwork for a Just World created the Discipleship Award to recognize individuals who had made significant contributions to faith-based justice and peace activities in Michigan. Over the years, three Grand Rapids Dominican Sisters were recognized for their advocacy by Groundwork. In 1990 Sister Helen LaValley was the recipient of the award. At the awards ceremony, the following was read:

> In 1972 Helen retired from teaching as Associate Professor of Chemistry at Aquinas College to begin a ministry of neighborhood development and pastoral work. Helen indicates that her "resistance" work began in the 1960s when she combined efforts with the United Farm Workers, actively supported the Civil Rights Movement, and joined ranks with Vietnam War resisters. In 1980 she chose to serve among the poor as a missionary in Guatemala. A year later, during one of the most violent periods in that country's history, she was kidnapped by the Guatemalan military and held in one of their prisons for five days before being released to U.S. authorities. In recent years her resistance has led her to oppose the arms race at nuclear sites around Michigan and the country.[22]

Sr. Helen LaValley, peace advocate, in 1986

In 1986 the United States Conference of Catholic Bishops issued two documents that further impacted the focus and direction of our communal journey towards social consciousness. The bishops' document, *To the End of the Earth*, emphasized the Church's mission to the poor and the powerless. The previously

---

21. The following members of the Grand Rapids Dominicans were on its board: Ss. Carmelita Murphy, Suzanne Eichhorn, Orlanda Leyba, and Ann Walters.

22. Groundwork for a Just World, Testimonial Dinner Program, Shrine of the Little Flower, Royal Oak, Michigan, April 29, 1990.

mentioned document, *Economic Justice for All — Catholic Social Teaching and the U.S. Economy,* made everyone more aware of the gems of Catholic social teaching and encouraged all to more fully integrate those teachings into their lives and ministries. As a personal response to this document, Sister Helen LaValley moved to Morton House Senior Housing in Grand Rapids and began the Social Concerns Committee at St. Andrew's Parish in the Grand Rapids downtown area.

Meanwhile, Sisters Carol Gilbert, Ardeth Platte, and Jackie Hudson, among others, were continuing their active resistance opposing nuclear weapons and war. They held vigils, made posters, carried banners, and did nonviolent direct action. Because of these actions, they were arrested, presented testimony in court, and served time in both county jails and prisons. As these and other Sisters, acting from an informed conscience, participated in acts of civil disobedience or resistance, the Prioress and Council took the prudent action of formulating a Congregational policy on civil disobedience. According to the policy, "A member can never be missioned to break a law. The members are not acting as agents of the Congregation, thus the Congregation does not bear any financial burden due to their action."[23] The policy on civil disobedience was enacted in January 1986 to protect the Congregation while insuring the civil and religious rights and personal conscience of the individual. The policy recognizes that the individual Sister's conscience is her highest moral guide, transcending even the requirements of Religious Life.

As individual Sisters acted in accord with their conscience on behalf of

Srs. Carol Gilbert, Jackie Hudson, and Ardeth Platte reunite after years of incarceration in federal prison for public protests against the stockpiling of nuclear weapons.

> The individual Sister's conscience is her highest moral guide, transcending even the requirements of Religious Life.

---

23. S. Teresa Houlihan, Oral History, 2008-2009, p. 1, Marywood Archives.

justice, so too did the corporation itself. In the 1984 Chapter, the Committee for Corporate Social Responsibility proposed that "stockbrokers that are working with the Congregation's investments . . . stay clear from investing in companies that deal with nuclear armaments."[24] The members of the Chapter further recommended that all of the Congregation's investments be reviewed to insure that companies invested in were not producers of military or nuclear weapons, were not damaging the environment, and otherwise were in accord with the Congregation's mission and vision policies. These principles and policies are now part of the official documents of the Congregation.

1988-1994 New Directions in Social Consciousness

In 1988 Sister Carmelita Murphy was elected Prioress. It became her responsibility, and that of her Council, to continue the legacy of the previous administrations, expanding the new direction toward social consciousness. The Dominican conference Doing Justice, held at Rosary College (now Dominican University) in River Forest, Illinois, in July 1988, was a huge boost. For six days Dominicans from the United States and around the world immersed themselves in prayer, study, social analysis, and theological reflection. Participants came from the United States, Canada, France, Ireland, Italy, Bolivia, Nicaragua, El Salvador, and the Philippines; twenty-nine Dominican women's Congregations, six provinces[25] of Dominican men, and members of the Dominican laity[26] were included among the participants in the conference. From the seeds germinated at this historic event, a global consciousness of doing justice in the Dominican family grew and flourishes to this day. A direct result of this conference was a twofold mandate: first, all Dominican Congregations of Women and Provinces of men were to appoint a Justice Promoter, and second, a male and female Justice Promoter from North America were to be elected to serve at an international Dominican level.

24. Proceedings from Chapter 1984.
25. Provinces in the Dominican Order are geographical regions and part of the government structure.
26. Dominican laity (not to be confused with Dominican Associates) are men and women, single or married, who make promises to follow the Rule of the Lay Chapters of St. Dominic.

In June 1989 the Congregational Nonviolence Committee was established with the following directive:

> The focus of this committee is to study ways to live nonviolently, working toward conversion of heart and continuing formation in a nonviolent lifestyle while witnessing to the values of the Gospel. The committee will promote educational processes regarding nonviolent lifestyle.[27]

Peace Pole on Marywood Campus

In the same year, a peace pole[28] was erected on the Marywood grounds as a public display of the Congregation's commitment to the ministry of the Holy Preaching on behalf of peace and justice. This committee served as the vehicle to energize ministerial directions. In a memo to the Nonviolence Committee dated March 16, 1990, the Prioress, Sister Carmelita, wrote:

> I come to you today for your suggestions and ideas. I think it would be most advantageous if I reflected with you on the efforts of the General Council to address the doing of justice in 1988-1994. It is obvious to me that there are a variety of forms in which we are making decisions that promote justice. There are: Central Committees such as Care of the Earth, Nonviolence, Women in Church and Society, Corporate Stance, Ministry Subsidy and others, which are clearly vehicles for addressing a broad spectrum of justice concerns. I believe the Central Committees are effectively and creatively moving the Congregation forward in the work of justice.[29]

---

27. Nonviolence Committee memo, June 7, 1989, Marywood Archives.
28. A peace pole is a monument consisting of a simple pole displaying the words "May Peace Prevail on Earth" in several languages.
29. Memorandum to members of the Nonviolence Committee from S. Carmelita Murphy

These committees were instrumental in continuing the communal dialogue on these issues that led to direct action. For example, after a year's study, five committees — Nonviolence, Hispanic, Simplicity of Life, Corporate Responsibility, and Care of Earth[30] — supported the recommendation of the Corporate Stance Committee[31] that the following boycotts be endorsed: California table-grape growers (for lacking humane working conditions for farmworkers regarding use of pesticides), General Electric (producer of engines for nuclear warheads), Coca-Cola products (for its complicity in supporting apartheid in South Africa), and Styrofoam products and packaging (for its environmental damage). This proposal was supported by members of the Congregation in their respective regions and was voted on and approved in April 1991.

In a *Grand Rapids Press* article featuring the boycott, Sister Carmelita Murphy is quoted: "We recognize the need to practice and to live justly with all peoples of the earth. . . . There is a connection between faith and action. There's the recognition that faith is embodied in social reality and that love of God must be affected in love of neighbor."[32]

The Bay City Times also carried an article on the boycott featuring Sister Maria Goretti Beckman. She was quoted, "If we are going to stand for anything as an Order of women, we have to first instill in ourselves that what we do every day affects generations to come."[33] This was to be the first of several corporate stances the Congregation espoused.

In 1992 as part of a Faith and Resistance retreat and subsequent acts of civil resistance, Sisters Jackie Hudson and Ardeth Platte were sentenced to six months' incarceration for a non-authorized entrance into Wurtsmith Air Force Base in Oscoda, Michigan. Sister Helen LaValley engaged in this act of civil resistance along with them, but, because she was eighty-two years old and legally blind, she was given 520 hours of community service. One can

> "There is a connection between faith and action. Faith is embodied in social reality and love of God must be affected in love of neighbor." Sister Carmelita

---

re: educational processes pertaining to justice making/justice issues, March 16, 1990, Marywood Archives.

30. The Care of Earth Committee began in 1989 with ten Sister members and one Associate member. The committee continues to educate and act on issues relative to justice and ecology.

31. A corporate stance is a deliberate public statement or action regarding an issue of concern taken by the Congregation after due study and discussion. A majority must approve a proposal for a corporate stance.

32. Judy Tremore, "Dominican Boycott," Grand Rapids Press, 1991 or 1992.

33. Connie Hawkins, "Dominican nuns boycott to change society," *Bay City Times,* May 25, 1991.

only imagine the quiet smile of a woman sentenced to community service after approximately sixty-two years of generous service to sundry communities. In the process of being given an alternate sentence, she had tea and a visit with the commander of the base.

In Deeds as Well as in Words — Investments

In the memo to the Nonviolence Committee of March 16, 1990, Sister Carmelita informed it of what was taking shape regarding corporate responsibility. She wrote:

> We actively promote our corporate responsibility through more stringent investment guidelines and stockholder action. [Sister] Maureen Geary has attended one meeting regarding proxy and will be attending a national meeting in June regarding stockholder action. Our social responsibility guidelines are very good, but we are scrutinizing them even closer regarding the South African reality.[34]

Currently, the Congregation uses three strategies in the exercise of corporate responsibility. The first is to channel investments toward socially responsible purposes. The second is to divert investments away from destructive uses. The third strategy may include retaining or buying shares in a company that has destructive or unethical practices in order to gain the right to file resolutions, attend shareholder meetings, educate on issues of difference, meet with the management, and vote proxies.[35]

Alternative investments were also set in motion during Sister Carmelita's years as Prioress. These investments were seen as concrete ways of fostering

---

34. Memorandum to members of the Nonviolence Committee from S. Carmelita Murphy re: educational processes pertaining to justice making/justice issues, March 16, 1990, Marywood Archives. At this time, countries around the world boycotted companies doing business in South Africa as a means of pressuring that government to end the practice of apartheid. In 1991, South Africa's president, F. W. DeKlerk, repealed the apartheid laws.

35. A Philosophy of Investments Policy Booklet: Guidelines for Investments, May 1983, Marywood Archives.

Social Consciousness and Ministry

justice by providing low-interest development loans to individuals or groups who would thus be empowered to more fully direct their own lives.

Focused Directions for Ministry

Every three years, a General Assembly of all the membership of the Congregation is held in August. Although primarily meant to be a unifying experience, it is also a time to share, discuss, and make recommendations to the Prioress and Council. In 1992 the General Assembly gave birth to four Direction Statements to guide the lives and decisions of the Sisters in the years ahead. These statements were wholeheartedly embraced by the Sisters. The spirited affirmation of these Direction Statements resulted in immediate implementation of programs. They were and continue to be instrumental in setting guidelines, priorities, and directions that have far-reaching effects as they continue to challenge social consciousness and ministry choices.

The four Direction Statements formulated in 1992 were expanded in 1994. Taken together, these statements commit the members to right and just relationships with each other, with the materially poor, and Earth herself. They also commit members to stand with women and children who are most often the recipients of violent and unfair treatment in the world. Additionally, the statements commit the members to living the common life and to collaborating with others to effect systemic change.

Direction Statements

1994-2000 Being Justice

While Sister Barbara Hansen was Prioress, conversation was underway that would eventually lead to establishing a living wage for all employees.

An article in the February 1998 issue of *Groundwork for a Just World* reads:

> Five years ago, the Grand Rapids Dominicans began to ask if we were giving our employees a "living just wage" or a "sustainable wage" as suggested by the Gospel and by the many social justice documents issued by the Church. It was a question that, as a Congregation of socially responsible investors, we were challenging other corporations to ask themselves. We found we had the same answer as other corporations. Our wages are competitive to the fair market value. Yet, we knew that a fair market wage does not always equal a "living just wage."[36]

The Direction Statements are to:

- **recognize and be open to the Holy in ourselves and one another of whatever culture and lifestyle**
- **affirm the need for community and renew our energy to live common life well**
- **stand in solidarity with those who are materially poor**
- **stand in solidarity with other women who have suffered from oppression and violence**
- **advocate for children in local, national and international communities**
- **collaborate with others to effect systemic change toward a just world**
- **foster a contemplative stance that all the earth is sacred and interconnected**

After grappling with the difficult questions of how to implement this as a policy for all Congregational employees, and considering the financial implications for the Congregation, the living just wage was embraced as policy. This was made possible by using money from the sale of the Albuquerque Nazareth property to endow the Living Wage Fund.

A unique opportunity to act on the Direction Statement to "walk with the materially poor" was realized on the Marywood Campus as the Prioress and Council considered how best to use a large underutilized two-story building on the east side of the property. The initial hope had been to use the building to house the Rose Haven Program, a transitional housing project operated by the Sisters of The Good Shepherd for women leaving a life of prostitution. This proposed use had to be abandoned in the face of opposition by some neighbors. After careful study and deliberation about another use for this residence, it was deemed to be an ideal house for women and children in need of temporary shelter. In April 1994 the Sisters began to explore this possibility through collaboration with The Salvation Army. Although the Board of the Neighborhood Association opposed this use as well,

---

36. *Groundwork for a Just World*, vol. 22, no. 4 (February 25, 1998). Marywood Archives.

other neighbors were supportive and the Board of Zoning Appeals approved the variance needed on February 16, 1995. The Congregation leased the building to The Salvation Army Booth Family Services for $1.00 per year and also provided an interest-free loan to fund the needed renovation. For over a decade the residence provided shelter and support for women and children until they were able to find permanent housing.

During the General Assembly of 1997 the Congregation proposed that work toward undoing the systemic sin of racism be undertaken in an intentional manner. Sister Barbara states: "Of course, the work had to begin in our hearts, in our own attitudes and beliefs."[37] A committee was formed, modules of materials for study and discussion were designed for the membership, and a gathering of Sisters, Dominican Associates, and guests from the civic community participated in a program: *Weaving the Tapestry of Our Lives: Healing Racism through a Celebration of Our Differences.* It takes a long time to undo the legacy of privilege, the luxury of ignorance of the other, and the assumption of the rightness of one's own way that is the inheritance of white middle-class Americans. The work was begun and continues to this day.

Sr. Barbara Hansen cuts the ribbon to dedicate the Family Lodge at the Marywood Complex.

The action of a corporate stance requires study, discussion, and a two-thirds majority vote of the Sisters on a particular issue. It is not lightly taken, nor easily done; rather, it is a public statement on a concern for justice according to the principles of the Gospel. Such a position is grounded in the ethical principles developed by Cardinal Joseph Bernardin in his position known as "Consistent Ethic of Life" or the "Seamless Garment Ethic." It is based on two fundamental principles or truths rooted in Catholic social teaching. These are: first, the intrinsic dignity, worth, and value of every human person; and second, that every human being is, by nature, a social creature. On this account, morally good acts, be they initiated by an individual or by society, contribute to human life or human flourishing, while morally evil acts diminish or destroy human life. Thus the Sisters not only realized that they had a sound basis for opposing capital punishment (the first issue studied for a corporate stance action), but they also expanded the vision about all life issues from the begin-

A corporate stance is not lightly taken, nor easily done.

---

37. *Dominican Futures,* vol. VIII, no. 32 (Fall 1999), p. 1.

ning of life (abortion) through childhood (violence inflicted by an individual or the state) to adulthood (violence, war, capital punishment, murder, suicide) and into end-of-life issues (assisted suicide, euthanasia).

This ethical position, which provides a sound basis for decision making, recognizes the role of circumstances in individual situations as well as avoiding "the one issue" mentality. From such a basis each Sister works for the issue or cause which resonates with her prayer and social commitment. Sisters have worked in pregnancy clinics, protested against abortion, supported new mothers in at-risk situations, rocked babies addicted to cocaine in hospital neo-natal units, and wrought sculptures depicting the tragedy of abortion.

Other Sisters have worked in support of access to affordable health care, in programs to eliminate hunger, in peace initiatives, in hospice ministry, in immigration reform, in efforts to halt human trafficking, in civic coalitions to end homelessness, and in many other programs to bring about a more peaceful and just society.

Another affirmation of witnessing to the moral significance of the Direction Statements was the 1998 construction of two houses in inner-city Grand Rapids. Sister Barbara Hansen explained the rationale for this decision:

> Aware of the push in Grand Rapids towards the healing of racism through the work of the Grand Rapids Area Center for Ecumenism (GRACE), our congregational commitment to that cause through the advocacy of the Committee on Racism, and because of our concern for more houses where communities of three to seven Sisters might live, we made the decision to look for real estate that might meet one or both of those purposes. The Jefferson Street houses, near downtown and in a mixed neighborhood, in a project for lower income families through ICCF (Inner City Christian Federation), put the Sisters into direct contact with a rich diversity of neighbors.[38]

Justice to the Ends of the Earth

Among the Sisters who have dedicated the ministerial witness of their lives to unmasking the evils endemic in nuclear weapons and the military-industrial

---

38. S. Barbara Hansen, e-mail to S. Orlanda Leyba, March 19, 2012.

complex are Sisters Carol Gilbert, Jackie Hudson, and Ardeth Platte. In 1993, Sister Jackie moved to the state of Washington to live in community with members of Ground Zero for Nonviolent Action. In 1995 Sisters Carol and Ardeth joined the faith-based community of Jonah House in Baltimore, Maryland. From these locales, the Sisters, either separately or together, witnessed to nonviolence as a way of life, based on Gospel values and a life of prayer, study, community, and ministry — Dominican essentials from which all derive strength. Armed with prayerful conviction, rooted in faithfulness to the nonviolent Jesus, and speaking truth to power, they bravely expose those powers that lead human and economic resources away from life-affirming engagements. In some instances, these public actions have led to arrests, incarceration, or extended probation, a price they willingly pay for their convictions. Over the decades of their service on behalf of peace, these Sisters have accumulated approximately eight years of incarceration in jails and prisons.[39]

November 1998 began a yearly witness at the gates of Fort Benning, Georgia, for Sisters Marie Rachael Guevara and Orlanda Leyba. Along with thousands of other protestors, they joined in the yearly vigil that called attention to this army base that trains soldiers from Central and South America at U.S. taxpayers' expense. Some of these same soldiers, upon graduating, have been implicated in killing Sisters, priests, and farmers who work to protect human rights and to secure and protect ancestral lands. On one occasion, the Sisters were detained, fingerprinted, photographed, and given a warning letter not to return to the base. Along with an increasing number of protestors, the Sisters, later joined by other Dominican Sisters and Associates, continue to hold vigils at the army base in hopes of discontinuing the practice of training foreign soldiers to torture and kill. The practice of expanding social consciousness and awareness of the dignity and rights of all of God's family continues.

In June 2000 Sister Orlanda Leyba, along with a delegation from other Dominican Congregations, traveled to Washington, DC, to lobby Congress

> The Sisters bravely expose those powers that lead human and economic resources away from life-affirming engagements.
>
> These Sisters have accumulated approximately eight years of incarceration in jails and prisons.

---

39. While serving time in jails and prisons, the Sisters become advocates and spiritual/emotional support for the women who were incarcerated with them. In 2006, Zero to Sixty Productions in Boulder, Colorado, produced an award-winning documentary film entitled *Conviction* about these three Sisters and their civil resistance to the proliferation of nuclear arms in the United States.

on behalf of the suffering people of Iraq. Wearing lapel pins that proclaimed "I have family in Iraq," the delegation made known the impact sanctions were having on the civilian population and attested to the family connection with the wider Dominican family. Not only are there many Dominican Sisters and Brothers in Iraq among the Christian populace which has been there since the thirteenth century, but there are many brothers and sisters of the human family, which give the connection a deeper message than the slogan.

And thus the Sisters journey, following in the footsteps of Saint Dominic, continually discerning where to plant their feet, how to identify and work to address injustices, and with whom they will continue to proclaim the Gospel through the *Holy Preaching*.

These blessed and graced-filled years, grounded in the wisdom of Vatican Council II and the foresight, good judgment, and judiciousness of the Sisters, unleashed the Spirit's blessing on their sacred journey toward social consciousness. The Spirit that propelled "the opening of church and convent windows" was the same impetus that enabled the Sisters to courageously commit their lives and resources to embracing social consciousness in myriad ways. The Sisters' vision and passion, applying Gospel principles and Catholic social teaching, identified those social ills to which they would give their lives. The Congregation blessed those efforts and has been, in turn, immeasurably blessed.

Sisters and friends go to New Orleans to help clean up after Hurricane Katrina (left to right): Sr. Jude Bloch, Sr. Mary Ann Ferguson, Sr. Therese Leckert (Dominican Sister of Peace), Sr. Barbara Hansen, Mary Ann Keough (friend), Sr. Mary Donnelly, Sr. Joan Alflen, Sr. Kathy Przybylski, Sr. Maria Goretti Beckman, Dr. Cynthia Thomas (friend and president of Dominican High School), and Jeanne Lound Schaller (friend).

Horizons Broaden and Ministries Flourish

*"Go into the whole world and proclaim
the Gospel to every creature."*
MARK 16:15

From the late 1960s to the end of the century the scope of ministries of the Grand Rapids Dominicans widened to include more diverse peoples over a larger geographical area. Where once ministry was confined to the parochial settings of Catholic parishes and hospitals, now in response to the teachings of Vatican Council II and the changes in the culture, the venue and array of services widened and became more inclusive. To use the metaphor from a pre-Vatican era, the Church Triumphant, singing "an army of youth flying the standard of truth," was no longer apt. The new metaphor for the Church began to look more like pilgrims on a journey, singing "All Are Welcome."

How can this transformation be explained and how did it happen in the Grand Rapids Dominican Congregation? Simple answers with single cause and effect propositions fall far short of explaining the complex reasons for change. A confluence of forces in Church, society, and social consciousness at least partially explains the broadening of horizons, the expansion into diverse ministries, and the transformation of the lives of the Sisters from an insular Catholic existence to a global presence ministering both inside the auspices of the Catholic Church as well as in the public sector.

In order to understand the significance of the convergence of forces and

Simple answers with single cause and effect propositions fall far short of explaining the complex reasons for change.

the subsequent change in worldview, it is necessary to revisit, for a moment, life before the sixties. It is important to note that the following experiences did not, for the most part, raise any concern or protest from the players. This was just the way it was.

The formative texts taught to newcomers in Religious Life in the 1950s and early 1960s reflected the civic and ecclesial culture of that time; they included readings from such writers as Jean Mouroux. "The community needs a head and this head is the man . . . who is the direct image and glory of God . . . a figure of him who was to come. . . . As to the woman her part is to obey. . . ."[1] The young initiate into religious life may have listened to Father Meloche in his tape recording in which he admonishes young women to imitate Mary the Mother of God, a woman "wrapped in silence." He advocates modesty of speech and docility to male guidance. "Giving way graciously" is the mark of a real woman, he says, and suggests that training begin early. "I think a little girl two or three years of age should be taught how to give up her toys to her little brother graciously."[2]

Each summer on the Feast Day of the Assumption of the Blessed Virgin Mary, August 15, the Sisters gathered in chapel to await their assignment for the next academic year. Following the assignments, there were smiles or tears depending on the content of the envelope; but there was never a question or resistance to the assignment. No one said anything; these were women who had been taught from an early age that their role in life was to be obedient and to accept without question what authority figures told them.

Converging Strands

In the background, changes were afoot in the country. Catholics, once treated with suspicion, were eventually accepted into the mainstream of American society. The election of John F. Kennedy, the first Catholic president, marked the coming of age for the American Catholic. For a variety of reasons, Catholic families began to follow the trend of the rest of America in having fewer children. As the postwar economic prosperity increased, more

---

1. Jean Mouroux, *The Meaning of Man* (New York: Image Books, 1948), pp. 204-5.
2. Father Meloche, "What it is to be a woman," tape recording in Aquinas College audio-visual collection, quoted by Mary Navarre, in "Woman Like Spring," accepted research paper in Aquinas Institute of Religious Studies (AIRS) program, July 24, 1972, unpublished.

Catholic families chose to move out of the core cities to more affluent areas where there were few Catholic schools.

Gradually the cost of education escalated with the rise of teacher salaries, fewer Sisters to subsidize the cost of faculty salaries, new technologies with expensive hardware, and desirable extra-curricular activities. In Religious Congregations the increase in the number of elderly Sisters no longer able to teach and the decrease in the availability of younger Sisters to replace them magnified the difficulty of staffing schools.

In the 1950s, Congregations of Women Religious began to delay sending young members into the classroom until they had completed their degree and certification requirements. At the same time, the states were raising their standards of education for teachers and "learning on the job" was becoming less feasible. More lay teachers needed to be hired to staff the schools, and they required higher salaries. It was diocesan policy that if a Congregation agreed to staff a school and did not have enough Sisters, the Congregation would pay the salary of the lay teachers. This became a significant financial hardship, and from the Congregation's stand-point, it was better to withdraw from a school than assume responsibility for lay teachers' salaries.[3] Thus, what had once been a financial burden for Religious Congregations became the responsibility of the parishes.

As more Catholic parents became affluent, they also began to assert more independence; some even saw an advantage to having their children interact with children from a variety of cultures and religious and ethnic backgrounds. For these reasons, among others (e.g., the passing of Proposal C by the Michigan voters which prohibited direct or indirect state aid to non-public schools), parish schools began to be replaced by religious education programs. These realities were only part of the converging forces that changed everything.

Another strand was the impact of Vatican Council II on the self-concept of vowed Religious as a "special group" in the Church, as well as the image of the Church herself. In the 1950s and early 1960s children in Catholic schools were taught that there were three options or "vocations" in life. The highest calling was to serve God wholly and completely through ordination as a priest for a man or as a member of a religious community for a woman. The second calling or vocation was married life — to which most were called.

---

3. Mona Schwind, *Period Pieces*, 1991, pp. 293-94.

The third possibility, and least prestigious, was a call to the single life. Those who chose the "highest calling" were assured of salvation — if faithful — and would receive "the hundred-fold" on earth. Their parents and family members too would be blessed for having given their son or daughter to the Church. Those who chose this "highest calling" lived in the world of the "sacred" which was distinguished from the world of the "secular." Following World War II, large numbers of children were born in the country and large numbers of Catholic children chose to enter the highest form of life — that of the priesthood or sisterhood.

The documents of Vatican Council II, in particular *Lumen Gentium* and *Gaudium et Spes,* chipped away at that dualistic thinking — dividing the world into sacred and secular — a concept that had been in place since the Middle Ages and even earlier. The remarkable eighth section of *Lumen Gentium* states:

> But the society equipped with hierarchical structures and the mystical body of Christ, the visible society and the spiritual community, the earthly church and the church endowed with heavenly riches, are not to be thought of as two realities. On the contrary, they form one complex reality comprising a human and a divine element. For this reason the church is compared, in no mean analogy, to the mystery of the incarnate Word.[4]

The document *Gaudium et Spes* clearly positions the Church *in* the modern world, not separate from it.

> The joys and hopes, the grief and anguish of the people of our time, especially of those who are poor or afflicted, are the joys and hopes, the grief and anguish of the followers of Christ as well. Nothing that is genuinely human fails to find an echo in their hearts. For theirs is a community of people united in Christ and guided by the Holy Spirit in their pilgrimage towards the Father's kingdom, bearers of a message of salvation for all of humanity. That is why they cherish a feeling of deep solidarity with the human race and its history.[5]

---

4. *Lumen Gentium,* 8. (For this and all references to Vatican II documents the reader is referred to the internet link: http://www.vatican.va/archive/hist_councils/ii_vatican_council/.)

5. *Gaudium et Spes,* #1.

Horizons Broaden and Ministries Flourish

This new view of the Church is a far cry from one described at the beginning of the 20th century when Pope Pius X wrote: "the one duty of the multitude is to allow themselves to be led, and like a docile flock, to follow the Pastors."[6]

Again in *Lumen Gentium* the entitled status of priests and vowed Religious is moderated with this passage on the priesthood of all baptized people:

> The baptized, by regeneration and the anointing of the Holy Spirit, are consecrated as a spiritual house and a holy priesthood, in order that through all those works which are those of the Christian man [sic] they may offer spiritual sacrifices and proclaim the power of Him who has called them out of darkness into His marvelous light. Therefore all the Disciples of Christ, persevering in prayer and praising God, should present themselves as a living sacrifice, holy and pleasing to God. Everywhere on earth they must bear witness to Christ and give an answer to those who seek an account of that hope of eternal life which is in them.[7]

And "everywhere on earth" was where the Dominican Sisters would find themselves as they embraced wholeheartedly the good news of these two seminal Vatican II documents.

There is one more document from Vatican Council II which offered a powerful strand in the confluence of forces bringing about the flourishing of diverse ministries and the broadening of the "tent stakes" of the ministerial world of the Sisters. In the document *Perfectae Caritatis,* the Council Fathers called for a complete renewal and adaptation of Religious Life in light of the modern world and its needs. In particular the document mandates Religious to return to Holy Scripture and to the unique charismatic gifts of their founders:

> The adaptation and renewal of the Religious Life includes both the constant return to the sources of all Christian life and to the original spirit of the institutes and their adaptation to the changed conditions of our time.[8]

---

6. http://www.vatican.va/holy_father/pius_x/encyclicals/documents/hf_p-x_enc_11021906_vehementer-nos_en.html (accessed November 9, 2012).

7. *Lumen Gentium,* #10.

8. *Perfectae Caritatis,* #2.

Following this statement, very specific principles are listed: study Scripture, delve deeply into the founding gift (charism) of your Congregation, update knowledge of current social conditions and adapt to these, and above all listen to and follow the Spirit of God in that renewal. Religious women and men took this decree promulgated by Pope Paul VI to heart and began the work of reviewing and renewing every aspect of their lives together.

And there was yet one more event that impacted the way the Congregation viewed ministry; it was a tragic one and particular to the Grand Rapids Dominicans. As Rome bustled with the excitement of final preparations for the opening session of the Second Vatican Council and cardinals, bishops, and *periti* (experts) made their way to Vatican City, the Dominican Sisters in Grand Rapids were immersed in "the night of our greatest sorrow."[9] Late in September 1962, seven Sisters went on a "color tour" to enjoy the changes in the autumn trees. In a terrible collision near Mesick, Michigan, five of those Sisters were killed and two were critically injured. The parish school, St. John the Evangelist in Essexville, Michigan, lost seven of its twelve Sisters in that dreadful moment. It was a very dark night indeed.

Funeral for five Sisters killed in an automobile accident; this tragedy was known as the "night of our greatest sorrow."

Immediately following the funeral, Mother Victor, the Prioress, began the task of reassigning Sisters to take the place of those who were dead or disabled. The task was complicated and arduous as Sisters covered for Sisters who were covering for Sisters. A Sister from another Congregation, Elkins Park, Pennsylvania, Dominicans, volunteered to take the place of a high school Sister in Grand Rapids so that Sister could go to Essexville to replace one who had died. Like rearranging pieces on a chess board, the changes and moving of personnel was complicated and depended on many factors, e.g., skills, experience, and family considerations, as three of those who died had blood sisters in the Congregation.

Dominican life has been for the sake of the mission since St. Dominic founded the order in the thirteenth century. This powerful impetus of ministry for the sake of Jesus' mission remained unchanged. But in this tragic moment, a shift took place in the sense of mission. This moment in time revealed that ministry meant more than

9. Schwind, p. 319.

Horizons Broaden and Ministries Flourish

working for an institution; it meant being part of a generous and loving Community engaged in the work of the Church. This moment too was a strand in the converging forces for what followed, and a foretelling of the pilgrim Church waiting in the wings of Vatican Council II. For in its unfolding, the web of connections beyond the Congregation became evident, and the willingness of Sisters to go wherever the need was great became apparent. The magnitude of loss felt among people far and wide was expressed by one woman's comment, "The whole church mourns."[10]

The fragility of life, the futility of certitude, the significance of the impending changes were expressed in the last letter of Mother Victor as she anticipated the end of her era and the beginning of a new moment in the history of Church and world:

> The rapid changes and continued progress of our times will take extreme poverty of spirit not to cling too much to the past. The present is our challenge and we must meet it as Dominic would were he here today! In short, Sisters, what you and I must do today to be witnesses to Christ in the world is: Find Dominic's tune for this nuclear space age; find what our witness must be and then adapt and translate Dominic's tune to these needs.[11]

These, then — culture, country, Vatican Council II, and an exceptionally tragic event — are some of the major strands that converged on the lives of Sisters living in the mid-sixties. The Sisters pondered all of this in their hearts. When they gathered for the General Chapter of 1966, they were ready to analyze, scrutinize, discuss, dissect, and debate during endless committee meetings. General Chapters, which had previously lasted only one week, were now extended over many weeks in the summers. Even special Chapters were called in between the General Chapters. And always, the goal was the same: to find that "tune" of our founder Dominic, and that message of the Gospel of Jesus, and so move forward into the "what next" of our lives together.

"The whole church mourns."

---

10. Schwind, p. 319.
11. Letter of Mother Victor Flannery, Feast of SS. Simon and Jude, October 28, 1964, Marywood Archives.

MINISTRY

Sisters Respond to the Converging Strands

All across the nation, Sisters began to ask for dispensations from their vows.

An unexpected response to the changes in the Church after Vatican Council II and the cultural transformation of the sixties was the exodus of many women from the sisterhood. All across the nation shortly after the close of Vatican Council II, Sisters began to ask for dispensations from their vows. They left for many reasons; some had been unhappy for years, but had been hindered by the disgrace connected with leaving. Any such shame fell away with the new view of Church and Religious Life. Some left because they couldn't think of a reason to stay. Others fell in love and left to get married, or to live a single life. Still others were swept up in the wave of those leaving. A few realized that their choice to join the convent had never really been a free one, but rather the fulfillment of parental or societal expectations. The Grand Rapids Dominican Sisters saw 208 Sisters leave between the years 1966 and 1972. The Directory for the year 1966-67 lists 857 Sisters.

Sr. Eileen Popp in pastoral ministry

Those who stayed had new options. For the first time ever, beginning in 1967, Sisters would be asked their preferences for assignments. They were asked if they wanted to return to their assignment or seek an alternative. They were asked if they were happy; and they were asked what skills or abilities they had that might be utilized. In other words, the Sisters were asked for their input regarding the apostolic work of their lives. They would receive their appointments after consultation and before August 15th to give them more time for the transition. It was a new moment, confusing for some, energizing for others.

The Sisters were called to be about the work of making peace, of doing justice, and of study to act responsibly as individuals and as a body.

An office for Personnel Services was established for the Congregation. Although her role was not fully developed, the director of Personnel Services was charged with the task of helping Sisters find suitable placements in ministry. The first director recalls, "It was pretty nebulous as to what it was going to be. It was new. . . . the role kept getting defined. . . . I owe a lot of people in our Congregation apologies for calling them at ungodly hours and so on and trying to get them to go to places. . . ."[12] The days of passive

12. S. Nancy Malburg, Oral History, July 29, 2009, Marywood Archives.

acceptance of an appointment were replaced with days of discussion, discernment, negotiation, and preparation.

Sisters took to heart the call by the membership to be about the work of making peace, of doing justice, and of study to act responsibly as individuals and as a body. They moved into positions as directors of religious education, pastoral ministers, or pastoral associates. Music teachers became parish liturgists and/or retreat directors; Sisters with administrative skills moved into positions as parish administrators — especially in areas where the shortage of priests was acute, such as northern Michigan and some places in New Mexico. Diocesan positions opened up in New Mexico, Michigan, and elsewhere. Sisters served in adult education, family life, Hispanic ministry, jail ministry, Christian service, vocations, diocesan personnel offices, religious education resource centers and bookstores, apostolate to persons with disabilities, ministry for the deaf, Native American ministry, midwifery, and hospital chaplaincy.

Sr. Rose Callahan, an advocate for religious education for all children

Sr. Joanne Toohey, far right, engaging with parishioners in ministry

Some Sisters moved out of the Catholic milieu and into the public sector — nursing in public hospitals, teaching in charter or public schools, in adult education programs, music, art, and programs to teach English to speakers of other languages. Sisters opted to work on behalf of peace and justice efforts at every level in any organization where their skills and the needs were a good fit. Sisters worked for The Salvation Army as counselors and advocates for unwed mothers. Others were administra-

Sr. Anne Francis Erndt ministering at the Bay Regional Medical Center in Bay City, Michigan

MINISTRY

Sr. Justine Kane, far right, instructing teachers on the integration of science and literacy

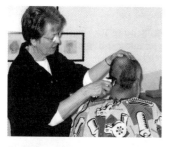

Sr. Marjorie Stein offers a free haircut to a client at the Heartside Ministry.

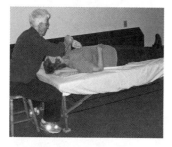

Sr. Mario Pavoni eases sore muscles through her ministry in physical therapy.

tors working on behalf of the homeless, for juvenile justice, or against the death penalty. Sisters in food service left their roles cooking in the convents and served as nutritionists and directors in public school cafeterias and nursing homes. Others became trained as hair stylists. Still others became pastoral ministers in parishes.

Some Sisters began their own ministries based on their talents and skills and the needs of people. Some of these include a specialized form of physical therapy, a consulting business for Religious Congregations and businesses, psychotherapy, pharmacy for low income people, therapeutic massage, and media services.

Sisters became known as authors, composers, and artists as they pursued their interests, developed their talents, and gave generously of their time and efforts — giving witness as members of the pilgrim Church described in *Lumen Gentium*.

Everywhere on Earth

Since their arrival in Michigan in 1877, the Dominican Sisters served primarily in Michigan and New Mexico with some years in Canada. With the new opportunities offered by Vatican Council II, Sisters began to fan out far and wide. The first major mission outside the United States was Chimbote, Peru. This foray into new mission territory was in response to a request in the early 1960s, wherein both the Master General of the Dominican Order and Pope John XXIII requested Religious

Horizons Broaden and Ministries Flourish

Congregations of women in the United States to send missionaries to Latin and South America.[13]

Sister Joan Williams began ministry in Honduras in 1998. She currently works in San Pedro Sula with Sister Doris Regan, a Dominican Sister of Peace. Together they work in religious education, prison ministry, and support for those suffering from HIV/AIDS. In speaking of their ministry in prison, Sister Joan says that they soon look beyond the crime to see the person and this generates mutual respect, appreciation, and gratitude.

After the fall of the Iron Curtain in 1989, countries where religion had been suppressed needed help to understand the changes in the Church since Vatican Council II — a reality that had bypassed them. The National Conference of Catholic Bishops in Washington, DC, maintained an Office to Aid the Catholic Church in Central and Eastern Europe for just this purpose. From 1993 to 1997, Sister Lucianne Siers worked in this office as the Coordinator of Volunteers to Central and Eastern Europe for the purpose of assisting in the efforts to rebuild the Catholic Church after the collapse of Communist governments. Several Grand Rapids Dominicans with family roots in Eastern Europe or with a desire to serve in this capacity volunteered for duty.

Specific instances of Sisters' initiatives in beginning specialized ministry include Sister Mario Pavoni's LOOKING IN, MOVING OUT, which utilized the Feldenkrais ® method of physical therapy; Sister Carmelita Murphy, LEAD, Inc., consultant to Nonprofit Organizations and Religious congregations; Sister Eva Silva, INNERWORK, Inc. psychotherapy; Sister Phyllis Klonowski, CRXP, a pharmacy for the underserved population; Sister Ann Norman, massage therapist; Sister Barbara Hansen, who works in public television; and Sisters Julia Nellett and Marge Stein, who are certified hair stylists.

In prison ministry, the Sisters look beyond the crime to see the person and this generates mutual respect, appreciation, and gratitude.

Sr. Joan Williams (holding the umbrella) serving in ministry in San Pedro Sula, Honduras

13. Schwind, pp. 307-8.

In 1993 Sisters Lucianne Siers and Brigid Clingman traveled to Romania for this purpose. First in Bucharest and then in Baia Mare, the Sisters worked with groups to teach the documents of Vatican Council II and to coach them in community building and communication skills.

Srs. Juliana and Elizabeth Barilla ministering to the people in post-Communist Hungary

In 1995 Sisters Carmelita Murphy and Phyllis Ohren traveled to the Czech Republic and to Slovakia to meet with Dominican Congregations who had stopped admitting new members in the 1940s. They began again to admit new members in the 1980s and were in need of "bridge builders" to help them develop processes for formation post–Vatican Council II.

Sisters Juliana and Elizabeth Barilla had maintained their ancestral language from their childhood years in Saskatchewan, Canada, where their parents spoke Hungarian. They spent several years teaching with the Greek-rite Catholic community in Hungary. They found the people eager and grateful for help in learning about Vatican Council II.

Sister Emeliana Judis had maintained fluency in the Lithuanian language from her childhood. Also well into her retirement years, she journeyed to her ancestral homeland where she too found people eager to update and understand the changes brought about by Vatican Council II.

Srs. Jean Reimer, Thomasine Bugala, and Jean Marie Jones ministering to the people of Russia

Sister Jeanne Marie Jones traveled to Riga, Latvia, where she worked for six weeks in 1995 to assist the seminary in organizing their library. A couple of years later, Sister Jeanne Marie, along with Sisters Jean Reimer and Thomasine Bugala, journeyed to the Diocese of Novosibirsk to assist in whatever ways they could and to offer pastoral support to the people there. Although their ministry was not long, they were changed by the witness of the long-suffering people and one hopes the benefit was mutual.

For many years, Sister Jeannine Kalisz had been a successful teacher in Michigan and New Mexico, but she was a woman with a missionary heart for more distant shores. Sister Jeannine chose to continue her work first in Chimbote, Peru, then in Guatemala, and finally in Papua New Guinea, where she joined her brother, Bishop Raymond Kalisz, SVD, for eight years by teaching and ministering wherever she was needed.[14]

Another Sister with a deeply missionary heart is Sister Jean Reimer, a compassionate skilled nurse with a gift for languages and a survivor of earthquakes and terrorists. Sister Jean was assigned to work as a nurse first in New Mexico then in California hospitals. While working in El Centro, California, in 1970, she asked if she could work in Mexicali, Mexico. Her work was sponsored by LAMP (Latin American Mission Program). The director of LAMP asked her to consider going to Guatemala to minister and also study Spanish.

Sister Jean served as a missionary in Chimaltenango, Guatemala, from 1971 to 1981. In April 1975 she was joined by Sister Jeannine Kalisz. On February 4, 1976, Sisters Jean and Jeannine survived a tremendous earthquake that killed over 2,000 people and destroyed entire villages.

After several months' recovery in Michigan, Sister Jean returned to Guatemala in 1977 as a pastoral minister for San Bernabe Parish in Acatenango, in the Diocese of Solala. Sisters Helen LaValley and Ann Porter joined her in the work of building faith communities. When the three Sisters came back to Grand Rapids for a home visit in 1980, they indicated that the political situation was becoming very tense. Hoping to enhance their personal safety, the Prioress, Sister Teresa Houlihan, and her Council asked them to attend a six-week Maryknoll program and then attach themselves to a Maryknoll team serving in Guatemala. After the six-week program, Sisters Jean and Helen chose to return to Guatemala (Sister Ann Porter opted not to return) to transfer all their ministries to the local leaders and then return to the United States.

Sr. Jeannine Kalisz ministering in Papua, New Guinea

Sr. Jean Reimer and friend in Guatemala

---

14. S. Jeannine Kalisz, interviewed by S. Mary Navarre, 2008, DVD format, Marywood Archives. S. Thomasine Bugala, Oral History, 2010, Marywood Archives.

About a week before they were to return to Grand Rapids, on November 19, 1981, the two Sisters were kidnapped and held for five days by Guatemalan military forces. There was great fear that they would suffer martyrdom as many had before them. In their captivity, they prayed to accept their death with courage. International pressure from the United States State Department and church groups brought about the Sisters' release. They returned to Grand Rapids on November 26, 1981, to the joyous ringing of the Marywood tower bell.

In their Guatemalan captivity, the Sisters prayed to accept their death with courage.

New Ministries within the Boundaries of the United States

In 1982 as a means of offering more diverse opportunities for ministry, the Grand Rapids Dominicans joined eighteen other Congregations (and over 10,000 Women and Men Religious) in the Ministry Resource Center, Inc.[15] Through the auspices of this national office housed in Chicago, the Sisters were encouraged to join with other Congregations of Women and Men Religious to go wherever the need was great and their skills were an apt fit. Through networking with this organization, Sisters began working in both the southeastern and southwestern regions of the United States.

Sister Angelina Abeyta, bilingual in Spanish and English, became a researcher for the Ministry Resource Center, Inc. Sister travelled throughout the Southwest on behalf of the organization. She identified dire needs in the twelve dioceses she visited, and she developed mobile teams of ministers to work in three Texas dioceses to develop lay ministry programs for the people of the areas. In response to the specific needs of women living in some areas of Texas, she moved to El Paso, where she coordinated a team working to better the lives of women living on the border between El Paso, Texas, and Juarez, Mexico. Known as the *Centro Mujeres de la Esperanza* (The Center for

Sr. Darlene Sikorski ministering in Louisiana

---

15. MRC "widens the options available to individuals and opens out the possibility of planned collaboration with participating congregations." Printed in *Chapter Matters,* June 15, 1982, Marywood Archives.

Women of Hope), this organization continues to work through education and advocacy to change structures that oppress women.

Sister Ellen Mary Lopez, born in Texas in a bilingual family, served the Hispanic population through her role as a pastoral minister in both Gratiot County in the Saginaw Valley and later in the Archdiocese of Detroit.

Two Sisters chose to work among the poor in Louisiana. Sister Darlene Sikorksi tutored Houma Indian and Cajun French women at the Community Development Center on the South Laforche Bayou in Galliano, Louisiana. Here women were tutored in literacy skills and earned their GED (General Educational Diploma). Sister Darlene summed up her ministry thus: "Working with these women is ministry at its best. They are here because they want to be, they are highly motivated, and they are capable, intelligent people — we're simply facilitating and guiding their learning."[16]

Sister Mary Martens, once a mathematics professor at Aquinas College, spent her later years working as a lawyer for the poorest people in Monroe, Louisiana. She assisted clients with civil law cases, such as those threatened with eviction or repossession of their homes, bankruptcy, and other civil and domestic problems. She found it rewarding to help her clients navigate through a legal system whose intricacies are more baffling than most due to the fact that the system is based on the Civil Code established by the French emperor Napoleon in 1804.[17]

While several Sisters left teaching for other types of ministry, educational ministry continued with Sisters taking new positions in the southern part of the United States — new territory for the Grand Rapids Dominicans. Sisters Edith Marie Schnell, William Mary Conway, Mon-

(Left to right) Sr. Jackie Bennett, Mrs. Jane Cook, and Srs. William Mary Conway and Monica Meyer prepare Workshop Way materials.

---

16. S. Darlene Sikorski, OP, *Tessera*, Spring 1991, p. 12.
17. S. Mary Martens, "Conversion of Heart," *Tessera*, Winter 1993, p. 11.

ica Meyer, Rosanne Szocinski, Lorraine Rajewski, Jackie Bennett, Joyce Ann Hertzig, Lucianne Siers, and Anthony Therese Pacek all found ministries in education in Louisiana, Georgia, Alabama, Texas, California, and Florida.

Some Sisters felt a call to work with indigenous peoples of the Native American tribes. Although there was a long tradition of ministry with the peoples of the San Juan Pueblo in New Mexico, expansion to other tribes and nations began with collaboration among Dominican Congregations. Sister Helen Bueche tutored children from the Cheyenne and Arapaho tribes in northwest Oklahoma. Sister Ann Porter served as pastoral associate and director of religious education at the St. Francis Mission in Sawmill, Arizona.[18]

Most recently, Sisters Margaret Hillary and Mary Louise Stauder minister in St. Ignatius, Montana, with the Salish people on the Flathead Indian Reservation.

Two Sisters with degrees in nursing offered their skills in midwifery and women's health in the southern states. Sister Rosemary Homrich assisted in the delivery of many babies as a nurse-midwife in the Mount Bayou area of Mississippi and Sister Linda Thiel served as a nurse in the Mud Creek Clinic in Grethal, Kentucky, where she worked with women who were victims of domestic violence.[19]

Nurse-midwife Sr. Rosemary Homrich, RN, celebrating with a new mother

Sister Sandra Delgado served in the field of adult education in the area of Kentucky known as Olive Hill. Sister Sandra later became a program consultant with the State Office of Adult Education in Frankfort, Kentucky.[20] Sister Evelyn Schoenborn was

---

18. S. Ann Porter, "On Holy Ground: Where God Is, Is Holy," *Tessera*, Spring 1991, p. 14. Mary Pat Beatty, Reminiscences from Sister Ann Porter. E-mail message to the author, June 28, 2011.

19. S. Rosemary Homrich, Oral History, Marywood Archives.

20. S. Sandra Delgado, "A Kentucky Mission-Adult Education," *Futures*, vol. III, no. 2 (Fall 1994), pp. 4-5. "Roman Catholic Diocese of Lexington, KY: Diocesan Hispanic Ministry Pastoral Plan 2003-2006," June 11, 2011, pp. 1-3. Sister Sandra Delgado still later became the first director of the newly established Office of Hispanic Ministry for the Roman Catholic Diocese of Lexington, Kentucky, August 15, 2000. The function of the office was to serve as a resource to parishes as they began to serve Hispanics in their area. A Hispanic pastoral center was set up in June 2001. In October 2001, the first class of Escuela de Ministerios (School of Ministry) graduated.

Horizons Broaden and Ministries Flourish

a companion to Sister Sandra and served as a pastoral visitor for persons in nursing homes.

Support for women, especially those economically disadvantaged, continued in places like Omaha, Nebraska, where Sister Dolorita Martinez directed the Omaha Archdiocesan Hispanic Ministry Office from 1989 to 1993. There she helped initiate the Esperanza (Hope) Project, where Hispanic women gathered for presentations and discussions on topics that were of particular interest to them. She also worked in the Pacific Northwest with underserved populations. In 1993 Sister Joan Alflen joined the Esperanza Project, adding a weekly art class in the basement of the convent. Alice Gutierrez, a lay woman, became co-director of the program, and has carried it forward to the present day.

Two other Spanish-speaking Sisters born and raised in the Saginaw, Michigan, area served populations in particular need of their gifts of cultural understanding and language fluency. Sister Lupe Silva was appointed Associate Vicar for Hispanics and then Vicar for Hispanics in Saginaw — a diocesan post she held from 1983 to 1988. She also served as a board member of the Michigan Farm Workers Coalition.

Sister Dorena Gonzalez, also fluent in the Spanish language, served as an interpreter for the poor in an Indian-Chicano clinic in Omaha, Nebraska.

Srs. Marguerite Cool and Jean Kramer help parents to develop needed skills in the Partners in Parenting program.

Ministry Ventures Closer to Home

In 1996 the Prioress and Council of the Congregation extended an invitation for members to envision new ministries. The establishment of the Ministry Fund afforded the possibility of new ministries to address social needs and capitalize on the gifts and talents of the Sisters.[21]

---

21. S. Barbara Hansen, "New Ministries Ventures," *Dominican Futures*, vol. VII, no. 3 (Fall 1998), pp. 1-2, Marywood Archives.

Several ministries, seeded by that initiative, flourish to this day in the Grand Rapids area. Some continue to be staffed by Sisters, while others have been transferred to capable lay leadership. The following is a summary of these initiatives.

Partners in Parenting, a dream of two Sisters with many years of experience teaching primary grades, continues to benefit children and parents throughout the Grand Rapids region. Sisters Marguerite Cool and Jean Kramer knew it was time to retire from classroom teaching and seek out new ways to fulfill their vocations as Dominicans. They had a dream based on a program called Systematic Training for Effective Parenting. A motor home was customized to serve as a mobile classroom; stenciled on both sides are colorful renditions of children of various ethnic backgrounds as well as the title of the program, *Partners in Parenting.* They have conducted parenting classes mainly in West Michigan, serving private and public schools, Head Start, and various social service agencies. The two also provide individual sessions for parents who request their help or are under court order to learn how to become better parents. "We've committed ourselves to working with women, men and children of diverse backgrounds to reach out to everyone," said Sister Marguerite. "People of all religions and cultures are in our classes. All are created by God and should be included. Everyone is welcome."[22] Over the years they have helped more than 8,000 parents enhance their skills in parenting and anger management through modeling positive behaviors, discipline, and stress reduction techniques. Their ministry began in 1999 and continues today.[23]

Grandville Neighborhood Library and the Grandville Academy of the Arts. In an area on the southwest side of the city of Grand Rapids known as Roosevelt Park, there was a neighborhood association with the determination to make the crime-ridden area a better place for its residents. In the 1990s the seeds were planted for a library and eventually an arts center to provide a much-needed resource for literacy and intellectual development. As a result of collaboration between the Roosevelt Park Neighborhood Association and

> "People of all religions and cultures are in our classes. All are created by God and should be included. Everyone is welcome."
> Sisters Jean Kramer and Marguerite Cool

> "Jesus' message was as simple as love your neighbor. There isn't a better way to do that than to provide opportunities to become the best image of God they can be. The arts are a good common ground for that."
> Sister Kathi Sleziak

22. "Sisters Go Mobile to Offer Program on Parenting Skills," *Faith Magazine,* April 2011, pp. 16-21. Ss. Jean Kramer and Marguerite Cool, "A Dream Come True," *Futures,* vol. VIII, no. 2 (Summer 1999), p. 4.

23. http://www.grdominicans.org/our-ministry/sponsored-ministries/partners-in-parenting (accessed November 9, 2012).

the Dominican Sisters, the library was dedicated on October 24, 1996. Sister Joan Pichette, the first librarian, served from July 1996 to May 2002. Sister Jeanne Marie Jones served from September 2002 until 2004. Today the library has expanded, moved to a larger site, and is staffed by capable lay persons.

Sister Kathi Sleziak was particularly interested in preventing youth violence. After some research, she learned that the arts are a key to prevention. Music, art, dance, and drama are all activities that build confidence and lead to better learning in school. Together with Mary Angelo, director of the Roosevelt Park Neighborhood Association, she brought the dream of an Academy for the Arts into a reality. The arts center opened June 30, 2001, in a primarily Hispanic and African American area of the city that was plagued by gang violence and high crime.

Sr. Kathi Sleziak with Andy and Mary Angelo: Mary and Sr. Kathi founded Grandville Avenue Arts and Humanities, Inc., which includes an arts academy and neighborhood library.

Sister Kathi Sleziak served as the director of the project from July 1, 1997 to 2002. Both the Grandville Avenue Neighborhood Library and the Grandville Avenue Academy for the Arts were later renamed Cook Arts Center and Cook Library Center after a generous donation of the Cook family.[24] For Sister Kathi, the academy springs from deeply held convictions of faith and justice. "This is religion to me. Jesus' message was as simple as love your neighbor. There isn't a better way to love your neighbor than to hold them up and provide opportunities to become the best image of God they can be. The arts are just a real good common ground for that."[25]

The W.O.R.D. Literacy Project started in 1998 with funding from the Congregation's Ministry Fund. W.O.R.D. is an acronym for Writing Opportunities Reading Discov-

Founders and tutors for the W.O.R.D. Project (left to right): Srs. Thomasine Bugala, Vera Ann Tilmann, June Martin, Joellen Barkwell, Mary Ann Ferguson, Ellen Mary Lopez, and Dolorita Martinez

---

24. Both Peter C. Cook, major benefactor, and Mary Angelo, director and promoter, had a strong affinity for this neighborhood where they had grown up.

25. Terri Finch Hamilton, "Art in the right place; Arts academy brings out the best in children, neighborhood," *Grand Rapids Press*, June 9, 2002, p. J1. Charles Honey, "Academy for the Angels: Dominican Sister's Vision for Arts Haven in Poor Neighborhood Becomes Reality," *Grand Rapids Press*, June 30, 2001.

eries. The proposal and grant request was written by Sisters June Martin, Ellen Mary Lopez, Thomasine Bugala, Vera Ann Tilmann, and Dolorita Martinez. The project aimed to provide an intergenerational program of services that work together to support English literacy, that is, the development of reading, writing, listening, speaking, technology, and social skills. There are two prongs to the project: English for Speakers of Other Languages and Homework Assistance and Skills Development.

Sr. Consuelo Chavez teaching English to speakers of other languages

The site for implementing W.O.R.D. was Steepletown, a low-income and largely Hispanic area in Grand Rapids, Michigan, that included the parishes of St. Adalbert, St. James, St. Mary, SS. Peter and Paul, and Sacred Heart.[26] (The name of the area reflects the numerous steeples from the many ethnic parishes there.)

The program of English for Speakers of Other Languages has benefited from the direction of three Dominican Sisters, Sisters Thomasine Bugala, Angelina Abeyta, and as of this writing, Carmen Rostar. The students come from many different countries, including Belarus, China, Dominican Republic, Guatemala, Panama, Mexico, Peru, Vietnam, Russia, Yugoslavia, Bosnia, and Croatia. The program continues to flourish in the west wing of Marywood on Fulton Street.

Homework Assistance and Skills Development (HASD) has been in operation since 1998 with Sister Vera Ann Tilmann as director. Sister Vera Ann had a dream to find ways to provide tutoring — especially to families who might not be able

Sisters teach in the W.O.R.D. project: (back row, left to right): Sr. Carmen Rostar, Director; Srs. Diane Dehn, Mary Courtade, Ann Norman, Doris Faber, and Jean Reimer; (front row, left to right): Srs. Margaret Kienstra, Janice Mankowki, Josine Schafer, and Patricia Kennedy

26. Notes from the original proposal for the W.O.R.D. program found in the Archives. S. Barbara Hansen, "New Ministry Ventures," *Dominican Futures*, vol. VII, no. 3 (Fall 1998), p. 2.

to afford it for their children. She knew that without strong literacy skills it is very difficult to make progress in any area of academics. Although Sister Vera Ann retired in 2011, the program continued under the capable leadership of lay persons.

Sr. Vera Ann Tilmann with children in the homework assistance program

The Family Literacy Program began in 1998 in an effort to advance learning among different generations of adults and children. Sister Joellen Barkwell directed this component for one year; she was followed by Sister Phyllis Supancheck, who directed the program from 1999 through 2002. The specific title was the Drop-In-and-Learn for children and the DiaLEARN program for adults. The children worked on reading, writing, board games, and computer skills. The adults learned to read and write in Spanish and in English.

Yet another ministry new to the Sisters was to unfold. *The Prayer and Listening Line at Marywood* was literally a dream of several Sisters who were retired from active ministry. Sister Eileen Popp said, "It came to me in a dream," when asked about the beginnings of the Ministry of the Prayer and Listening Line. In 1989 Sister Eileen was to celebrate her Golden Jubilee as a Dominican Sister. Jubilees, anniversaries, and special birthdays are always good times to ask, "What should I do with the rest of my life?"

The Prayer and Listening Line 2000 (standing, left to right): Srs. Karen Thoreson, Eileen Popp, and Emeliana Judis, (seated, left to right) Srs. Lois Schaffer and Elizabeth Barilla

For Sister Eileen and her two classmates and friends, Sisters Karen Thoreson and Emeliana Judis, who had similar dreams, that dream took form as a ministry for those seeking spiritual assistance through prayer and a listening presence.

Who called the Prayer and Listening Line?[27] Christians, Jews, and Muslims; the churched and the unchurched; men, women, and children; those in financial, medical, or spiritual crisis; those with a crisis in personal or family relations; those in need of housing, work, health care, community, or love; the lonely, anxious, ill, heartbroken, or grieving; those who sought success in studies, job searches, or special projects; those seeking God.

As the ministries of the Dominican Sisters of Grand Rapids diversify and flourish and as their horizons broaden far beyond the familiar, much changes or so it seems. One thing, however, remains the same — that is the undying conviction among the Sisters of who they are and what they are about. As stated in the Constitution of the Grand Rapids Dominicans:

> We undertake with courage, confidence and joy the work and the risks involved in bringing about the *"new creation"* of the Risen Lord. Within our means and relying on God's help, we prepare ourselves to engage in any role necessary to promote justice, to empower the powerless and oppressed, to teach the unknowing and to sustain the efforts of all who seek to live fully human lives.[28]

And so we do.

---

27. As of this writing, the Prayer and Listening Line has ceased operation.
28. *Constitution & Statutes*, #14, p. 6.

CONCLUSION

The View from Here

Don't roll our love
In musty parchment
and prison us with
Ancient manuscripts,
Or speak of us
In past tense,

. . . .

See us now,
Loving in this living day,
With beating hearts
Against the warm breast
Of this decade.[1]

SUZANNE ZUERCHER, OSB

---

1. Suzanne Zuercher, OSB, *I Don't Expect an Answer* (Nashville: Winston-Derek Publishers, 1991), p. 65.

CONCLUSION

Although written decades ago, the message of the poem holds true today. We are not yet ready to be spoken of in the past tense. Our hearts still beat in this decade. To the question of the future of Religious Life, the best answer is the one given in the title of the collection of poems by Sister Zuercher — *Don't Expect an Answer*. No one really knows the future of Religious Life. Fewer women are entering and remaining in Congregations of whatever kind — more traditional or more contemporary. The large numbers of entrants of the 1950s and early 1960s were an anomaly of the postwar generations. Except for a time in the twelfth century with the phenomenon known as the Beguines, the numbers of women entering any kind of communal or religious life have always been few. Yet a few nuns sent as missionaries to America built the schools and hospitals that laid the foundation for a robust Catholic presence in the United States. They went where the "harvest was great, and the laborers few." Small numbers, few possessions, few corporate responsibilities enabled those early pioneers to nimbly move wherever they were called to serve.

But that was then; where do we stand now?

We are resourceful, intelligent, prayerful, and pastoral women; known for our friendliness, appreciated for our "down to earth" ways in daily life and our soaring liturgical celebrations when we gather to praise, to bless, and to preach. This then is our story of how we lived from 1966 to the present time, navigating the enormous changes of Church, culture, and our own Religious lives. It is a story that needs to be told by those who lived it.

It has been my privilege to bring a unified narrative voice to the storytelling of the Sisters who wrote essays, answered e-mails, engaged in conversations, did research, and offered resources for this story. Those who observed from afar have written histories of Women Religious in the United States; but there is a danger in the story told by others, as the author Chimamanda Ngozi Adichie reminds us. The story as told by others, she says, "creates stereotypes, and the problem with stereotypes is not that they are untrue, but that they are incomplete.... The consequence of the single story is this: It robs people of dignity. It makes our recognition of our equal humanity difficult. It emphasizes how we are different rather than how we are similar."[2]

For Sisters, too, there is a danger of the story told by others. Some have

---

2. See TED conference 2009; available here: http://www.youtube.com/watch?v=D9Ihs241zeg.

Conclusion

written of us as victims of a hierarchy, double-crossed in the words of one author.³ Others, in films and television, portray a view of Sisters as naïve and childlike; ruler-wielding classroom tyrants; or quaint and irrelevant do-gooders out of touch with the real world.

Still others tell the story of Women Religious whom they perceived to have "lost their way," becoming "radical feminists," out of line with their role as consecrated women in the Catholic Church.

This latter assessment, along with the drop in numbers entering Religious Life, fueled two Vatican-based investigations of Congregations of Women Religious in the United States in 2008. The first of these was the Apostolic Visitation by the Vatican's Congregation for Institutes of Consecrated Life and Societies of Apostolic Life. This action evoked incredulity, astonishment, and angst in the hearts and minds of many in the United States and across the world. Thousands of people from all walks of life, every religion, and many nations voiced support for Sisters and dismay that their lives were being questioned by the Vatican. The results of the assessment were submitted in 2012 with the report of Mother Mary Clare Millea, ASCJ, to Archbishop Joseph Tobin. Although the final report may never be made public,⁴ Mother Millea stated the following in a press release at the conclusion of her work:

> As a religious myself, I am keenly aware of our history and vital role in the Church in the United States. I also see the joys and hardships of religious life daily in my own community. But as I learned of and observed firsthand the perseverance of the religious in the United States in their vocations, in their ministries and in their faith — and witnessed the fruits of their service — I have been both inspired and humbled. Although there are concerns in religious life that warrant support and attention, the enduring reality is one of fidelity, joy, and hope.⁵

For Sisters, too, there is a danger of the story told by others.

---

3. See Ken Briggs, *Double-Crossed: Uncovering the Catholic Church's Betrayal of American Nuns* (New York: Doubleday, 2006). Although he does portray an accurate accounting of events, most Sisters do not claim to be victims of the clergy.

4. The report of the Apostolic Visitation was completed December 16, 2014, online: http://press.vatican.va/content/salastampa/en/bollettino/pubblico/2014/12/16/0963/02078.html

5. Press release January 9, 2012, found at: http://www.apostolicvisitation.org/en/materials/close.pdf.

CONCLUSION

Also in 2008, the Vatican Congregation for the Doctrine of the Faith (CDF) announced a Doctrinal Assessment of the Leadership Conference of Women Religious (LCWR). Eighty percent of the Congregations of Women Religious in the United States belong to this organization. While acknowledging the LCWR's laudable promotion of social justice issues, the investigators felt that failure to promote the official Church position on various issues was serious enough to necessitate the appointment of an Archbishop and two delegate Bishops to oversee the workings of the LCWR for five years. As of this writing, the issue has not been entirely resolved. Both the Apostolic Visitation and the Doctrinal Assessment of the LCWR elicited enormous publicity for Women Religious in this country. This was an unfamiliar experience for most. Although disheartened by the implications of impropriety, the Sisters were also amazed and encouraged by the outpouring of gratitude and acknowledgement from the people who had come to know and appreciate them and their service over the decades. They responded to the assessment with a reasoned hope that dialogue about the issues would resolve the misunderstandings therein.

*   *   *

In these pages, the story is told by those who lived it. For me, as the narrator, the view is somewhat like the rider who pauses at the top of the Ferris wheel. The view is panoramic, stunning, even breathtaking. What do I see?

I see that most Sisters go about their work of teaching, healing, preaching, comforting, visiting the sick and imprisoned; administering and providing pastoral services in parishes without priests; advocating for the disadvantaged, counseling, offering spiritual direction, caring for each other and for Earth, tending libraries and archives; writing and creating works of art that illuminate and reflect God's own creativity. In a word, most Sisters are about serving Jesus' mission, and do not see themselves as victims, naïve, or irrelevant. Investigations and assessments flare up, come and go, but what sustains and strengthens the Sisters in their living remains a deep prayer life, study of and reflection on Scripture, and the strength that comes from shared community and service.

I see that the courage and faith, the risk-taking and fortitude of the Sisters following the post-Conciliar changes were not unlike that of the first

What sustains the Sisters in their living remains a deep prayer life, study of and reflection on Scripture, and the strength that comes from shared community and service.

Conclusion

Dominican Sisters who left the familiar security of their Bavarian home for the unknown shores of New York City; and then again left the frontier town of Traverse City to heed the call to yet another home in Grand Rapids, Michigan.

I see that the integrity of those who study and sign corporate stances, petition for a more just government, make phone calls and write Congress for laws protecting the most vulnerable, or serve time in prison on behalf of a hope for a nuclear-free world is not unlike those early Sisters who signed the request to relinquish their privileged status as second order Dominicans in order to be third order Dominicans — active, apostolic, and less prestigious.

I see bravery in those who travel alone or with one other to administer parishes in remote places where no priest is available. They are not unlike the risk-takers who boarded a train for the unknown lands of the southwestern United States; or, conversely, left the secure family and familiar culture and language of the southwest for the cold and strange land of Michigan; or boarded a plane for the distant shores of Chimbote, Peru, San Pedro Sula, Honduras, or other lands far from home.

I see a few women, including widows and mature singles, who respond to the call to join an active apostolic Religious Life. Since the late 1970s, women who choose to enter Religious Life are more likely to have graduated from college. Some have postgraduate degrees and many have their professional careers underway.

And I see the phenomenon of hundreds of lay women and men responding to the charism and values of Congregations of Women Religious and making promises of commitment to the charisms of a given Order through Associate Life or through comparable arrangement. In either case, the call is to a deeper spiritual life and a commitment to the mission of Jesus.

Much has changed since 1966. The visual signs of habit, horarium, status, common work, prescribed prayer, relationships with the world itself — all have changed for most of the Sisters, and in the words of Yeats, have "changed utterly" — yet the "terrible beauty remains." It is the beauty of life given to God — a life lived with simplicity and detachment from material goods; a life in the quest for the living God, in the messiness of human attachments; a life of personal responsibility informed by a mature Christian conscience and vowed to deep listening, discernment, and cooperation with those vested with authority.

CONCLUSION

Finally, this is the story of the life of seasoned veterans serving in the ministry of Jesus who know full well that both cross and the hope of resurrection await those who "bear witness to the truth" and who commit themselves to "save and not to judge, to serve and not be served."[6]

From the vantage point of fifty years, one sees beauty, both terrible and serene, and always in the distance — the shadow of the cross. The stitches of the tapestry have held. As each member once stitched a fragment to make a beautiful whole, and each whole tapestry reveals the vast tableau of seasons and the liturgical year, so the members of the Congregation have held together, have not fragmented, but rather continue to pray and study together, to love each other in Community and serve generously with the gifts each brings to the mission of Jesus. Together the individual Sisters constitute that "joyful sisterhood based on the shared blessings of faith and the mutual enjoyment of the lives and gifts of the others."[7]

One sees beauty, both terrible and serene, and always in the distance — the shadow of the cross.

6. *Gaudium et Spes*, #3.
7. *Constitution & Statutes*, #24, p. 7.

APPENDIX 1: WORKING ASSUMPTIONS FOR THE HISTORY PROJECT TASK FORCE

(Adapted from the COR [Claiming Our Roots] Team of Sisters, Servants of the Immaculate Heart of Mary, Monroe, Michigan)

1. All history is grounded in fact.
2. History in all its forms is interpretive.
3. History can be constructed from all forms of media; written, oral, visual, and audio sources.
4. Construction of history can employ educated guesses.
5. We will be conscious of our own biases.
6. We will meet for extended collaborative sessions throughout the project.
7. We will make decisions based on consensus.
8. Resources needed for the project will be available to the committee.
9. Material produced will be well researched and communally critiqued.
10. We will not personalize criticism of our individual work.
11. We will employ constructive criticism of individual and communal work.
12. We will offer and use our gifts for individual tasks and communal sub-committee needs.
13. We will hold in confidence sensitive materials and discussion. What is discussed in the committee stays in the committee.

APPENDIX 2: STATEMENT OF POLICY AND INVESTMENT OBJECTIVES

The Sisters of the Order of St. Dominic of Grand Rapids
October 28, 2005
Revised February 2006
Revised May 2011
Revised March 2013

V. SOCIALLY RESPONSIBLE INVESTING

Motivated by the desire to use economic power responsibly, the Congregation strives toward integrity of investment policy and procedure. Integrity embraces and includes a high degree of moral and ethical sensitivity to social responsibilities; demands managerial competence, financial expertise, and careful research; and requires the exercise of responsible judgment in matching investment growth and income values with an acceptable risk-reward ratio.

The General Council will work in collaboration with the Conference on Corporate Responsibility of Indiana and Michigan (CCRIM), the Interfaith Center on Corporate Responsibility (ICCR) and other appropriate groups in evaluating investment opportunities. The Prioress or her delegate shall exercise the right to vote proxies. The General Council may choose to own equities and fixed income securities in companies that perform poorly in social responsibility ratings for the purpose of applying pressure, as a shareholder, to correct this situation.

Responsible stewardship requires knowledge and expertise in the investment field and the time to research changes in the economy. Therefore, the General Council shall employ Managers to administer major portions of the funds available for investment. These Managers, selected for high repute and competent performance, are accountable to the General Council. The Managers shall be advised of the Philosophy of Investments and Guidelines for Investment and strive to carry out the objectives of the agreement in all details.

The Congregation uses three strategies in its exercise of Corporate Responsibility.

(a) It channels investments toward socially responsible purposes. In particular, it considers investments in corporations which:

manifest responsible stewardship of the earth's resources and engage in environmentally sound practices

respect the dignity of the human person in employment practices, humane work environments and in production of safe and healthy products

utilize corporate profits responsibly as with profit-sharing and just wages for employees

encourage and foster the hiring and advancement of women and minorities

are operating or investing in the post-apartheid South Africa, are promoting equal rights of all citizens regardless of race and are contributing to the building of just social structures

are engaged in conversion away from military-oriented research, development or production.

(b) It diverts investments away from destructive uses. In particular, it refrains from investing in businesses which:

manufacture nuclear weapons

are among top 25 weapons contractors

own nuclear power facilities

develop or produce biological or chemical weapons

produce tobacco and/or tobacco products with revenues greater than 3%

APPENDIX 2

produce abortifacients; perform embryonic stem cell or fetal tissue research

ignore World Health Organization recommended practices in under developed countries

lend money to and/or refinance loans for regimes whose policies and practices repress the political, economic and religious rights of its citizenry

do not attain satisfactory Community Reinvestment Act ratings

produce pornographic materials or services

(c) It is an activist investor. It may:

retain/buy shares in companies which have destructive or unethical practices in order to gain the right to file resolutions

attend shareholder meetings

meet with the management over issues

vote the proxies

write letters to encourage positive movements and to educate on issues of difference

APPENDIX 3: LISTS

Chapters and Elections of Prioress and Council by Year

1966 *Fifteenth General Chapter*, election of Srs. Aquinas Weber (Prioress), Letitia VanAgtmael (Vicaress), James Rau (Councilor), Mary Sullivan (Councilor) Marjorie Vangsness (Councilor)

1967 Second Session of the *Fifteenth General Chapter*

1969 *Chapter of Affairs*, published *Religious Life: a Lived Reality*

1970 Summer Session of the Chapter of Affairs

1972 *Sixteenth General Chapter*, election of Srs. Norbert Vangsness (Prioress), Wanda Ezop (Vicaress), Letitia VanAgtmael (Councilor), Thaddeus Kowalinski (Councilor), Bernice Garcia (Councilor), published vol. 2 of *Religious Life: Lived Reality*

1974 *Chapter of Affairs*, First Session

1975 Second session of the *Chapter of Affairs*, published *Supplement to Religious Life: Lived Reality*, vol. 2

1976 *Seventeenth General Chapter*, election of Srs. Norbert Vangsness (Prioress), Aquinas Weber (Vicaress), Elizabeth Eardley (Councilor)

1980 *Eighteenth General Chapter*, election of Srs. Teresa Houlihan (Prioress), Phyllis Ohren (Vicaress), Patrice Konwinski (Councilor)

1984 *Nineteenth General Chapter*, election of Srs. Teresa Houlihan (Prioress), Carmelita Murphy (Vicaress), Patrice Konwinski (Councilor), Joan Thomas (Councilor)

1988 *Twentieth General Chapter*, election of Srs. Carmelita Murphy (Prioress), Barbara Hansen (Vicaress), Margaret Schneider (Councilor), Jarrett DeWyse (Councilor)

1994 *Twenty-first General Chapter,* election of Srs. Barbara Hansen (Prioress), Ann Walters (Vicaress), Dolorita Martinez (Councilor), Lisa Marie Lazio (Councilor)

2000 *Twenty-second General Chapter,* election of Srs. Maribeth Holst (Prioress), Diane Zerfas (Vicaress), Mary Brigid Clingman (Councilor), Darlene Sikorski (Councilor)

2006 *Twenty-third General Chapter,* election of Srs. Nathalie Meyer (Prioress), Maureen Geary (Vicaress), Joyce Ann Hertzig (Councilor), Mary Navarre (Councilor)

2012 *Twenty-fourth General Chapter,* election of Srs. Maureen Geary (Prioress), Sandra Delgado (Vicaress), Lucianne Siers (Councilor), Mary Ann Barrett (Councilor)

BIBLIOGRAPHY

Abbot, Walter M., SJ, general ed. *Documents of Vatican Council II*. New York: Herder & Herder, 1966.

Albuquerque Journal. May 24, 1999. Albuquerque, New Mexico.

Aquinas Magazine. Spring 1983. Aquinas College, Grand Rapids, Michigan.

Beyenka, Barbara, trans. *Rule of St. Augustine*. Sinsinawa Press, 1996.

"The Chimbote Foundation: A Bridge of Love and Hope," a brochure of the Catholic Diocese of Pittsburgh. Spring 2011.

Conn, Sarah A. In *Ecopsychology: Restoring the Earth and Healing the Mind*, ed. T. Roszak. Sierra Club Books, 1995.

Constitution and Statutes. Grand Rapids: Sisters of St. Dominic, 1990.

Delio, Ilia, OSF. *The Emergent Christ*. Maryknoll, NY: Orbis Books, 2011.

Dominican Leadership Conference. "Unless They Be Sent: A Theological Report on Dominican Women Preaching," November 1997.

Dominican Liturgical Commission. *Dominicans at Prayer*. Parable Conference for Dominican Life and Mission, 1983.

Dominican Praise: A Provisional Book of Prayer for Dominican Women. Dominican Sisters, St. Mary of the Springs, Columbus, Ohio; The Sisters of St. Dominic of Akron, Ohio; Sisters of the Order of St. Dominic of Grand Rapids, Michigan; The Sisters of St. Dominic Congregation of the Most Holy Rosary, Adrian, Michigan, 2005.

Eberle, Gary. *Going Where We Are Needed*. Grand Rapids: Aquinas College, 2013.

Faith Magazine. April 2011. Diocese of Grand Rapids, Michigan.

Fiand, Barbara, SNDdeN. *Where Two or Three Are Gathered: Community Life for the Contemporary Religious*. New York: Crossroad, 1992.

———. *Living the Vision: Religious Vows in an Age of Change*. New York: Crossroad, 1990.

Gaillardetz, Richard. "The State of the Church." In *Reflections on the State of American Catholicism Today*. From the Murray/Bacik lecture series. University of Toledo Press, 2011.

Grand Rapids Dominican Sisters. "Cloths of Heaven: The Liturgical Tapestries of Dominican Chapel/Marywood." *Dominican Futures,* vol. XVI, no. 1 (Winter 2007).

———. "A Dream Come True" *Dominican Futures,* vol. VIII, no. 2 (Summer 1999): 4.

Hardesty, Nancy A. *Inclusive Language in the Church.* Atlanta: John Knox Press, 1986.

Kennelly, Karen M., CSJ. *The Religious Formation Conference 1954-2004.* Silver Spring, Maryland, 2009.

Kline-Chesson, Kathleen. "The Living Word: Dance as a Language of Faith," http://www.religion-online.org/showarticle.asp?title=1106.

Kozak, Pat, CSJ, and Janet Schaffran, CDP. *More Than Words.* Rocky River, OH: Creative Offset Printing, 1986.

Lortie, Jeanne Marie, OSB. *Gracious Living.* Duluth: Priory Press, 1970.

Marywood Archives, 2025 East Fulton, Grand Rapids, Michigan.

Meehan, Chris. "A New Moment: Renovated Chapel at Marywood Viewed as a Symbol of Renewal." *Grand Rapids Press,* September 21, 1985.

Miano, Peter J. "Pilgrimage or Tourism." *The Society for Biblical Studies Newsletter,* 30 September 2009, http://www.sbsedu.org/L3_e_newsletter30.9.09PilgrimageTourismB.htm.

Mouroux, Jean. *The Meaning of Man.* New York: Image Books, 1984.

O'Connor, Paschala. *Five Decades: History of the Congregation of the Most Holy Rosary, Sinsinawa, Wisconsin, 1849-1899.* Sinsinawa Press, 1954.

O'Rourke, Kevin. *New Laws for Religious.* Chicago: Cross and Crown, 1967.

Osiek, Carolyn, RSCJ, general editor. *Anselm Academic Study Bible.* Winona, MN: Anselm Academic, Christian Brothers Publication, 2013.

Petit, Ian, OSB. "The History of the Charismatic Renewal," http://www.dentoncatholic.org/history.html.

Religious Life: Lived Reality. Vol. 1. Grand Rapids: Sisters of the Third Order of St. Dominic of the Congregation of Our Lady of the Sacred Heart Marywood, 1969.

Religious Life: Lived Reality. Vol. 2. Grand Rapids: Sisters of the Third Order of St. Dominic of the Congregation of Our Lady of the Sacred Heart Marywood, 1974.

Remen, Rachel Naomi, MD. *My Grandfather's Blessings: Stories of Strength, Refuge and Belonging.* New York: Riverhead Books, 2000.

Bibliography

Schneiders, Sandra. *Buying the Field.* New York: Paulist Press, 2013.

Schwind, Mona. *Period Pieces.* Sisters of the Order of St. Dominic, 1991.

Starn, Orin. "Maoism in the Andes: The Communist Party of Peru-Shining Path and the Refusal of History." *Journal of Latin American Studies,* vol. 27, no. 2 (May 1995).

Teilhard de Chardin, Pierre. *Divine Milieu.* New York: Harper & Row, 1960.

Thompson, Margaret Susan. "History of Women Religious in the United States." Audio CDs. Now You Know Media, 2009.

Tugwell, Simon, OP. *The Nine Ways of Prayer of St. Dominic.* Dublin: Dominican Publications, 1978.

United States Conference of Catholic Bishops, Bishops' Committee on the Liturgy. *Environment and Art in Catholic Worship.* November 1977.

Vatican website: http://www.vatican.va/archive/hist_councils/ii_vatican_council/

Vicaire, M. H. *Saint Dominic and His Times.* New York: McGraw-Hill, 1964.

Vidmer, John. *Praying with the Dominicans.* New York: Paulist Press, 2008.

Wessels, Cletus. *The Holy Web: Church and the Universe Story.* Maryknoll, NY: Orbis Books, 2000.

Western Washington Catholic Charismatic Renewal "Burning Bush Pentecost Novena," http://www.wwccr.org/pentecost/burning_bush.htm.

Wussler, Marilyn, SSND, MS. "Don't is a Four Letter Word." *Human Development* 10, no. 1 (Spring 1989).

Zuercher, Suzanne, OSB. *I Don't Expect an Answer.* Nashville: Winston-Derek Publishers, 1991.

GLOSSARY

Angelus Prayer said three times each day commemorating the Incarnation.

Annals Annual written account of convent events submitted to the Congregation's Central Office at the end of the school year.

Apostolic Refers to the ministry of Sister, i.e., teaching, nursing, social work, counseling, etc.

Apostolic Year One of two years of novitiate — the one in active ministry is the apostolic; the other is the canonical year.

Area Government structure, often regional, begun in 1984 to facilitate participation and communication.

Assembly (General) Meeting of the whole membership every three years.

Associates Non-vowed women and men who desire to practice Christian faith in the spirit of the Dominican Sisters, and go through a process to become a member of Associate Life.

Baltimore Catechism Standard text for religious education (1885-1960s), summarizing Catholic belief and doctrine in a question/answer format. Students memorized much of the catechism.

Bread for the World Alliance of Christians urging the nation's decision makers to enact policies to end hunger at home and abroad.

Canon Regular Priest who lives in community under the Rule of St. Augustine, and shares property in common. St. Dominic was a Canon Regular in Osma de Burgos, Spain.

Canonical Year A novice must spend one year in contemplation and study under the supervision of an appointed director to discern her vocation, learn about the life, and make a free choice to take vows.

Chapter A meeting of members of a religious congregation to elect leaders, review the life of the congregation, and set direction for the future.

Chapter of Affairs A special Chapter wherein members meet to address current affairs or business of the congregation but not to elect leaders.

Charism The particular characteristic, work, and spirit of a religious institute.

Charismatic Renewal A prayer style initiated in 1967 among some Catholics which includes faith healing, glossolalia (speaking in tongues), and emotional expressions of spontaneous prayer.

Cloistered Literally enclosed, referring to rule of enclosure whereby nuns did not leave their convent except for extraordinary reasons. This enabled them to live a life of prayer and contemplation separate from the secular world.

Code of Canon Law Set of rules governing every aspect of the Roman Catholic Church; the 1917 Code of Canon Law was revised in 1983 following Vatican Council II.

Compline The night prayer of the official canonical prayer of the Church; it completes the day.

Coordinator An elected or appointed Sister in a local convent who coordinates the living of the Sisters and acts as a liaison with the central offices of the Congregation.

Council In this context, usually refers to those elected to assist the Prioress in her responsibilities to lead the Congregation for a given term.

Council of Trent An Ecumenical Council held in Trento, Italy, in 1545-1563. It was a major reform council embodying the counter-reformation, establishing dogma, decrees, creeds, and catechism.

Diocese An administrative district under the supervision of a bishop.

Discernment A process whereby an individual seeks to determine God's will through prayer, detachment, and the counsel of others.

Divine Office Also known as the Liturgy of the Hours, it is the recitation of certain prayers at fixed hours according to the order prescribed by the Church.

Doctrines The compilation of teachings that the Catholic Church requires the faithful members to believe.

Dogma Doctrines that the Catholic Church teaches are revealed by God and are therefore irrefutable.

Dominican Days Annual celebration during the first week of August when members gather to celebrate their founder St. Dominic and the Jubilee celebrants of that year.

Don Virgil Michel A Benedictine monk from St. John's Abbey in Collegeville, Minnesota, who was a leader of the liturgical movement in the United States.

Ecclesial Pertaining to the Catholic Church as a community of believers.

Ecumenical Literally "universal." May refer to one of the 21 Councils the Church has called since A.D. 325 or it may refer to the movement toward unification of all separated Churches in Christendom.

Extraordinary Chapters A gathering of members/member delegates held to formally attend to the business of the Congregation, but not to elect new leadership.

Friar A male member of the Dominican Order; he may be ordained or not.

Gathering Days See Dominican Days.

General Chapters Meeting at regular intervals (commonly every six years) to elect leaders and review the quality of life of the Congregation.

Gregorian Chant Liturgical music of the Roman Catholic Church used to accompany Latin texts of the Mass and the Divine Office. It is usually both monophonic and unaccompanied, and it dates from the Middle Ages.

Heresy Denial of a Church doctrine by a baptized member or the belief in a doctrine contrary to revealed truth.

Holy See Official residence of the Pope in Rome, along with administrative offices, tribunals, and departments.

Homiletics The branch of study in theology that treats content and delivery of sermons, homilies, or other religious discourse.

Horarium/Horary Antiquated term for the hourly schedule for each day in the life of a nun.

Hymnody Having to do with singing or writing hymns, i.e., songs of praise to God.

Incarnational Refers to the embodiment of God; the Incarnation is the name given to God's taking on of human form in the person of Jesus.

Lauds Morning prayer of the official canonical prayer of the Church.

LCWR Acronym for the Leadership Conference of Women Religious.

May Crowning Catholic custom popular in the past and still practiced by some today whereby Mary, the Mother of God, is honored in the month of May by prayers, a procession, and placement of a wreath of flowers on the head of a statue of Mary.

Monasticism A way of life characterized by seclusion, prayer, contemplation, keeping a strict rule. Some monastics engage in outside apostolic activity, while others do not leave the monastery except for extraordinary purposes.

Motherhouse Central headquarters of a religious order of women, often, but not always, including the name of the city of the headquarters, e.g., Grand Rapids Dominicans.

Mother General Elected or delegated head of a Congregation of Women Religious.

Moto Proprio A special papal edict.

NETWORK A national Catholic social justice lobby committed to the global movement for justice and peace through the principles of Catholic social teaching. It was begun in 1971 by 47 Catholic Sisters. Membership is open to all.

Novitiate May refer to a place, or a period of time, wherein a woman desiring membership learns what it means and discerns her vocation.

Office of the Dead A prayer in the Divine Office cycle to be said for the repose of the soul of a deceased member.

Office, The Divine Also known as the Liturgy of the Hours or the Breviary, it is the official set of public prayers prescribed by the Church.

OP Acronym for Order of Preachers, the initials following the name of a woman or man who is a member of the Dominican Order.

Pacem in Terris Literally "Peace on Earth"; this encyclical of Pope John XXIII issued on April 11, 1963, was unique in its address to all, not just to Catholics, and its statement that every person has the right to life, to bodily integrity, and to the means for the development of life.

Papal Encyclical A letter sent by the Pope and addressed to Catholic bishops or to a broader audience.

Pax Christi USA A peace movement begun in France after WW I and started in the United States in 1971; consisting mostly of Catholic laity, Religious, and clergy and committed to working for peace for all humankind, witnessing to the peace of Christ.

Perfectae Caritatis The document issued by Vatican Council II which deals specifically with Religious Life in the Church. It was promulgated on October 28, 1965.

Pilgrim People The Pastoral Constitution on the Church in the Modern World, *Gaudium et Spes,* and the Dogmatic Constitution on the Church, *Lumen Gentium,* both use the metaphor of pilgrimage to convey the idea of the Church as a people on a journey toward God.

Practicum Part of a course of study wherein the student is supervised in the practical application of the theories studied, e.g., student teaching.

Prioress The head of a Congregation of Women Religious in the Dominican tradition.

Psalmody A collection of psalms or a composition of psalms for singing.

Psalter A book containing the Book of Psalms, often with musical settings.

Purgatory An intermediary state after death where a soul undergoes purification before admittance into Heaven.

Regensburg/Ratisbon A city in Bavaria, Germany (historically Ratisbon), from which in 1853 four nuns immigrated to America. These four were the foundation of twelve Dominican Congregations. Grand Rapids is one of these twelve.

Sacraments A ritualized outward sign entrusted to the Church to bestow grace. The seven official sacraments mark significant milestones in life.

Stations/Way of the Cross A devotional practice where pilgrims meditate on the suffering and death of Jesus by pausing at 14 stations, each depicting a moment in the last hours of Jesus' life. Specific prayers are said at each station.

Superior Head of a convent of Sisters.

Triune God Catholic belief in the mystery of the Trinity, i.e., there are three persons in one God. They are the Creator (Father), the Redeemer (the Son), and the Holy Spirit sent to earth by God on Pentecost.

Vatican Decree An official document from the Holy See having the force of law.

Vespers The evening prayer of the official canonical prayer of the Church.

Vicaress The councilor elected to assist the Prioress and to take her place if she is incapacitated.

Way of the Cross See Stations of the Cross.

INDEX OF NAMES

Abbott, Walter M., 64-65
Abeyta, Angelina, 59n11, 272, 278
Adichie, Chimamanda Ngozi, 282
Adrienne (Kindergarten teacher), 161
Alflen, Joan, 258, 275
Alflen, Laurena, 34, 36, 159n15
Amman, Elizabeth, 221
Ancona, Gus, 47
Anderson, Catherine, 132
Andres, Innocence, 213, 215-16
Angelo, Andy, 277
Angelo, Mary, 277
Ankoviak, Connie, 11
Atencio, Emilia, 87, 202
Austin, Gerard, 78

Barilla, Elizabeth, 104, 270, 279
Barilla, Juliana, 104, 270
Barkwell, Joellen, 132, 277, 279
Barnett, Jim, 167
Barrett, Mary Ann, xiv, 11, 163, 179
Beatty, Mary Patricia, xiv, 156, 243n11, 274n18
Beckman, Maria Goretti, 245n15, 245n16, 251, 258
Benedict, 51, 234
Bennett, Jacqueline, 142n10, 178, 273-74
Bermudez, Francisco Morales, 222
Bernardin, Joseph, 255
Berrigan, Daniel, 234
Beyenka, Barbara, 118
Birchmeier, Margaret Mary, xiv-xv, 212n3, 212n4, 213-15, 216n7, 216n8, 218n11, 219, 221, 223, 226-28
Birkman, Jean Marie, 67n2, 75n17
Bishop, Alphonsine (Elizabeth), 206
Bloch, Jude, 154, 258
Bockheim, Lillian (Gerarda), 214, 216-17, 221-24, 226-28

Bowler, Killian, 142n10
Boyle, Paul, 73, 79
Bray, Theresa, 127
Brechting, Mary Catherine, 84, 104
Breitenbeck, Joseph, 41, 73, 102
Briggs, Ken, 283n3
Brousseau, Nancy, 178, 234-35
Brown, Janet, 47, 135, 155
Brown, JoAn, 231
Bryan, Thomas Estelle, 202
Buchan, Kim, 44
Bueche, Helen, 142n10, 200-201, 274
Bugala, Thomasine, 186-87, 270, 271n14, 277-78
Bukowski, Arthur, 13, 184
Byrne, Cecile, 96

Callahan, Rose, 160, 267
Calvin, John, 234
Carmody, Lenora, 73, 129n16
Catherine of Siena, 165-66, 234
Chavez, Cesar, 240, 241n5
Chavez, Consuelo, 202, 278
Chavez, Sylvia, 241n5
Chenicek, Barbara, 37-39, 43, 48
Clare, 234
Clarke, Mark, 232-34
Clingman, Mary Brigid, 166-67, 245, 270
Colloton, Paul, 47, 233
Conn, Sarah A., 151-52
Conway, William Mary, 273
Cook, Jane, 273
Cook, Peter C., 277n24
Cool, Marguerite, 153, 275-76
Cosmao, Vincent, 85n30
Courtade, Mary, 278
Coyne, Margaret William, 141
Coyne, Nancy, 15
Culkin, Ann, 70

INDEX OF NAMES

Cushing, Richard, 211n2

Davey, Joanne, 86
Davis, Mary Constance, 78
Dehn, Diane, 155, 195, 278
DeKlerk, F. W., 252n34
Delgado, Sandra, 66, 274-75
Delio, Ilia, 152
DeRycke, Laurice, 232
DeWyse, Jarrett, 39, 85, 102, 231-32
Diana d'Andalo of Bologna, 27
Diego, Bishop, 27
Doherty, Catherine de Hueck, 77
Dominguez, Ada, 202
Dominic, 9, 12, 16, 23, 25-28, 51, 99, 121, 129, 164-65, 182, 195, 203, 232-33, 238n1, 258, 264-65
Donnelly, Mary, xv, 98, 176, 258
Downes, Norena, 204
Dubay, Thomas, 72, 79

Eardley, Elizabeth, 36n4
Easley, Linda, 192-93
Eberle, Gary, 140n5
Eckhart, Meister, 234
Edison, Thomas, 192-93
Ehr, Carolyn, 154
Eichhorn, Suzanne, 20, 247n21
Elemowu, Roseline, 116n1
Elizabeth (cousin of Mary), 28
Emanuel (baby boy), 229
Engbers, Susan, 44
Erlandson, Marguerite, 160n17
Erndt, Anne Francis, 267
Erno, Robert Ann, 84
Ezekiel (prophet), 234
Ezop, Wanda, 159

Fabbro, Amata, 6-7, 13-14, 123n6, 146n19
Faber, Doris, 278
Falkowski, Alice, 157
Farnsworth, Ann Michael, 106
Farrell, Pat, 117n2
Fedder, Mary Jane, 232
Ferguson, Mary Ann, 178, 258, 277
Fiand, Barbara, 147, 149
Fifelski, Constance, 244n14

Flannery, Victor, xx, 61, 109, 119-20, 211-13, 264-65
Frahm, Bede, 14-15, 72n14, 110-11
Francis of Assisi, 234
Friedan, Betty, 78
Fujimori, Alberto, 225
Fyffe, Donna, 231

Gaillardetz, Richard R., 243-44
Galante, Joseph A., 93n5
Galka, G., 5n5
Gallagher, Joseph, 64
Gallmeier, Deborah (Teresa), 147, 159n15
Gancarz, Helen, 157
Gannon, Eileen, 81
Garcia, Bernice, 147n20, 154-55, 201-2, 204, 207
Garcia, Maria Teresita, 213, 218, 222
Geary, Maureen, 121, 173-76, 246n17, 252
Geib, Jim, 192, 194
Gelderloos, Sally Schad, 155
Georgeff, Fran, 160n17, 161, 165-66
Gilbert, Carol, 241n5, 245n15, 246n20, 248, 257
Goeldel, Regina Mary, 153
Gonzales, Angelina, 202, 206
Gonzalez, Chela, 95
Gonzalez, Dorena, 275
Goyette, Francis Borgia, 206
Grinstead, Ruth Beckman, 155, 157
Guevara, Marie Rachael, 257
Gumbleton, Thomas, 79
Gussin, Gabriel Joseph, 221
Gutierrez, Alice, 275
Gutierrez, Gustavo, xvi, 80-82
Guzmán, Abimael, 224-25

Hackett, Estelle, 47, 57
Hale, Carol, 154
Hall, Bridget, 13
Hamilton, Terri Finch, 277n25
Hanley, Philip, 78, 80, 101
Hansen, Barbara, 21, 46, 66, 121, 148, 171, 231-32, 234, 236-37, 253, 255-56, 258, 269, 275n21, 278n26
Hardesty, Nancy A., 8n15, 9n19
Haring, Bernard, 79
Harmer, Catherine, 127

Index of Names

Hartman, Katrina, 85
Hathaway, Millie, 157
Hauser, Agnes Leo, 110-11
Hawkins, Connie, 251n33
Hayward, Ann Banner, 97
Hefferan, Roberta, 135
Heille, Edward, 160n17
Heille, Gregory, 8-9, 20, 30, 40-46, 232
Heins, Alison, 160n17
Heiskel, Ann Frederick, 78
Heitz, Janet Marie, 15, 111
Heitz, Stephanie, 127, 178
Herald, Chris, 74
Hertzig, Joyce Ann, 71, 246n20, 274
Heydens, Don, 44
Hilkert, Cathy, 20
Hillary, Margaret, 5, 74, 127, 146n18, 243n11, 274
Holmes, Marilyn, 178
Holscher, Kathleen, 205n13
Holst, Maribeth, 121, 169, 222
Homrich, Veritas (Rosemary), 213, 216, 274
Honey, Charles, 277n25
Houlihan, Teresa, 7, 19, 29, 37-38, 42, 81, 84, 121, 127, 132, 156, 172, 242, 243n9, 247, 248n23, 271
Housewert, Linda, 159
Hronek, Madelyn (Marie George), 154
Hruby, Norbert, 120, 184-85, 192
Hudson, Jackie, 142n10, 143, 178, 241, 245n16, 248, 251, 257

Ibáñez, Armando P., 176, 177n37

Jacokes, Lee, 186, 187n3, 231
Jane of Aza, 27, 164
Janowiak, Mary Lucille, 159n15
Jaramillo, Eileen, 201-2
Joanna (witness of Resurrection), 28
John (apostle), 28
John XXIII, 12, 203-4, 268
John the Baptist, 28
Joncas, Michael, 33n18
Jones, Jeanne Marie, 241, 270, 277
Jordan of Saxony, 26
Judis, Emeliana, 270, 179-80

Kaiser, Margaret (Francis Bernadine), 155

Kalisz, Jeannine, 218, 270-71
Kalisz, Raymond, 271
Kane, Justine, 268
Kane, Madeleine, 159, 160n17
Kania, Karen, 154
Karasti, Rose, 246n20
Keating, Anne, 186n2
Keller, Valerie, 159n15, 160n17
Kelly, Robert, 47n25
Kennedy, Diane, 163
Kennedy, John F., xix, 260
Kennedy, Patricia, 15, 278
Kennedy, Robert F., xix
Kennelly, Karen M., 106n8
Keough, Mary Ann, 258
Kienstra, Margaret, 278
King, Martin Luther, Jr., xix, 240, 243
Kline-Chesson, Kathleen, 10n21
Klonowski, Phyllis, 39, 127, 269
Konwinski, Patrice, 37, 73
Korson, Peter Mary, 200
Kowalinski, Thaddeus, 126
Kowalski, Georgiana, 213
Kozak, Pat, 7n14
Kozal, Jarek, 34
Kozal, Patricia, 188n4
Kramer, Jean, 275-76
Kreul, Ron, 179
Kroondyk, Cassandra, 160n17
Krushchev, Nikita, 107
Kuhn, Maggie, 79
Kulczyk, Charmaine, 160-61
Kulhanek, Emma, 39
Kuppers, Peter, 196
Kusba, John Therese, 202

LaBell, Elaine, 6, 90, 141n8
Lakoff, Robin, 29
Lalonde, Bertrand, 60
Larkin, Ernest, 73
LaValley, Helen, 243n10, 245n16, 247-48, 251, 271
Lazio, Lisa Marie, 46, 127, 132
Leannah, Lucille, 202
Leckert, Therese, 258
Ledrick, Dorothy, 160n17
Lesinski, Martha, 44
Lewis, Albert, 46

INDEX OF NAMES

Leyba, Orlanda, xv, 127, 199, 202, 247n21, 256n38, 257
Lincoln, David, 47
Loehnis, Laura (Marie Frances), 155
Logue, John Cassian, 219-22
Lopez, Ellen Mary, 71, 273, 277-78
Lortie, Jeanne Marie, 69-70
Lozier, Donald, 78
Luke (evangelist), 13
Lynch, Leonard, 230
Lythgoe, Anne, 170n32

Madoush-Pitzer, Max, 42
Maez, Herman Marie, 211-12
Malburg, Nancy, 59n9, 147, 266n12
Mankowski, Janice, 278
Martens, Mary, 273
Martin, June, 277-78
Martinez, Dolorita, 46, 137, 177, 199, 246n20, 275, 277-78
Mary (Blessed Virgin), 12, 28, 260
Mary (mother of James), 28
Mary Magdalene, 28
McAllister, Robert, 68, 70-71, 78
McCann, Francetta, 177
McDonald, Mary Ellen, xvi, 20-21, 82
McDonnell, Graham, 186
McDonnell, Irene, 85
McElroy, Megan, xvi, 17
McGee, Thomas Marie, 68-69
McKenzie, Jessica, 179
McKenzie, John L., 79
McLuhan, Marshall, 78
McNerney, Charlene, 154
Mead, Margaret, 78
Meehan, Chris, 42n17
Mehr, Aloysius, 73
Meloche, Father, 260
Merrienboer, Edward van, 85, 246
Meyer, Monica, 273-74
Meyer, Nathalie, 95, 121
Miano, Peter J., 49n29
Micaela (adopted baby), 227
Michel, Dom Virgil, 41
Michelangelo, 165
Micka, Mary Anne, 157
Milan, Patricia, 142n10, 142n11
Milhaupt, Jean (Maris Stella), 37-38, 154, 185

Millea, Mary Clare, 283
Miller, Marie Celeste, xv
Mische, Gerald, 80
Mohr, Julia, 44
Mondragon, Charlotte, 11, 201-2
Montreuil, Genevieve, 84
Moore, Ray, 213
Moraczeski, Albert, 45
Moss, Eileen, 156
Mouroux, Jean, 260
Mrozinski, Phyllis, 177
Murphy, Carmelita, 8, 19-20, 40-43, 84, 86, 121, 127, 159n15, 163-65, 167, 231-32, 247n21, 249-52, 269-70
Murray, Jane Marie, 47, 57
Murray, John Courtney, 58
Myerscough, Angelita, 73

Navarre, Mary, xvi-xvii, 44, 84, 127, 260n2, 271n14
Neal, Marie Augusta, 79
Needham, Aline, 72n14
Neiman, Judi (Thomas Francis), 157
Nellett, Dominica, 15
Nellett, Julia, 15, 269
Nelson, R. Paul, 189, 194
Neville, Richard, 67n3
Newton, Elaine M. (Rose Karl), 153n6
Norman, Ann, 269, 278
Nouwen, Henri J. M., 86
Novakoski, Mary Ellen, 127
Nugent, Carole, 161

O'Connor, John, 120
O'Connor, Mary Paschala, 76n21
O'Donnell, Rosemary, 5n4, 10-11, 85
Ogren, Michelle, 233
Ohren, Phyllis, 20, 37, 246n20, 270
Okolocha, Kate, 116n1
Oosdyke, Mary Kay, xvii, 85
O'Rourke, Kevin, 73-74, 76
Orsy, Ladislas, 58, 73, 79
Ortega y Gasset, José, 197
O'Toole, Marie Benedict, 49
Otway, Mary Ann (Gregory Ann), 154

Pacek, Anthony Therese, 274
Parks, Lyman, 192

Index of Names

Paul (apostle), 151
Paul VI, 64, 240, 264
Pavoni, Mario, 268-69
Pawlikowski, John, 46
Penet, Mary Emil, 105
Peter (apostle), 12
Petit, Ian, 13n26
Pettersch, Carl, 189
Pichette, Joan, 277
Pinten, Joseph, 184
Piorno, Francisco, 227
Pius X, 263
Pius XII, 105, 211
Plamondon, Maxine, 15, 111-12
Platte, Ardeth, 86, 243n10, 245n15, 248, 251, 257
Poole, Stafford, 73
Popp, Eileen, 13, 68, 90, 266, 279-80
Popp, Gilbert, 13
Porter, Ann, 68, 271, 274
Post, Emily, 69
Przybylski, Kathy, 258

Quinn, Frank, 30n14
Quinn, William, 67

Rahner, Karl, 58
Rajewski, Lorraine, 155, 202, 274
Rau, James, 72n14, 192-93
Regan, Doris, 167, 269
Rego-Reatini, Michelle, 8-9, 30, 44n21, 46, 232
Reid, Barbara, 103
Reimer, Jean, 39, 127, 179, 246n20, 270-71, 278
Remen, Rachel Naomi, 209
Ridley, Susan, 241, 243
Rodriguez, Therese, 73, 137, 202
Romero, Ann Perpetua, 202
Roos, Jules, 213-14
Rostar, Carmen, 278
Rover, Dominic, 71-72
Ryan, Marie Joseph, 246n20
Ryan, Marybride, 66, 241n6

Salazar, Marie Bernarde, 81
Sanchez, Elizabeth, 217, 222
Sandoval, Betty, 215

Scanlon, Joan, 168-69
Schafer, Josine, 278
Schaffer, Lois, 279
Schaffran, Janet, 7n14
Schaller, Jeanne Lound, 258
Schaub, Geneva Marie, 97
Schillebeeckx, Edward, 58
Schiltz, Rita, 37-39, 43, 48
Schlichting, Jan, 30
Schneider, Margaret, 231-32
Schnell, Edith Marie, 85, 241n5, 245n15, 273
Schoenborn, Evelyn, 132, 274-75
Schoenherr, Richard, 73
Scholastica, 234
Schrems, Kateri, 84, 164-65
Schwartz (gym teacher), 230
Schwind, Mona, 76n20, 109n10, 196n1, 261n3, 264n9, 265n10, 269n13
Searle, Mark, 45
Selik, Edith Mary, 219-21
Shalda, Anne Monica, 157
Shangraw, Phil, 160n17
Shaw, Joseph E., 57
Sheahan, Maureen, 15
Siciliano, Jude, 20
Siers, Lucianne, 81, 104, 269-70, 274
Sikorski, Darlene, 272-73
Sills, Gretchen, 16, 20
Silva, Eduardo, 201-2
Silva, Eva, xvii, 199n4, 200n5, 200n7, 201-2, 269
Silva, Lupe, 21, 246n20, 275
Silva, Rafelita, 201-2
Silvia, Ken, 15, 111
Sleziak, Kathi, 74, 179, 228, 276-77
Smith, Virginia, 40-41, 45-46
Solomon, Denise, 11
Spencer, Judy Karafa, 157
Starn, Orin, 224n15
Stauder, Mary Louise, 274
Stein, Dolores, 15
Stein, Marjorie, 39, 268-69
Steves, Blanche, 49
Stokes, Edward J., 73, 78
Suenens, Leon Joseph, 52, 57, 60-61
Sullivan, Kathleen, 154
Supancheck, Phyllis, 279

Switzer, Carmelita, xvii–xviii, 47n25, 81, 157, 172–73, 236
Szocinski, Rosanne, 274

Taft, Bill, 179
Teilhard de Chardin, Pierre, 151
Thelen, Donna Jean, 105
Thiel, Agnes, 125, 189
Thiel, Linda, 274
Thielen, Ann, 126, 206
Thomas Aquinas, 51, 54, 58–59, 164
Thomas, Cynthia, 258
Thomas, Joan, 39, 87, 101, 127, 132, 159n15, 178, 191
Thomas, Margaret, 127
Thompson, Clara, 78
Thompson, Margaret Susan, 239n2
Thoreson, Karen, 13, 96, 279–80
Tillard, J. M., 79
Tilmann, Jean Paul, 192–93
Tilmann, Vera Ann, 178, 277–79
Timm, Marie Elegia, 71
Tobin, Joseph, 283
Tobin, Mary Luke, 234
Toohey, Joanne, 267
Tracy, Susanne, xviii, 153, 163n22, 165n25, 166n26, 166n27, 173n34, 177n38, 177n39, 244
Tremore, Judy, 251n32
Trenshaw, Cynthia, 160n17, 161–62
Troy, Gabriel, 227
Tugwell, Simon, 11, 54n3
Turcios, Max, 208n16

Untener, Ken, 20–21

Vaccaro, Mary, 159, 160n17, 161
Valerio, Edemia (Aurora), 39, 68, 216–17
Vanderbilt, Amy, 69
Vangsness, Norbert (Marjorie), 36n4, 60, 82–83, 121, 125, 218, 240–42, 246n20

Vest, Joseph, 46, 232
Vicaire, M. H., 23n1, 28n11, 53n1
Vidmer, John, 26n9
Viesnoraitis, Marie Dominica, 211-12, 214, 218
Vitalino (clinic director), 167

Walraven, Sandra, 155
Walters, Ann, 46, 148, 179, 247n21
Webb, Ann, 159n15
Weber, Mary Aquinas, xx, 6, 36n2, 36n4, 61–63, 69n5, 73, 77, 78n23, 120, 123, 130–31, 139–42, 192–94, 238, 240
Welsh, Janet Johnson, 155
Welty, Eudora, 197
Werner, Honora, 166
Wesley, John, 234
Wessels, Cletus, 151
Westerman, Ann, 178
Wieber, Ann Terrence, 15, 157
Williams, Joan, 137, 167–68, 269
Williams, Michael, 192–93
Willits, Ann, 83, 162
Wilson, Charles, 199, 230
Wittenbach, Alice, 147
Wojkowiak, John Mary, 141
Wolff, Madeleva, 99n2
Woodhouse, Arthur, 120
Wozniak, Teresa, 86
Wright, David F., 25n8
Wussler, Marilyn, 139n4

Yousufzai, Malala, 112n13

Zacarelli, Herman, 15, 111
Zerfas, Diane, xviii, 46–48, 159–60, 233, 236
Zinn, Carol, 81
Zuercher, Suzanne, 281

INDEX OF SUBJECTS

abortion, 256
accident, of seven Sisters, 264-65
action, and contemplation, 80-83
Acts of the Apostles, and the Charismatic Renewal, 12-13
adaptation, 66, 68-69, 75, 263-64; in the Dominican Order, 23-24; in governance, 123; in ministry, 182
aggiornamento, 12, 66, 68, 137
Ancash earthquake, 220-22
Annual International Balloon Fiesta, 208-9
Apostolic Visitation, assessment by, 283-84
apostolic year (Apostolic Novitiate), 93-95
apprenticeship, 98-99
Aquinas College, 181, 183-95; and AIRS, 100; and the Charismatic Renewal, 13; discussion in, 60-61; summer programs at, 66-67, 77-79; as teaching preaching, 20; and theological study, 58
Aquinas Institute of Religious Studies (AIRS), 11, 99-101, 190-91; in the canonical year, 93; and the CDN, 174-76; and the Preaching Certificate, 20; and World Order, 80
Aquinas Reading Clinic, 189
Aquinas Summer School without Walls, 188
Aquinata Hall, 48-49, 135
Area Coordinators, 127
Areas, structure of, 126-28
arrests, of Sisters, 245, 248, 251-52, 257, 272
art, 176-77
Asilo (home for the aged), in Chimbote, 213, 221-22
assessment, of Women Religious, 282-86
assignments, ministry, 123-24, 260, 266-68
Associate, 92
authority, 133; as a circle, 124-25; sources of, 121-22

Balloon Fiesta Park, 208
Baltimore Catechism, 1, 57
Baptism, 4; and holiness, 65; and names, 92-93
Beguines, 234, 282
Big Gray Book, 30
birth ledgers, of *Maternidad*, 225-26, 229
boycotts, for social justice, 251
"bride of Christ," 65, 113

call, to the Religious Life, 139
calling, 261-62
Call to Action, 241-42
Candidate, 92
canonical year (Canonical Novitiate), 93-94
Canon Law, renewal through, 73-77
Career Action Program, 188
Care of Earth Committee, 85, 250-51
catechesis, in Chimbote, 217-18
Catholicism: in Aquinas College, 183-84, 187; changes in, 260-62
Center for Women of Hope, 207n16, 272-73
Central America. *See* Latin America
Central Committees, 84
Centro de Obras Sociales, 210-29
Centro Mujeres de la Esperanza, 207n16, 272-73
certifications: academic, 98-101; of nurses, 110; of teachers, 107-8
Challenge of Peace, The, 243-44
change, renewal in, 61-63
Chapel of the Word, 48
chaplain, new, 39-41
Chapter of Affairs, 130-31; renewal of, 66-68
chaqwa, 224-25
chastity, reframing of, 91
children: and DCM, 231; housing for, 254-55

307

INDEX OF SUBJECTS

Chimbote, Peru, ministry in, 210-29, 268
Christ Life Series, 57-58, 63
Church, as the Pilgrim People of God, 3-4, 259
Church Militant, 3
Church Triumphant, 259
civil disobedience: Congregational policy on, 248; *See also* protests, Sisters' involvement in
civil rights movement, 240
clinic, outpatient, in Chimbote, 213, 216, 219-22
Closer Union Committee, 171
clothing: buying, 122-23; issues of, 140-42; in Peru, 212-13
colectiva, travel by, 211
collaboration, 162-80; with the Salvation Army, 231, 254-55; in study, 52
Collaborative Dominican Novitiate (CDN), 93-94, 172-76; and expanding community, 116-17
collegiality, principle of, 123-24, 131, 137, 203, 220
"Come and See," 198
Co-Membership Committee, 159-60
Commission on Latin America, 211
commissions, 130-32
Committee for Corporate Social Responsibility, 249
Committee on Governance, 126
committees, 130-32
commonality, 115
Common Dominican Novitiate. *See* Collaborative Dominican Novitiate
communication, 130-31; benefits of, 147; with former members, 158; verbal, 135-36
community, intentional, 142-44, 147; *See also* life, common
Community Concern Days, 82
Community Life. *See* life, common
Community Living Agreement, 124
Compline, 136
conflict resolution, 136, 138, 140
Congregation, meetings of, 34-35
conscience, as highest moral guide, 248
consciousness, social, 238-58
"Consistent Ethic of Life," 255
Consitution and Statutes: on clothing, 142; on the common life, 134, 144; on Congregation direction, 121; and the Gathering Days, 130; on ministry, 280; on prayer, 35; on study, 53, 98; revision of, 61, 76-77
Constitution on the Sacred Liturgy, 58
Constitution retreats, and preaching, 19-20
contemplation, and action, 80-83
contemplative life, primacy of, 72
Continuing Life Development Committee, 84
convents, traditional, 118-19, 125
Conviction (film), 257n39
Cook Arts Center, 276-77
Cook Library Center, 276-77
cooperation, in Chimbote, 218
Coordinating Committee on Common Life, 145
Coordinators, vs. Superiors, 124-25, 144
Corporate Stance Committee, 250-51
corporations, and social justice, 245-46, 249, 251-53
coup, in Peru, 218-22
creation: connectedness of, 151; and the New Mexico landscape, 197-98; as revelation, 32
crime, around Aquinas College, 191-93
culture, differences of, 201-2
curriculum: of AIRS, 190-91; of Aquinas College, 183-87
customs, of the common life, 134-49
Czech Republic, ministry in, 270

dance, liturgical, 10-11
daughter of justice, 113
deconstruction, of past practice, 87-88
Decree on the Renewal of Religious Life. See Perfectae Caritatis
degrees, academic, 98-113
departure, from Religious Life, 96-97, 153, 265
Detroit/Windsor Refugee Coalition, 245
DiaLEARN, 279
Dies Irae (Day of Wrath), 33
Dignitatis Humanae, 131
dignity, human, 131-32, 146, 255-56
Directed Studies Program, 188
Direction Statements, 86-87; and the Gen-

Index of Subjects

eral Assembly, 128-29; and the Marywood campus, 231; and relationships, 147-48; and social justice, 253-54, 256
Director of Liturgical Life, 46-47
Director of Novices, 96
Directory of Former Members, 155
Discipleship Award, 247
discussion, use of, 60-61
dispensation: principle of, 145; and study, 55
disputatio, 127
distress, emotional, 148
Divine Office: in English, 5-6; vs. Little Office, 23-24; and manual labor, 53
Divino Afflante Spiritu, 75
Doctrinal Assessment of the Leadership Conference of Women Religious, 284
Dogmatic Constitution on the Church. See *Lumen Gentium*
Doing Justice, 240-41, 249
Dominican Alliance, 116, 168-71
Dominican Associate Life, 158-62
Dominican Center at Marywood, 230-37
Dominican Chapel/Marywood, opening of, 42-45
Dominican Conference on Justice, 246
Dominican Formation Conference, 172-73
Dominican Futures, 133
Dominican Institute for the Arts, 176-77
Dominican Land Company, 206-8
Dominican Leadership Conference (DLC), 168-71; and preaching, 17-19
Dominican Praise, 30-32
Dominican Sisters Conference (DSC), 116n2
Dominican Sisters International, 117
Dominican Volunteers USA, 179
Don't Expect an Answer, 282
Drop-In-and-Learn, 279
"Duquesne weekend," 12-13

Earth, as holy, 151
earthquake, Ancash, 220-22
Eastown, 191-94
Eastown! A Report on How Aquinas College Helped Its Community Reverse Neighborhood Transition and Deterioration, 193
Eastown Neighborhood Association, 193

Ecclesia Militans, 3
Ecclesiae Sanctae, 56, 64, 121
Economic Justice for All, 243-44, 248
ecumenism, 45-46
education: continuing, 188-89; expanding ministry of, 273-75; ministry of, 276-79; motive for, 99; in New Mexico, 203-5
elderly, the, programs for, 79-80
El Niño, 223-25
Emergent Christ, The, 152
Emeritus Program, 189-90
Encore, 188
"Encounter with the Word," 163
English, 199; in prayers, 5-7
English as a Second Language, 186-87
Enkindling Life, 79
Environment and Art in Catholic Worship, 37
Esperanza (Hope) Project, 275
ethics, and social justice, 255-56
etiquette, feminine, 69-70
Europe, Eastern, ministry in, 269-70
evaluation, of Novitiates, 95
experience, renewal through, 76-77

faith, knowledge of vs. living the, 57-58
Faith and Resistance, 242-43, 251
family, of origin, 137-39
Family Literacy Program, 279
Family Lodge, 231, 254-55
Federation of Dominican Sisters U.S.A., 170-72
femininity, true, 68-72
filia justitia, 113
film, as a medium of knowledge, 78
flooding, in Peru, 220-21
Focus on the Present, 79
Focus on Your Future, 79
Fontbonne College, 110-11
food, in New Mexico vs. Michigan, 198
Food Research Center, 111
Food Service Directors, housekeepers as, 111
food service ministry, 110-12
forgiveness, and former members, 156
Formation, 89-97
"Formation of Community," 77-78
Fort Benning, protests at, 257

INDEX OF SUBJECTS

freedom, 130-32
Freedom House, 245
friendships, as allowed, 146-47
frugality, of some Sisters, 138
"Fuji Shock," 225
"Fulfillment of Feminine Personality in the Religious Life," 68-72

Gathering Days, 129-30
Gathering of Dominican Artists, 176-77
Gaudium et Spes, 56, 64-65, 262
General Assembly, 128-29; and Direction Statements, 253-54
General Chapters, 119-21; renewal through, 66, 72-74
gestures, in prayer, 26-27
Global Concerns Committee, 82, 242
God, expansive concept of, 8
Gospel: and liberation, 80; and social justice, 240
governance: of Aquinas College, 187; between Chapters, 121-26
Gracious Living, 69-70
Grand Rapids, Eastown neighborhood of, 191-93
Grand Rapids Area Center for Ecumenism (GRACE), 45-46
Grandville Avenue Academy for the Arts, 276-77
Grandville Avenue Neighborhood Library, 276-77
Great Peruvian Earthquake, 220-22
Groundwork for a Just World, 247
Ground Zero for Nonviolent Action, 257
Guadalupe Hospital, 206
Guatemala, ministry in, 271-72

habit, Dominican, 140-42; in Peru, 212-13
healing, pursuit of, 85-86
Heartside Pride Cleansweep, 194
Hispanics, ministry among, 272-73, 275
hobbies, need for, 71, 79
holiness, 65; as the path, 4
Holy, the, encountering, 147-48, 231-32
Holy Cross Catholic School, 203-4
Holy Preaching, 238, 240, 244, 250, 258
home visits, 120

Homework Assistance and Skill Development (HASD), 278-79
homiletics, courses on, 20
Honduras, collaborative ministry in, 167-68, 269
horary. *See* schedule
hospitality: and DCM, 232-33, 235-36; in New Mexico, 198-99
hospitals, in New Mexico, 205-6
housekeepers, 110-12, 136; and retreats, 14-15
houses, in inner-city Grand Rapids, 256
humanities, the, studies in, 107-9
Hungary, ministry in, 270
hygiene, in Chimbote, 217

ICEL, 29-30
identity: Dominican, 15-16; as a Sister, 90
INAI Studios, 37-38
Inclusive Lectionary, The, 8
inclusivity, in AIRS, 101
individual, the, in the whole, 151-52
Individually Designed Education for Adults (IDEA), 188
infants, care of, 213-16
INNERWORK Psychotherapy and Counseling, 207n16
In Pilgrimage, 82
Institute for Renewal and Christian Leadership, 77-79
International Commission on English in the Liturgy (ICEL), 8-9
Into the Streets, 194
investments, policy of, 245-46, 252-53
Iron Curtain, fall of, 269-70
itinerancy, importance of, 55

Japan, and ESL, 186-87
Jefferson Street houses, 256
Jonah House, 257
Jubilarians, 129
justice, social, 280-81, 285
Justice Promoter, 246, 249
"Justice Shall Come!," 85

Kentucky, ministry in, 274-75
labora, study as, 55
laboratory, medical, in Chimbote, 219-20

Index of Subjects

laity, the, and AIRS, 190-91; and Aquinas College, 184-85; and the Chimbote catechetical program, 218; formal association with, 158-62; relationships with, 152-53
"La Madruga," 208n16
Lamaze, in Chimbote, 226, 228-29
Land of Enchantment. *See* New Mexico
Lands of Dominic, Pilgrimage to, 84, 164-66, 168
landscape: of New Mexico vs. Michigan, 197-202; of Peru, 211-12
language, inclusive, 7-10, 29-30
Latin, 199
Latin America: ministry to, 166-68; as needing ministers, 210-11, 269
Latin American Mission Program (LAMP), 271
Latvia, ministry in, 270
leadership, during change, 61-63
Lectio Divina, 235
Liberation Theology, 80-82
life, common: concentric circles of, 150-80; customs of, 134-49; introduction to, 115-17; structures of, 118-33
listening, empathic, 148, 279-80
literacy, ministry of, 277-79
Lithuania, ministry in, 270
liturgy: reform of, 57-58; as the "work of the people," 47-48
Liturgy of Eucharist, 25
Liturgy of Hours, 25, 29-31
liturgy team, 39-42, 45-48
living singly, 145-46
Living the Word retreats, and preaching, 19-20
Living Wage Fund, 254
Louisiana, ministry in, 273
love: altruistic, 91; and the common life, 148-49; of neighbor, 72; study as, 51
Lumen Gentium, 56, 64-65, 262-63, 268

Marywood Academy, 230-31
Marywood Campus, 135
Marywood Health Center, 135
Maternidad (Maternity Hospital), 213-15, 219-27
Maternidad de Maria, 222

mathematics, studies in, 107
media, regulated use of, 54
medicine, ministry in, 109-10
meetings: Area, 126-27; house, 124-25
Mellow D's, 178
members, former, 153-58
Methodist Mission School, 203-4
midwives, in Chimbote, 213-15
milagros, 199
minister, music, 40-41, 46
ministry: assignment of, 123-24, 260, 266-68; changes in, 259-80; in Chimbote, Peru, 210-29; collaborative, 167-69; introduction to, 181-82; in New Mexico, 196-209; preparation for, 98-99; and social consciousness, 238-58; and study, 103-5; volunteer, 179
Ministry Fund, 206-8, 275-76
Ministry Resource Center, Inc., 272
miracles, in New Mexico, 199
mission: and collaboration, 169; and ministry, 264-65
Mission and Ministry, 133
Missionary Society of St. James, 211, 216
Mississippi, ministry in, 274
monasticism, 136-37; enclosed, 55
money, personal, 122
Montessori School, 161, 230-31
Motherhouse, 135
Mothers' Club, in Chimbote, 217
music, 178; in congregational meetings, 34-35; of New Mexico vs. Michigan, 202; and prayer, 2
mystics, praying with, 234-35

name, change of, 90-93
National Catholic Educational Association, 105
National Defense Education Act (1958), 107
National Leadership Conference of Women Religious (LCWR), 240
Native American tribes, ministry among, 274
Nazareth Sanatorium, 205-6
Nebraska, ministry in, 275
neighborhood, of Aquinas College, 191-94
NETWORK, 241-42

INDEX OF SUBJECTS

New Mexico, ministry in, 181-82, 196-209, 268
New Mexico Community Development Loan Fund (NMCDLF), 207n16
News and Notes, 133
newsletters, 133
Nine Ways of Prayer, 26; and liturgical dance, 11
non-governmental organization (NGO) status, 81
Nonviolence Committee, 250-52
Novice, 92
Novitiate, 92-97, 172-76
Nun in the World, The, 52, 57, 60-61
nurses, Sisters as, 109-10
nursing, in Chimbote, 210-29

O Antiphons, 32
obedience, 91, 260; new meaning of, 203
obedire, 91
Office of Hispanic Ministry, Lexington, KY, 274n20
Office of the Dead, 32-34
Office to Aid the Catholic Church in Central and Eastern Europe, 269-70
O Lumen, 6
Option for Justice, 242-43
Option for Justice Committee, 85
orphans, ministry to, 226-28
Orphan's Court, in Chimbote, 226-27
Osher Lifelong Learning Institute (OLLI), 189

Pacem et Terris, 203-4
Parable Conference, 16, 83-84, 162-68; and expanded community, 116; and preaching, 19
parenting, classes in, 276
participation, in governance, 122
Partnership for Global Justice, 81
Partners in Parenting, 276
Pastoral Constitution on the Church in the Modern World. See Gaudium et Spes
Pax Christi, 242-43
peace pole, 250
Perfectae Caritatis, 4, 56, 63-66, 74, 132, 137, 203, 263
perfection, pursuit of, 4, 55-56, 68, 87

personality, renewal of, 68-72
Personnel Services, 266-67
Peru, ministry in, 210-29, 268
Philosophy of Investments Policy, 245-46
pilgrimage, and prayer, 49-50
Pilgrimage to the *Lands of Dominic,* 84, 164-66, 168
Pilgrim People of God, 65
poor, the: and the Ministry Fund, 206-8; ministry to, 210-29
Posta Medica. See clinic, outpatient, in Chimbote
Post-Conciliar Commission for Religious, 56
Postulant, 92
poverty, 138; evangelical, 91
praxis, 57-58
prayer, and DCM, 232-37; Dominican emphases in, 22; and Dominican traditions, 32-35; as ecclesial, yet innovative, 23-26; as incarnational, 26-27; introduction to, 1-2; ministry of, 279-80; new moments in, 3-21; new places for, 36-50; and women, 27-32
Prayer and Listening Line at Marywood, 279-80
"prayer and work," 51, 55
preaching: through the arts, 177; Holy, 238, 240, 244, 258; and the Parable Conference, 163; and study, 55; and women, 16-21
prenatal care, in Chimbote, 214-16, 226, 228
preparation, ministerial, 98-99
priesthood, of all baptized people, 263
Prioress: and Area structure, 126-27; authority of, 121-22, 133; election of, 119-20
Project Unite, 194
Promoters of Justice, 85
Proposal C, 102, 125, 261
Protestants, working with, 203-5
protests, Sisters' involvement in, 240-48, 256-58
psalter, inclusive, 8-9, 29-30
psychology, 78; and personality renewal, 68-69

race, 201n8
racism, work against, 255
Rapport, 133

312

Index of Subjects

rebellion, of Guzmán, 224-25
reception, 90n3
reconciliation: and former members, 156; with New Mexican Protestants, 204-5
Reid, Barbara, accomplishments of, 103n6
relationships: and "encountering the Holy," 147-48; outside the Congregation, 152-53
Religious Life: A Lived Reality, 24, 68
Religious Life: definition of, 67-68; departure from, 96-97, 153, 265; reasons for entering, 139; renewal of, 73-77; transition in, 83
Remembering, Reaching, and Responding, 156
renewal: and change, 61-63; in study, 66
"Renewal through General Chapter," 72-73
renovation, of the Chapel, 36-39
ressourcement, 66
retirement, 79-80
retreats, annual, 14-15; and DCM, 235-36
reunion, with former members, 153-58
revelation, through prayer, 9-10
Romania, ministry in, 270
Rule of St. Augustine, 54, 76
Rule of St. Benedict, 55

sacred, vs. secular, 65, 262
Sacrosanctum Concilium, 10, 58; celebration of, 233-34
Saginaw Summer Institute, 58-59
salaries: as living just wage, 253-54; of nurses, 109-10; of teachers, 106, 108, 261
Salvation Army, collaboration with, 231, 254-55, 267
Salve Regina, 6, 33-34
"San," the, 205-6
schedule: daily, 136, 146; of prayer, 5, 25-26
schools: cost of, 261; in New Mexico, 203-5
science: and relationships, 151-52; studies in, 107-9
Scripture: and the Parable Conference, 163; and the Spirit, 13-14; study of, 74-75, 103, 263-64; and women's roles, 28
"Seamless Garment Ethic," 255
Second National Congress of Women Religious in Peru, 212, 218
secular, vs. sacred, 65, 262
seculars, in the Chapter room, 120-21

Self-Study, of Aquinas College, 185-87
Sendero Luminoso (Shining Path), 224-25
service: and Aquinas College, 194; in New Mexico, 209; women's role in, 77-78
Service Houses, 194
Shining Path, 224-25
Shoshone Indian Nation, protests with, 245
Siena House, and the CDN, 176
silence, 54
Sister Formation Conference, 58, 105-6
Sixteenth General Chapter, on prayer, 24-25
Slovakia, ministry in, 270
Social Justice Committee, 240
Social Works Center, 210-29
Sonia and Sofia (newborns), 223
sources, the, return to, 66
Southwest Creations Collaboration (SCC), 207n16
Soviet Union, and education, 107
Space Race, and education, 107
Spanish: 199-202; Scripture in, 7
Spirit, the: and the Charismatic Renewal, 12-14; responding to, 234-35
Spiritual Direction Practicum, 235
Spiritual Exercises of Ignatius Loyola, The, 235
Spiritual Formation Program, 234-35
Spiritual Intercession Specialist Teams for the Enhancement of Human Resources (S.I.S.T.E.R.), 148
Sponsa Christi, 65, 113
Stations of the Cross, 33
St. Elizabeth Shelter (Santa Fe), 208n16
St. Mary's College, Notre Dame, 99n2
St. Paul Seminary, 100; and theological study, 58-59
St. Pius X High School (Albuquerque) Tuition Assistance, 207n16
structures, of the common life, 118-33
study, academic, 98-113; and Area structures, 126-27; introduction, 51-52; renewal through, 64-88; and social analysis, 239; as transforming the community, 53-63
subsidiarity, principle of, 122-24, 131, 137, 203, 220
Summa Theologica, 54, 58-59

Summer Institute, and the Direction Statements, 86-87
Summer Study Program, in Fanjeaux, France, 195
Superior, 136-37; authority of, 203; living without, 142-43; vs. Coordinators, 124-25, 144

tapestries, seasonal, 38-39
task forces, 130-32
teachers, Sisters as, 105-8
Team for Justice, 245
Tessera, 133
tetanus, 216
theology, study of, 58-59, 98-105
Total Religious Education Center (TRE), 205
To the Ends of the Earth, 247
tours: of Central America, 166-67; *Lands of Dominic*, 84, 84, 164-66, 168
tracks, in DCM programs, 232-33
traditions, training in, 96
"twenty year plan," 106-7
twins, in Chimbote, 215

uniformity, 115, 136-37; vs. unity, 56-57, 90
United Farm Workers, 241
United Nations, 80-81
unity: through Area structures, 126; and newsletters, 133; vs. uniformity, 56-57, 90
University of Louvain, exchange studies at, 102
Upward Bound, 189-90

values, Dominican, and Aquinas College, 194-95
Vatican Council II, 3, 32-33, 92, 130-31, 146; and adaptation/*aggiornamento*, 24, 29; as broadening the base, 150-53, 179-80; and collegiality and subsidiarity, 220; and the common life, 115-16, 133; and Formation, 95-96; and General Chapters, 119-21; and governance, 122-23; and the laity, 218; and liturgy, 10-11; and ministry, 203, 212, 259-68; and personal maturity, 139; and prayer, 1-2; and Protestants, 204; and renewal, 64-88; and social consciousness, 238-40, 258; on the Spirit, 12; and study, 51-52, 56-63, 98, 102-3, 113
venia, 120
Veritas, 232
vernacular, importance of, 7
Vespers, 136
Vietnam War, 240
visits, home, 120
vocations, 261-62
Voluntary Surgical Contraception, 225
volunteers, 179
vows, the, 91
Vulgate, 75

weapons, nuclear, 208, 256-57
Weaving the Tapestry of Our Lives: Healing Racism through a Celebration of Our Differences, 255
welcome: in the Dominican Chapel/Marywood, 43-45; *See also* hospitality
Well Baby Clinic, 222, 226
W. K. Kellogg Foundation, and Eastown, 193
Whatever Happened to . . . ?, 155
What Ivan Knows That Johnny Doesn't, 107
wholeness, 151-52; pursuit of, 85-86
Wholistic Living Committee, 84-85
women: and DCM, 231; housing for, 254-55; and prayer, 27-32; role of, 68-72, 260
"Women Searching and Thirsting," 156-58
W.O.R.D. Literacy Project, 277-78
world, the: being in touch with, 71-72, and the Church, 262-63
World Order, seminar on, 80
"wounded healers," Sisters as, 85-86
Writing Opportunities Reading Discoveries Literacy Project, 277-78
Wurtsmith Air Force Base, protests at, 244-45, 251-52

Year of the Liturgy, The, 45
"You Are Special," 178
Young Professed, 92